The Novel in Nineteenth-Century Bengal

Becoming Readers in Colonial India

Sunayani Bhattacharya

BLOOMSBURY ACADEMIC
NEW YORK • LONDON • OXFORD • NEW DELHI • SYDNEY

BLOOMSBURY ACADEMIC
Bloomsbury Publishing Inc
1385 Broadway, New York, NY 10018, USA
50 Bedford Square, London, WC1B 3DP, UK
29 Earlsfort Terrace, Dublin 2, Ireland

BLOOMSBURY, BLOOMSBURY ACADEMIC and the Diana logo
are trademarks of Bloomsbury Publishing Plc

First published in the United States of America 2023
This paperback edition published 2025

Copyright © Sunayani Bhattacharya, 2023

For legal purposes the Acknowledgments on pp. viii–x constitute
an extension of this copyright page.

Cover design: Eleanor Rose
Cover image: Islam Pracharak from the Bangiya Sahitya Parishad library,
Kolkata © Sunayani Bhattacharya

All rights reserved. No part of this publication may be reproduced or transmitted
in any form or by any means, electronic or mechanical, including photocopying,
recording, or any information storage or retrieval system, without prior
permission in writing from the publishers.

Bloomsbury Publishing Inc does not have any control over, or responsibility for,
any third-party websites referred to or in this book. All internet addresses given
in this book were correct at the time of going to press. The author and publisher
regret any inconvenience caused if addresses have changed or sites have
ceased to exist, but can accept no responsibility for any such changes.

Library of Congress Cataloging-in-Publication Data
Names: Bhattacharya, Sunayani, author.
Title: The novel in nineteenth-century Bengal : becoming readers in
colonial India / Sunayani Bhattacharya.
Other titles: Novel in 19th-century Bengal
Description: New York : Bloomsbury Academic, 2023. |
Includes bibliographical references and index. |
Summary: "Examines a history of reading practices in 19th-century
Bengal at the intersection of Sanskrit and Perso-Arabic aesthetics,
British colonial pedagogy, and the rise of Bengali novels"– Provided by publisher.
Identifiers: LCCN 2022058990 (print) | LCCN 2022058991 (ebook) |
ISBN 9781501398469 (hardback) | ISBN 9781501398506 (paperback) |
ISBN 9781501398483 (ePDF) | ISBN 9781501398476 (eBook) |
ISBN 9781501398490 (eBook other)
Subjects: LCSH: Books and reading–India–Bengal–History–19th century. |
Bengali (South Asian people)–Books and reading. | Bengali fiction–Appreciation.
Classification: LCC Z1003.5.I5 B47 2023 (print) | LCC Z1003.5.I5 (ebook) |
DDC 028/.909541409034–dc23/eng/20230123
LC record available at https://lccn.loc.gov/2022058990
LC ebook record available at https://lccn.loc.gov/2022058991

ISBN:	HB:	978-1-5013-9846-9
	PB:	978-1-5013-9850-6
	ePDF:	978-1-5013-9848-3
	eBook:	978-1-5013-9847-6

Typeset by Integra Software Services Pvt. Ltd.

To find out more about our authors and books visit www.bloomsbury.com
and sign up for our newsletters.

For the women who taught me to dream of criss-cross greens

Contents

Acknowledgments	viii
Introduction: Establishing the Problem—Reading as Practice	1
1 Breaking the Cycle of Bad Readers: Battala Literature, Colonial Pedagogy, and the Idea of Education	45
2 Becoming a Reader: Letters, Reviews, and Memories of Reading	87
3 Dear Reader, Good Sir: The Reader and Bankim's Novels	115
4 Another World of Reading: Hossain and Islamic Bengali Prose	147
Conclusion: The Novelty of Reading	185
Bibliography	199
Index	212

Acknowledgments

The roots of *The Novel in Nineteenth-Century Bengal* lie in the bookshelves of my childhood home, and in the many *bajarer tholis* next to the shelves overflowing with paperbacks that my father had bought during his work trips. They lie in the well-worn copies of Enid Blyton's *Malory Towers* from which I got the idea that all lucky kids had midnight feasts with ham sandwiches and root beers. I tried both much later in life—not everything you read in books is true. They lie in the hardbound *Reader's Digest* book that my grandmother owned, and which I feared because it had a picture of a large gorilla. They lie in my grandfather's *Collected Works of Sherlock Holmes* which I had read and reread so often that the spine barely held together. They lie in a copy of a French textbook with a red cover whose name I cannot recall but which I will forever associate with learning the French alphabet in Seychelles.

Somewhere amidst this collection of books, I learned that reading is a fraught affair. It wasn't enough to put words together, to get the grammar right, and to understand what the marks on the page meant. I learned that there are good books and bad books, good readers and bad, and that much as I imagined myself alone with my books, I was a part of a much larger structure that determined who read what and how. Even without midnight feasts in a boarding school, I was lucky enough to have mostly unsupervised access to books far outside the limited school curriculum. But what did these books mean to those who knowingly and unknowingly let me read them? What did my grandmother see in *Reader's Digest* that prompted her to spend a sizeable sum on that book of natural wonders? As it sat next to her Political Science textbooks, did she see in it the possibilities of a world outside her quotidian life, or was it something she bought because of the discount she got as a subscriber to the magazine? What was her relationship to that book, and how did she read it?

These are the scenes this book conjures up as it asks: how and why do people read the way they do? *The Novel in Nineteenth-Century Bengal* explores these questions in the context of nineteenth-century Bengal as each chapter tells the story of a different kind of reading. I look for traces left by readers in the books they read, in the magazines they subscribed to, in the letters they wrote, and through it, I try to recreate that sense of wonder they might have felt as they read the opening lines of *Durgeshnandini* with Jagatsingha riding across an open field into the storm.

Acknowledgments

The book began as my dissertation in the Department of Comparative Literature at the University of Oregon, and along the way I have accrued debts of gratitude that I cannot hope to repay. I want to thank my mentors foremost for inspiring me and for believing in ideas that, to me, seemed so unformed. To Michael Allan, I owe so much of what is contained in this book today. I thank him for his intellectual and personal generosity, for his extraordinary insights, for teaching me the value of a good argument, and his friendship. I thank Sangita Gopal for her guidance, her thoughtful engagement with literary history, and for sparking the thought that readers could be the subject of a study. I thank Paul Peppis for his constant support and encouragement, and for being an incredible reader. I thank them for modeling what it means to be a scholar, for being willing to read endless drafts, for the hours of conversations, and so much more.

I want to thank Saint Mary's College of California for the institutional, professional, and personal support I have received. To my colleagues, thank you for welcoming me with open arms, and for giving my work a home. I am grateful for the support I received from Molly Metherd and Kathryn Koo as chairs of the English Department. Thank you Marilyn Abildskov, Elisa Findlay Herrera, Robert Gorsch, Rosemary Graham, Brenda Hillman, Jeannine King, Emily Klein, Hilda Ma, Lisa Manter, Meghan Sweeney, Yin Yuan, and Matthew Zapruder. I have been fortunate enough to have been surrounded by the most incredible students. I thank them for their collegiality and intellectual curiosity which has helped shape this book.

I am grateful for the institutional support I have received along the way. I thank the Provost's Office for the Provost Research Grant which allowed me to travel to Kolkata and Mumbai during the summer of 2019. The archival work necessary for Chapter 4 was conducted during that trip. I was able to complete a draft of the dissertation thanks to the Himes Memorial University of Oregon Doctoral Research Fellowship which I received in 2015.

The book has benefited from the insights provided by the anonymous reviewers, from questions and comments received at panels at the American Comparative Literature Association, and from audiences at Diamond Harbour Women's University and Aliah University. I thank my editor, Amy Martin, at Bloomsbury Publishing, and Hali Han for their support and professionalism throughout this process. Excerpts from Chapter 3 first appeared as Sunayani Bhattacharya, "How Not to Read Like a Victorian: Reimagining Bankim's Reader in Nineteenth-Century Bengali Novels," in *Comparative Literature* 73:1 (2021), 84–109. I thank Duke University Press for permission to publish this material here.

Acknowledgments

I have made some incredible friends in this journey without whose camaraderie this work would not have been possible. Thank you to all who made Villard Hall and Eugene feel like home. Thanks especially to Elizabeth Howard, Andrea Gilroy, Shaun Gilroy, Jenny Odintz, and Tera Reid for countless nights of Doctor Who, Sherlock, and brownies. Thank you Arunima Bhattacharya for not only being the "other" Bhattacharya on campus but for all the love and support. Thank you Suhasini Sanyal Saxton, Philippe Bou Malham, Reza Motamedi, and Aida Salketic for an international cohort that turned into lasting friendships. To Baran Germen, Yvonne Toepfer, and Palita Chunsaengchan, thank you for being my family in Eugene and beyond.

Thank you Vedita Cowaloosur and Akshya Saxena for thinking through the various iterations of this project and reading innumerable drafts. Their friendship has been invaluable as I have sought to bring this book to fruition.

I have been formed by Jadavpur University's Department of English in more ways than one. I thank my professors and mentors for the foundation they provided in the discipline which gave me the confidence to travel across disciplines. They gave me the freedom to read without the strictures of exams or syllabi. Jadavpur also gave me lifelong friends whose love and support I am thankful for. Thank you Srijani Ghosh, Saumava Mitra, Arundhati Ghosh, and Azeem Hussain for being there from the start.

Thank you Swapan Chakravorty for inspiring this book, for telling me where to go looking for obscure essays by Bankim, for teaching me how to read theory, for showing me how it's done.

Tayana Chatterjee and Priyanka Chowdhuri, thank you for being the kind of best friends only sisters can be. To them I owe so much in love and friendship.

To my family—I am everything because of you. Every word in this book is a result of years of sacrifice you chose to make, a result of the love and confidence you have given me to pursue my dreams. Poli and Chandrima, thank you for your unconditional support, and for believing in me when the chips were down. Ma, Baba, this one's for you. Ma, you are, and always will be, my first reader, my harshest critic, my staunchest supporter. Baba, you are my rock. Thank you my furry friends for showing me the richness of life, the beauty of pausing to throw springs in the midst of all the practicality of this world. Zach, thank you for your love and companionship. Without you, this book would not be. Finally, Gora, thank you for being the best part of me.

Introduction: Establishing the Problem—Reading as Practice

I. The Novelty of Reading

In 2015, the Association of Publishers in India and the Federation of Indian Publishers commissioned Nielsen, a global research firm, to study the burgeoning publishing industry in India. The *Nielsen India Book Market Report: Understanding the India Book Market* aimed at gathering information about one of the fastest growing reading publics in the world, and at documenting the reading preferences of the twenty-first-century Indian reader. When the report was released at the Frankfurt Book Fair, India was found to be the second largest consumer of English language books, and the sixth largest print book market globally. Nielsen Book India identified over 9,000 registered publishers, and noted the presence of thousands of unregistered publishers catering to both English and bhasha[1] readers.[2] The numbers, when broken down, reveal a market that consumes over 55 percent of English language texts, the majority of which are school and college textbooks, and professional books. However, Indian readers choose to read fiction in languages other than English, as more than 50 percent of the fiction sold in India are bhasha texts.[3] In fact, the most sought-after genre, after study preps and job preps, is "general and literary fiction," as an article in *India Today* notes.[4] The sheer number of readers—not to mention the

---

[1] Indian vernacular languages: the use of the word "vernacular" is contentious, primarily because of connotations of regionality or secondariness, and while "vernacular" has been recuperated by several scholars, I prefer using the term "bhasha," which translates to "language" from Sanskrit.

[2] https://www.nielsen.com/eu/en/press-releases/2015/the-nielsen-india-book-market-report-2015-understanding-the-indian-book-market/.

[3] Vinutha Mallya, "Nielsen Values Indian Publishing at $3.9 Billion" https://publishingperspectives.com/2015/10/nielsen-values-indian-publishing-at-3-9-billion/, 2015.

[4] https://www.indiatoday.in/pti-feed/story/indian-book-market-to-touch-739-billion-by-2020-survey-522296-2015-12-01.

3.9 billion dollar industry—continues to make the Indian book market look very attractive to publishers and investors alike as both are keen on understanding not merely *what* the Indian reader reads, but *how* they read. The question of *how* has become even more pertinent in the last five years as India has seen incredible growth in access to the internet; more and more publishers are choosing online retailers to distribute their product while simultaneously noticing the readers' propensity for reading online, mostly on their smartphones.

What stands out in the discourse surrounding the Indian book market is the rhetoric of newness and novelty. The *Nielsen India Book Market Report* is touted to be the *"first-of-its-kind,"*[5] an attempt to study, document, and understand what is largely seen as an unregulated market with little to no history of formally reporting its numbers. The sense of excitement in being able to tap into a vast, emergent reading public is palpable in Nielsen Book India's own summary of the study, as well as in the response of the publishing industry and news media. As articles in several leading Indian news magazines note, Nielsen's endeavor represents a turning point in the history of publishing in India; the frequent use of words such as "potential," "maturing," and "growing" undergird both the study itself and the market it examines. The book trade is seen as emerging from an informal, chaotic past where it was held back by difficult distribution systems, a fragmented publishing industry, long credit cycles, and rampant piracy. A key factor in this narrative of a newly emerging industry is readers who are seen in the same light as the book market—they are becoming more literate, more of them are becoming literate, they are developing a taste for more than just pragmatic professional texts and entrance exam test preps, and they are willing to spend more time reading widely.[6] Reading, one is led to believe, is finally becoming fashionable in India as more individuals have the money and time to spend on the act of reading. The importance of the reader is not lost on Thomas Abraham, the managing director of Hachette India, who suggests a need to "build readership" to complement an increase in the numbers of new titles released, and to be attentive to readers now reading online, and reading in new ways.[7]

---

[5] https://www.nielsen.com/eu/en/press-releases/2015/the-nielsen-india-book-market-report-2015-understanding-the-indian-book-market/.

[6] *Publishing Perspectives, India Today, Nielsen India Book Market Report, The Hindu*, to name only a few news outlets reporting on this issue.

[7] https://www.thehindubusinessline.com/blink/cover/how-the-indian-publishing-industry-is-set-to-evolve-in-the-coming-decade/article30469070.ece: in an interview with Anish Chandy, 2020.

Introduction 3

Yet the remarkably new achievements of 2015 are far from new. As early as 1855, James Long undertook the first such survey of the print market in Bengal in *A Descriptive Catalogue of Bengali Works Containing a Classified List of Fourteen Hundred Bengali Books and Pamphlets, Which Have Issued from the Press during the Last Sixty Years, with Occasional Notices of the Subjects, the Price, and Where Printed.*[8] Long's work shares startling conceptual and methodological similarities with Nielsen's *Indian Book Market Report,* as both are interested in dividing the market into books read for pleasure and textbooks, and further into the language of publication, cataloguing in the process a market both imagine as burgeoning but uncharted. The *Catalogue,* however, takes a more generous view of readers than Nielsen; in the Preface to the work, Long suggests that "Popular Literature is an Index to the state of the popular mind," thereby relying on Bengali readers to serve as adequate barometers of the book market.[9] While Long is interested only in the Bengali publishing industry, given the centrality of nineteenth-century Bengal in establishing and developing the Indian book trade, both his *Catalogue* and the *Indian Book Market Report* are well matched in their scope and ambition. My point in noting this similarity is not to identify a certain myopia in the current Indian book market, nor to make a claim for conflating Bengal and India. Rather, my interest lies in noticing that as early as 1855, the reader and their practices of reading are indexical of trends in publishing. Questions such as who reads what, how does the reader read, how do they learn to read new genres, and how this information can be useful to all those involved in the production, distribution, and consumption of books can be found at one of the first sites of commercial publication in modern India— nineteenth-century Bengal under British colonial rule.

This book argues that nineteenth-century Bengal affords a signal moment in history when the aesthetic and political upheavals caused by British colonial rule allow one to isolate practices of reading. As one looks closer, these practices

---

[8] As Long himself remarks, his *Catalogue* is by no means the first of its kind; he acknowledges Henry Miers Elliot's *The History of India,* Friedrich von Adelung and D. A. Talboys' *A Historical Sketch of Sanscrit Literature,* Aloys Sprenger's *Catalogue of the Arabic, Persian and Hindustany Manuscripts,* and Joseph Garcin de Tassy's *Histoire de la littérature hindouie et hindoustanie (The History of Literature of Hindi and Urdu),* as undertaking similar projects in various Indic languages. Long is unique in focusing on Bengal and on Bengali works.

[9] Long also had a less salutary reason for documenting the book trade in detail. Following the Indian Rebellion of 1857, the Government felt it necessary to discipline some of the vernacular presses which were seen as publishing seditious material. Long presented his report to the Government of India in 1859, thereby providing the latter access to a comprehensive list of printers and publishers operating in Bengal.

can be found buried in a complex network of readers, authors, professional and amateur reviewers, and publishers and printers. *The Novel in Nineteenth-Century Bengal* tells the story of these practices of reading, now largely forgotten by literary history, which draw on the Bengali reader's quotidian familiarity with Sanskrit and Perso-Arabic aesthetic paradigms to grant them access to the newly emergent genre of the Bengali novel. As they read early Bengali novelists such as Bankimchandra Chattopadhyay and Mir Mosharraf Hossain, they are compelled by the disruptive forces of colonization to choose *how* they are to read a genre whose originary model is in a language that is not a part of their lived experience, and one which they can barely read or speak. This work documents their choice to read like a Bengali living in a world in which Sanskrit, Perso-Arabic, and their attendant traditions form not a distant past, but coexist, albeit contentiously, with the everyday present.[10]

Near the end of *Nabhel nāyikā* (*The Novel Heroine*), a popular late-nineteenth-century Bengali satire, the protagonist's husband Haradeb warns the general public of the perils of introducing one's wife to novel reading. "Save your money," he exclaims as he leaves for work—where he will be abused by his white master—"because buying bad novels will only turn your wife into a cheap romance loving animal."[11] The satire brings together questions of genre, taste, and morality in a microcosmic representation of late-nineteenth-century anxieties surrounding the reading of novels. The conclusion is deceptively simple—the man very publicly berates the woman for becoming influenced by novels and neglecting her domestic duties—but it confounds literary history since the genre is barely a couple of decades old at the time of *Nabhel nāyikā*'s publication. The text's anonymous author assumes Haradeb's wife to be a reader capable of (mis)reading the novel's aesthetic and ethical codes, but how does she

---

[10] At this juncture, I would like to note that *The Novel in Nineteenth-Century Bengal* consciously moves away from discussing English language experiments in novel writing, even though one of its central subjects, Bankim, began his career as a novelist by writing in English. I explicitly bracket this history for two reasons. The first—English was a language available only to a few Bengalis, and while the rate of literacy was itself fairly low, the rate of English language literacy was even lower. Thus, to discuss the role of English as a literary language with any degree of robustness would necessarily restrict the book's argument to a minority of Bengalis. What I find more attractive is to observe the presence of English as a minor language alongside Bengali, Sanskrit, Persian, Urdu, and Arabic as languages which had a much larger readership. English was often the language of the state, and as such had considerable cultural capital, but in the realm of literature, it was at best a secondary presence for most Bengalis. The second reason why I wish to distance my argument from the role of English is to ensure that this book is not merely rehearsing the well-known claim that English language and literature definitively shaped the Bengali novel, or that the latter was predominantly a response to the presence of the former in nineteenth-century Bengal.

[11] *Nabhel nāyikā*, translation mine.

Introduction   5

gain that knowledge in such a brief span of time? How does she learn to read
the novel genre, and what does her reading practice look like, given that the
emergence of any practice of reading often appears to blend seamlessly into a
culture's practices? What are the historical and ideological forces contributing to
the formation of her reading practice?

In conversation with debates in postcolonial studies and global Anglophone
studies, *The Novel in Nineteenth-Century Bengal* urges one to move away from the
perception that reading is a universal faculty, capable of being transported from
one location to another, and then made to suit the socio-political conditions it
has been transposed onto. Thanks to the efforts of a number of scholars, we have
now become quite familiar with the argument that the conditions producing the
Bengali novel were unique to its site of production, and that the materiality of
the book acquired forms significantly different from those of Victorian texts.[12]
Yet our perceptions of the generic contours of the novel itself remain constricted
to a historically conditioned lack—the Bengali novel, coming as it did after
the Victorian form, follows in the latter's footsteps, and is read along lines
imported from Victorian Britain.[13] In what follows, I propose a different way of
conceptualizing the relationship between the Bengali reader and the novel, one
which prioritizes their experiences as participants in a thriving book market,
over narratives of external influence, comparison, and imposition. What happens
when we engage with the Bengali reader not in terms of how they are like or unlike
the Victorian reader, and, via the reader, encounter the Bengali novel as a genre
responding to local pressures rather than a desire to emulate the British model?
What happens when we take the efforts of colonial institutions such as the Fort
William College in hollowing out Bengali to replace it with Enlightenment ideals
so as to create a modern language as a precursor to conversations animating
the field of the global Anglophone?[14] Ultimately, this book claims that reading
is not a universal practice, but rather highly localized, specific, and often non-
transferable, and it is only by approaching reading thusly that we can understand
what it means to read something at a particular time and place in history.

---

[12] For example, Abhijit Gupta demonstrates how the early print versions of *Annadāmangal* had added
to them certificates of purity assuring the Hindu reader that the ink used to print the text was mixed
with holy water from the Ganges ("Popular Printing and Intellectual Property in Colonial Bengal").

[13] Note, for example, Ulka Anjaria's work on realism in the modern Indian novel, and the emphasis
on realism being of a different nature in these novels, rather than these texts having a different
conceptual paradigm. I discuss this in greater detail in Chapter 3.

[14] I have here in mind Akshya Saxena's *Vernacular English* and her brilliant work on demonstrating the
role played by English in the Indian literary imaginary in the twentieth century.

Rethinking the practice of reading also allows us to begin to undo the narratives co-opting the Bengali novel within the project of Hindu nationalism. The pioneering role played by Bankimchandra Chattopadhyay in creating the genre in Bengali, when placed alongside his investment in imagining a Hindu nation, and his influence over Bengali literary history, has effectively wedded all discussions of the novel in nineteenth-century Bengal to those of nation and citizen formation. The trope of the Bengali novel as foundational to a national literature continues to have currency in postcolonial studies, and in the work of scholars working on South Asian literary production. This book gestures away from the consolidating and purifying tendencies of national literature—and from that current within postcolonial studies—suggesting instead that the Bengali novel in the nineteenth century is enmeshed in too diverse a fabric of reading practices to be assimilable into any narrative of national literature. That such a relationship between the novel and the nation appears teleologically inevitable by the end of the nineteenth century stands witness to the hegemonic rise of Hindu nationalism in response to colonial violence. *The Novel in Nineteenth-Century Bengal* takes on the task of revealing this systematic erasure of competing histories by reading the Bengali novel along with those readers whose practices disappear by the turn of the century.

II. The Journey of the Printed Book

The book as an object arrived in India well before the popularity of the novel in nineteenth-century Bengal, and the large publishing industry feeding this need for ever-newer novels. Yet from the moment of its arrival in Goa in 1556 till the founding of the Mission Press in Serampore in 1800, the colonial book[15] circulated very little by way of trade. Most of the publication was funded by either Christian missions or the colonial government, and even then, this activity was restricted to coastal India.[16] The conditions for commercial publication—and here I am following the lead of book historians—became available only after the Battle of Plassey in 1757 when the East India Company defeated Siraj ud-Daulah, the last independent Nawab of Bengal, and soon after established the

---

[15] I draw this definition and history from Abhijit Gupta's "Popular Printing and Intellectual Property in Colonial Bengal," as well as from *Print Areas*, a volume coedited by Gupta and Swapan Chakravorty.
[16] Gupta, Graham Shaw in *A Companion to the History of the Book*, 2007.

Introduction   7

three Presidencies or administrative centers at Calcutta, Bombay, and Madras. This allowed the colonial government to consolidate its administrative power, which led to a rapid increase in the scale of printing. As several scholars, including Priya Joshi, Abhijit Gupta, and Graham Shaw note, by the time Long published his 1855 *Catalogue*, print had gone from virtually non-existent to a thriving industry, with over forty-six indigenous and colonial presses in Bengal alone. Compared to the other Presidencies and Goa, the development of print technology in Bengal received not only religious impetus, but more importantly political momentum from the East India Company since it was the site of the first Presidency and also of the Company's first decisive victory over Islamic rule. Bengal, as the Company's first political and commercial center, saw the rise of commercial publications at a rate not matched by other parts of the subcontinent till the 1870s, and by the first two decades of the nineteenth century—thanks to the efforts of indigenous and European printer-publishers—the printed book became accessible and socially acceptable to a significant number of people in the region. A large body of texts, both secular and religious, in Bengali, English, Persian, and Sanskrit vied for a share of a growing book market as producers and distributors of books saw the opportunity to create a reader who would soon have preferences as to whether they wanted to be entertained or educated.

The story of this burgeoning print industry rests on a foundation intertwining the development of modern Bengali and of print texts in Bengali, and as I discuss later in this section, the consequences of this marriage of language and print are far reaching. The argument that I counter here seeks to create an origin story for modern Bengali that aligns it with the development of European vernaculars— the language acquires its current form with the coming of print modernity, and in its modern form becomes a vehicle for rational thought. Following this logic, texts produced in modern Bengali, and readers of the same, are folded into the world of Enlightenment reason. As you will see, this narrative is propagated by Bengalis and British alike, and remains unchallenged by most contemporary postcolonial scholars of the region.[17] What is left behind—deliberately obscured—are alternate histories of the Bengali language, its texts and their readers, and it is this history that I wish to recuperate. I focus on two institutions, Fort William College and the Mission Press, whose interpretation of Bengali as a

---

[17] Most recently in Tapti Roy's *Print and Publishing in Colonial Bengal* (2019) in which she presents a masterful study of the print history of *Vidyāsundar*, an early modern Bengali text, but her argument rests upon this very history of modern Bengali that I wish to challenge.

language extends far beyond the nineteenth century and the context of colonial Bengal. It becomes *the* definitive story of modern Bengali and it naturalizes 1800 as year when Bengali is effectively severed from its premodern past and set on the path of Anglicization.

For the first hundred odd years of British presence in the region under the aegis of the East India Company, Bengali was seen as merely the language of the locals with little to no administrative or literary standing. Those honors went to Persian, the court language, and to Sanskrit, the language of Hindu philosophy and aesthetics. Bengal had been under Islamic rule from the thirteenth century onwards, variously governed by the Delhi Sultanate, the Mughal empire, and the Pathans, and as part of the Persianate world, Bengali elites and those with administrative or literary aspirations were fluent in Persian, regardless of their religious affiliations.[18] Alongside this, Sanskrit served as the other significant language, and given the number of Hindu rulers governing locally while paying obeisance to the Islamic empires, Sanskrit maintained its position of prominence.[19] Bengali did not receive much courtly patronage, and remained a marginal language for the ruling classes while simultaneously being the language of daily use for the majority in the region. The rich body of work being produced in Bengali, including ritualistic and secular texts, was mostly relegated to the status of folk production, and given the power of Persian and Sanskrit, it was difficult for the vernacular to be acknowledged as anything other than a provincial language.

With the coming of the European traders and missionaries from the sixteenth century onwards, Bengali gained more visibility, but only because these groups realized that neither Sanskrit nor Persian gave them any purchase when it came to trading with or proselyting the masses; to engage with the average Bengali in any profitable way, the Europeans had to learn the Bengali language. As early as the seventeenth century, the Portuguese had already created a Bengali grammar, and consolidated a list of useful words and phrases, and the Portuguese missionaries in particular had considerable success in printing books in Bengali. They printed several Bengali books both in Bengal and in Lisbon, including pamphlets on

---

[18] For a detailed discussion on the Hindi-Urdu, Persian-Sanskrit split see Jennifer Dubrow's *Cosmopolitan Dreams* (2018), and Francesca Orsini's *Before the Divide* (2010).

[19] What I document here is restricted to Bengali print history and European receptions of the language. By the late nineteenth century, the narrative that Bengali lacked any aesthetic or political texts prior to the mid-1800s is successfully reversed by several Bengali scholars including Ramgati Nyayratna, Surendranath Sen, and Haraprasad Sastri, to name only a handful.

Introduction   9

Christian doctrines and a book of catechisms.[20] These efforts, however, paid little
if any attention to extant Bengali socio-literary manuscripts, and concentrated on
producing a Bengali suitable for the dissemination of Christianity, thus creating
a gap between the language as seen by the Europeans and the language as used
by the Bengalis. This process of hollowing out Bengali to fill it with European
knowledge was later perfected by the British who sought to create a Bengali
language that was Bengali in form but European in content. Yet this history of
Portuguese experimentation with Bengali is now mostly forgotten in favor of
British efforts at modernizing Bengali, and this forgetting is in no small part
a result of the systematic erasure of Portuguese presence in Bengal following
the Battle of Plassey. In 1757, the East India Company gains decisive control of
the region, reducing both the Mughals and the Portuguese to mere shadows.
In order to consolidate this power, the Company colludes with local nawabs,
uses considerable force and money, and simultaneously disavows Portuguese-
led experiments in Bengali and the singular hold of Persian over legal and
economic affairs. They focus on seemingly rescuing Bengali from the dark ages
so as to make it a vehicle fit for the Company and its affairs in the region. Bengali
for them becomes the *tabula rasa* on which they would leave their mark, and
through which they would establish their ascendancy in Bengal.[21]

    This story of creating a language that could help the Company profit from
the region more effectively, and of standardizing the Bengali script inadvertently
creates the material and cultural conditions facilitating the introduction of
novels and novel reading in Bengal. I say inadvertently because the start of
this story shows no signs of this possible outcome, as indeed of any outcome
other than producing a set of British officials trained in the local languages
and customs. Richard Wellesley, the governor-general of Bengal from 1798 to
1805, founds Fort William College in Kolkata in 1800 to commemorate his
victory over Tipu Sultan of Mysore. Not coincidentally, this is the same year the
Mission Press is founded in Serampore by the Baptist preacher William Carey,
John Marshman, and William Ward. The simultaneous efforts of the College

---

[20] The fascinating history of early print history in Bengal led by the Portuguese is well documented.
See Sajani Kanta Das' *Bāṅglā gadya sāhityer itihās* (1946), Suniti Kumar Chatterji's *The Origin and
Development of the Bengali Language* (1926), Surendranath Sen's *Prachin Bangala Patra Sankalan*
(1942), and M. Siddiq Khan's "The Early History of Bengali Printing" (1962), to name only a few.

[21] This narrative is by no means unique to Bengal; evidence of similar linguistic acquisitions by
the British can be seen across the Indian subcontinent during the eighteenth and the nineteenth
centuries. Tamil, in the Madras Presidency, and Marathi, in the Bombay Presidency, for example,
are also marked by the Company's desire for economic and political supremacy in these regions.

and the Press conjoin the language with its print history in such a way that it becomes nearly impossible to tell the story of the one without the other. Both the College and the Press are part of Wellesley's efforts to give the Company a more presentable, polished façade via an investment in the literatures and languages of India, alongside Latin and Greek. The College in particular is a result of Wellesley recognizing the need to reverse the Company's image as purely profit-seeking, and is one of the earliest embodiments of Britain's civilizing mission in colonial India. Warren Hastings, the first governor-general, had attempted something similar through the Royal Asiatic Society (1784), but the Society's focus had been predominantly on Sanskrit and Hindu culture, and Bengali didn't really get much of an impetus at that time.[22] Given the proximity to the Battle of Plassey, Hastings had good reason to give William Jones, the founder of the Asiatic Society, considerable freedom in studying a language and religion that could ostensibly dent the prestige of Bengal's Islamic heritage. By 1800, however, Wellesley had the comfort of relative stability in the region, and the College opened with classes in Hindi, Arabic, and Persian, with Bengali being added in 1801.[23] Carey was invited to teach Bengali to British officials, and to aid in the creation of Bengali as a codified, standardized, and modern vernacular.

In order to accomplish the second task, Carey along with his fellow Mission Press colleague, John Marshman, gathered manuscripts from various parts of Bengal to get a better understanding of the language as it existed. Carey had already been doing this for several years as a representative of the Baptist mission, but now he was an employee of the College and had financial and administrative support.[24] What Marshman and Carey discovered dismayed them; they found that in order to teach Bengali, they needed to first create a teachable language, given the supposedly abject state of Bengali. Marshman captures their mood well in his description of Bengali literacy at the turn of the nineteenth century:

> If they [the Bengalis] can write at all, each character, to say nothing of orthography, is made in so irregular and indistinct a manner, that comparatively few of them

---

[22] The Calcutta Madrassa (1781) and the Hindu Sanskrit College in Benares (1791) also made significant contributions toward fashioning India as a profitable subject of study.

[23] The history of the College is complex and makes for interesting study in its own right. For more on the founding of the College, its internal politics, and the role of the educator-administrator, see Kopf.

[24] Carey's *Memoir* (1836) by his nephew Eustace Carey, also a Baptist missionary, documents the early troubles Carey had in communicating with Bengalis and in finding the resources to help support the mission. The document provides a close, if unintentionally humorous, look at Carey attempting to speak Bengali, imagining his success, and only later realizing that his audience had not understood a word of what he had said.

Introduction   11

can scarcely wade through that which has been written by themselves after any lapse of time. If they have learned to read, they can seldom read five words together, without stopping to make out the syllable ... even when the writing is legible.[25]

As one of Carey's biographers George Smith notes, Marshman was not alone in his perception of Bengali; Carey himself undertook several trips to centers of learning across Bengal, including Nadiya and Bhatpara, and lamented that the whole of Bengali culture had produced a mere forty manuscripts.[26] Much has been written of Thomas Babington Macaulay's now infamous *Minute on Indian Education*, but his conclusions about the inadequacy of Indic languages appear fairly tame when placed against those of Marshman and Carey who served as sources informing Macaulay and his contemporaries. Dismayed but not disheartened by his findings, Carey undertook the task of compiling a Bengali dictionary during his tenure at Fort William College, and created several works in Bengali and Sanskrit, most of which was printed by the Mission Press.[27] These were then adopted as textbooks at the College, and the vernacular as imagined by the British was born at the conjunction of these two institutions. The impact of Fort William College and the Mission Press on Bengali language and literary history can be gauged from the plethora of presses and institutions that sprang up following the success of this combination, and were often headed by the College's professors. Thus, for example, John Gilchrist, who taught Hindi at the College, set up his Hindustani Press, charging the College for the funds required, J. Lavandier established his press in Bow Bazaar,[28] and Rammohan Roy founded his Unitarian Press. The College also played a signal role in conceptualizing what standard or official Bengali would look like. Under Carey's direction, the Bengali that was initially championed by the learned elites was the Sanskritized *sādhu bhāṣā*,[29] but later, thanks to Ram Ram Basu's influence, the standard form of Bengali became *ādālatī bhāṣā*[30] which was more colloquial, less pedantic, and Persianized.[31]

---

[25] As quoted in Kopf, "Fort William College and the Origins of the Bengal Renaissance," 298 (1961).
[26] Smith, *Life of William Carey* (1885), 12.
[27] Carrey's *A Dictionary of the Bengalee Language* is published in 1825 by the Mission Press, and in this he also builds on Nathaliel Brassey Halhed's 1778 tome *A Grammar of the Bengal Language* published in Hooghly.
[28] Part of European quarters in colonial Kolkata.
[29] Formal language.
[30] Court language.
[31] Kopf, 301; the transition is best explained by Ram Ram Basu's training as a Persian scholar, adept at the official uses of the language of the Mughal courts.

The story we get, then, is this: in order to train the Company's officials to be more effective, the College instructs them in the local language, which in this case is Bengali. However, once the College's professors embark on this project, they realize that there is no language that can be adequately taught; what exists is too fragmented, too poorly formed to lend itself to teaching, and it must be first codified into a language. In order to perform this act of collating and standardizing, the few extant manuscripts are collected and replaced with a modern, stable, and teachable print archive. Thus modern Bengali must first be formed, then textbooks teaching this language be written, and then this newly created language be taught such that the textbooks can be read more easily, and more texts be produced. There is a vicious circularity to this narrative that not only helps consolidate its authority but also gradually disperses other possible histories. Both British and Bengali linguists participate in this process as the College has in its employ not only Carey, but also scholars such as Ram Ram Basu, Mrityunjay Vidyalankar, and later Iswarchandra Vidyasagar,[32] who create some of the earliest Bengali language textbooks. One of the most significant products of this collaboration is Vidyasagar's Bengali primer *Barnaparicay* (1855) which is still in use to introduce children to Bengali.[33] This narrative of constructing Bengali from a seemingly chaotic mass of barely legible manuscripts is a powerful one, so much so that it is largely accepted by Europeans and Bengalis alike, and it forms the substratum of the cultural awakening—often referred to as the Bengal Renaissance—that takes place in nineteenth-century Bengal. The same individuals employed by the college, including Ram Ram Basu, Mrityunjay Vidyalankar, Vidyasagar, and those like Rammohan Roy who find themselves opposing the College while accepting the tenets of Enlightenment philosophy, go on to be leading figures of the Bengal Renaissance, weaving this story of modern Bengali into the fabric of literary-cultural history. Paradoxically, an institution whose original mission was to create effective civil servants and a press which sought to first and foremost publish texts to spread Christianity create the conditions for the transition of Bengali from the language of semi-literacy to that capable of producing high art.

As a product of the Enlightenment itself, the College and the Press fashion Bengali and its early print texts in the mold of European vernaculars such as

---

[32] The Bengalis were referred to as the *munshis*, a Persian word meaning writer or secretary, while the British were the professors.

[33] Vidyasagar's association with the College is yet another aspect of this story that deserves its own work. For more see Bhattacharya.

Introduction 13

English; the arrival of print modernity infuses into the vernacular the ideologies of the Enlightenment; and what lacked reason and method is now accorded with both. Modern Bengali as taught at the College has a dictionary, a comprehensive grammar, standardized spelling and font, and, in short, is cleansed of its past by the application of a rational, scientific approach. *Barnaparicay* is a perfect example of this Europeanization of Bengali. Even though it is published a year after the dissolution of the College, and bears the imprints of Vidyasagar's training in Sanskrit, the primer is based on the pedagogical principles of George Coombe, a prominent figure of the Scottish Enlightenment. Yet another primer, Akshay Kumar Dutta's *Cārupāth*, published in 1853, is similarly informed by Coombe and Scottish pedagogical practices.[34] Given this provenance, it becomes easier to understand why when the Bengali reader is later introduced to a genre as European as the novel, they are imagined to be reading like their Victorian counterpart, or why when Bankim writes *Durgeśnandinī*, he is soon after awarded the moniker "Scott of Bengal," asserting his likeness with the Scottish novelist, Walter Scott. If the language and its primers and textbooks are produced under the shadow of Enlightenment modernity, then it stands to reason that literature written in the same language will bear more than a passing resemblance with European genres. Thus readers who gain literacy through these textbooks and the methods embedded in them can naturally be expected to read within this ideological framework, or at least be more susceptible to it.[35] Purged of its past, Bengali is constructed as being born of British intervention—a lack of Mughal patronage and an uncomfortable relationship with Sanskrit led Bengali to appear as a product of British entrepreneurship. Nearly a century and a half later, when scholars revisit this period as an object of study, this story of modern Bengali leads to claims of a radical rupture between pre- and modern Bengali, and the need to perceive Bengali authors and readers as restricted to either appropriating or rejecting elements of European literary history, such as realism.[36] Thus

---

[34] The relationship between primers for children and Enlightenment philosophy is a profound one. Both *Barnaparicay* and *Cārupāth* imagine early childhood education in decidedly scientific and rational terms, and while this discussion is the subject of another work, it is worth noting the centrality of these primers in determining the form of modern Bengali language.

[35] This origin story also partly explains why cheap popular presses, also known as *battalā* presses, gain such a bad reputation during the nineteenth century. These presses, operating outside the ambit of the elite or the *bhadralōk* classes, are more aligned with folk aesthetic and literary traditions, and as such do not suffer from the compulsions of Enlightenment ideals. They offer a plausible counternarrative, and thus have to be actively rejected by both the *bhadralōk* and the British.

[36] Here I refer to scholars such as Sudipta Kaviraj, Tithi Bhattacharya, and Ulka Anjaria. I discuss this in greater detail with reference to Bankim in Chapter 3 of this work.

what is set in motion so as to create more effective administrators culminates in a unidirectional trajectory of Bengali literary history toward an inevitable comparison with mostly its British counterpart, and a sense of dreadful secondariness.

This is a difficult history to counter, not least because it is rendered invisible to the point where it becomes a part of the fabric of Bengali literary history. Yet what this weaving ignores are readers who consume texts for a variety of reasons without being mindful of mainstream narratives about a language's provenance. As one turns to the ephemeral act of reading, and to the relationship between readers and texts produced in nineteenth-century Bengal, it becomes evident that the form modern Bengali was to take was by no means predetermined by either the Company, the Crown, or the Bengali intelligentsia, and the latter's efforts produced at best one among many possible ways of conceptualizing this language. For example, there existed alongside Fort William College's version of Bengali, the more colloquial form of the language as used by Kaliprasanna Singha which freely mixed Persian and Arabic words with more Sanskritized ones. Readers of cheap *battalā* publications spoke and read a Bengali that was deemed vulgar by *bhadralōk* Bengali, but the condemnation did little to dent the popularity of *battalā* Bengali. A significant portion of these cheap presses catered to readers of *musalmānī bānglā* (Islamicized Bengali) which was yet another version of the language widely spoken by lower-class Muslims. The language of the *andarmahal* (lit. inner quarters of a house, the domain of women) found its way into prose and poetry alike, making frequent appearances in Bankim's and *bankimī* novels. As the following section shows, the language as envisioned by the College and the Press, and as embraced by the predominantly Hindu Bengali elite, was merely the language of a small section of the upper classes. Such a multitude of Bengalis leads one to believe that a variety of readers existed who paid little, if any, attention to the official linguistic efforts of the state. The vast majority of Bengalis were used to reading different versions of the language, and to see the former as anything more than a contender among many for the title of modern Bengali would be historically inaccurate at best and presentist at worst. Thus when one looks at practices of reading, modern Bengali is seen as developing under a patchwork of rubrics. Despite the concerted efforts of the College and the Press, neither the language nor its readers are under the singular aegis of European Enlightenment, and how Bengali readers read print texts—or indeed how authors produced these texts—demonstrate their allegiance to a variety of literary and aesthetic frameworks. In what follows, I look at the *battalā* book

Introduction   15

industry as one of many possible sites where these frameworks find expression
in cheap, popular publications, and examine how the mass production of print
works allows for a comfortable coexistence of reading practices that both predate
the arrival of print and are engendered by the technology.

Examining the role of *battalā* presses in fostering a variety of reading
practices is one way of understanding how there was no inevitable progression
toward European modernity in Bengali literary history; Bengalis across the
social spectrum read by mixing old and new genres, relying on the familiar to
make sense of the new, while using the latter to rethink their relationship to
the former.

III. Setting the Stage

It is impossible to tell the story of the Bengali reader without talking about
battalā. The vernacular presses of *battalā* have rightfully been the subject of
several book length studies,[37] so what I present here is neither comprehensive
nor exhaustive. Rather, I wish to look briefly at some of the more popular genres
of books published by these presses to understand what the average Bengali
reader chose to consume and, through that, begin to think about how they
read at the moment of the novel's inception and popularity. By the middle of
the nineteenth century, Bengali readers' primary source of print material was
neither the College and the Mission Press' affiliates, nor the various highbrow
presses run by the Bengali intelligentsia.[38] Instead, we find ourselves deep in
the heart of Kolkata's native town, in the area colloquially known as *battalā*
in the Chitpur-Ahiritolla neighborhood. In 1857, the majority of the forty-six
vernacular presses mentioned in Long's *Returns* are *battalā* presses, with this

---

[37] Goutam Bhadra's *Nyarā battalāye jāye k'bār* (2011), Sukumar Sen's *Battalār chāpā o chabi* (1984),
Sripantha's *Battalā* (1997), Anindita Ghosh's *Power in Print* (2006), and Adrish Biswas and Anil
Acharya's *Bāngālir battalā* (2013), to name only a few.

[38] Here I am thinking of presses such as Tatwabōdhinī founded by Debendranath Tagore, serving
as the mouthpiece of the Tatwabōdhinī Sabhā, or Jogendrachandra Basu's Bangabāsī press which
aimed at publishing conservative Hindu ideas, or the Sanskrit Press which was set up by Vidyasagar
which printed popular children's texts such as *Barnaparicay* by Vidyasagar himself, and Madan
Mohan Tarkalankar's *Śiśu śikshā* (1849). These presses sought to reform both the Bengali reader
and the language by cultivating more refined religious, aesthetic, and political tastes through
their publications. The products of these presses were journals such as Bankim's *Bangadarśan* and
Reazuddin Ahmad's *Islām Pracārak* which positioned themselves as clear antagonists of the *battalā*
publications, and indeed sought to rescue the Bengali reader from what they perceived to be the ill
influences of cheap mass publishing.

16 *The Novel in Nineteenth-Century Bengal*

number going up to over seventy by the time we come to the 1875 *Bengal Library Quarterly Report*.[39] *Battalā* printer-publishers[40] like Ashutosh Ghosal running the Victoria Press or Gopalchandra De of Puran Prakash Press published plays, medical treatises, mythological stories, society scandals, and books in *musalmānī bānglā*, copies of which they sold in the thousands.[41]

While the presses themselves were concentrated in Kolkata's northern reaches, the book trade extended to all over Bengal as publishers established well-developed networks to both spread word of and distribute their wares. There were few formal shops at this time as most *battalā* publishers ran their business out of their homes. They printed their address, along with the name of the press, on the book's cover or title page, thus informing readers where to go if they wish to buy a copy. Readers living far from the city could also rely on the itinerant bookseller who ferried books from the city to the various *muffasils*, allowing rural Bengal regular access to print texts.[42] Following the Postal Act of 1854 which introduced uniform postal rates in most parts of British India such that postage was determined by the weight of the package alone, regardless of the distance the package had to travel, these readers could also order books via mail. *Battalā* booksellers were some of the first to take advantage of these postal reforms when they included postal rates alongside advertisements for available titles in the texts they publish. The books themselves were priced such that Bengalis across social strata could afford to buy them.[43] Some of these books, notably editions of "*Vidyāsundar*," were produced as collector's items with full page lithographic illustrations, however more often than not, as in the case of satires, *battalā* publications tended to be cheaply produced on poor-quality paper, intended to be read rather than displayed.

---

[39] The Press and Registration of Books Act of 1867 required that a copy of every print title published in British India be submitted to the India Office. Every quarter, local newspapers published a list of all titles from the region, which came to be known as the Quarterly Lists. One such list compiled by the Bengal Library—and published in the *Calcutta Gazette*—covers the quarter ending in March 1875, and this is referred to as the *Bengal Library Quarterly Report*.

[40] The two roles frequently merge from the middle of the nineteenth century onwards.

[41] *Quarterly Reports*, 6.

[42] There prevalence was such that they even find special mention in Bankim's essay "A Popular Literature for Bengal," in which he ascribes to them the task of waking the Bengali reader from his [sic] somnolence.

[43] For comparison, 1 rupee could buy 31.65 *seer* (one *seer* is approximately equal to three pounds or one and a half kilos) of rice in Bengal in 1861, and the average income of the lower and middle classes (including agricultural and non-agricultural laborers, professionals, and artisans) ranged between Rs. 69.92 and 109.68 per annum in 1873 (Kabir, "Wages and Cost," 22). *Battalā* books, when the publisher retained the copyright, usually cost 1 or 2 annas on average (Long, *Descriptive Catalogue, Returns*). While a few annas were a substantial amount, it was well within the budget of the average Bengali.

Introduction   17

The *battalā* industry, although dominated by, was not exclusively Hindu; there were a number of Muslim presses whose numbers increased as the century progressed. Of these, ones that regularly published in Bengali were Mohammad Derasulla's Mohammadi Press and Rahmani Press (the latter catalogued by Long).[44] Alongside them, Hindu presses also published *musalmānī bānglā*, Arabic, Persian, and occasionally Urdu texts. The majority of the works, however, were published in Bengali, although the form of the language ranged from the colloquial (satires, sketches) to the highly Sanskritized (the Hindu epics), and *musalmānī bānglā* as an amalgamation of Bengali, Persian, Arabic, and Urdu. Both Hindu and Muslim presses followed in the footsteps of early-nineteenth-century print-entrepreneurs such as Gangakishore Bhattacharya and Bhabanicharan Bandopadhyay, as they capitalized on pre-print tastes while also catering to the novelty of print.[45] Thus, for example, the consistent popularity of almanacs in both Long's *Returns* and the *Quarterly Reports* attests to the ease with which this pre-print genre was appropriated by the new medium. Bengalis, already accustomed to handwritten almanacs in the form of *punthis*, now had the opportunity of buying a copy for themselves for as little as one and a half annas, and in far more compact and portable a form.[46] These almanacs often functioned as nineteenth-century versions of yellow pages—they contained lists of auspicious dates, names, and addresses of government officials, share prices, and shipping lists, to name only a few things. Alongside almanacs, *battalā* also made brisk trade in versions of *Rāmāyana* and *Mahābhārat*, various *śāstras*, *paurānik kāhinī*,[47] and *mangal kābyas*[48] such as Bharatchandra's *Annadāmangal* (1752–3). Varied as they were, what these genres had in common was the reader's familiarity with them in the manuscript or *punthi* form, and a desire to see the recognizable recast in the more affordable, and novel, print medium. *Annadāmangal*, and in particular the section titled "*Vidyāsundar*," was the first to transition from the handwritten *punthi* into print when Gangakishore published

---

[44] Sen, *Battalār chāpā o chabi*, 62. *Battalā* had its counterpart in Dhaka's *ketāb patti* (book market) in the Chakbazar neighborhood, and like the Kolkata-based publishers, *ketāb patti* too specialized in *musalmānī punthis*. Sripantha's brief but illuminating section on *ketāb patti* in his book *Battalā* is a good starting place for scholars of nineteenth-century Dhaka's book industry.

[45] See Chapter 1 for a detailed discussion of Gangakishore and Bhabanicharan, and their role in socializing the print book.

[46] Medium of currency, with 16 annas making up 1 rupee. Even almanacs that cost double, such as Sideshwur Ghose's *Almanac* sold 9,000 copies in 1855 (*Descriptive Catalogue*, 62).

[47] Tales from the *puranas*.

[48] Early modern Bengali religious poems celebrating the indigenous deities of rural Bengal, such as Manasa, Chandi, and Dharmathakur, and their assimilation into Vedic mythology.

18   *The Novel in Nineteenth-Century Bengal*

a version of the text in 1816. From here on, *"Vidyāsundar"* remained one of the most profitable text published by *battalā* presses till the end of the nineteenth century, documenting how both producers and consumers of Bengali print literature relied on texts and practices of reading that existed long before print modernity.[49] During the second half of the nineteenth century, Islamic legends, advice manuals, and tales of the Prophet were just as popular as the Hindu texts. The *qissās* and *dāstāns* of the Perso-Arabic tradition made their way into print as *battalā* presses published multiple versions of *Yusuf-Zuleikhā, Dāstān-e-āmir Hāmzāh*, or the *Adventures of Amir Hamzah, Qissā-e Gul-e bakavali*, and *Qissā-e Hātim Tāi*. Alongside this, we find tales from the Battle of Karbala printed in both prose and verse forms.[50] Unlike the Hindu texts, the majority of the Islamic works retained the form of the *punthi* in print till the end of the nineteenth century. In this they were unique among *battalā* texts as the print medium merely swapped the handwritten for the machine printed without altering the physical form of these texts.[51]

While quasi-religious texts with a porous boundary between print and manuscript were the mainstay of the *battalā* book industry, works that were exclusive to print also did good business. The most popular of these were satires or *prahaśan* which became an outlet for the working classes to condemn what they saw as the moral laxity of the more respectable *bhadralōk* or middle class.[52] So popular were these satires that in the twenty years between Long's *Returns* and the *Quarterly Report*, the genre goes from being non-existent to having between 1,000 and 2,000 copies published every quarter.[53] Produced on cheap, flimsy paper bound in yellow or pink covers, these satires appealed to

---

[49] Sukumar Sen captures the popularity of Bharatchandra's work in *Battalār chapa o chobi*, noting how *"Vidyāsundar"* is the first illustrated text published by the *battalā* presses, and it continues to accumulate more illustrations through the course of the nineteenth century (30–5).

[50] These texts are discussed in detail in chapter where I look at them in light of the first Islamic Bengali novel, Mir Mosharraf Hossain's *Biṣād Sindhu*.

[51] For an account of *punthis* in Islamic literature see Abdul Khaer Shaik's *"Musalmani" Punthi Sāhitya* (2016); Epsita Halder's "Reading the 'Cheapness' of Cheap Prints: Karbala Narrative in the Early Print Culture" (2015) provides a compelling discussion of the relationship between a rise in Islamic socio-religious reform and the prevalence of Islamic religious texts during the second half of the nineteenth century.

[52] As Anindita Ghosh and Tithi Bhattacharya rightly point out, however, class here functions not as an economic category but rather a moral one—what the satires attack is the very foundation of gentility from which *bhadralōk* such as Bankim and Michael Madhusudan Dutt criticize the common as obscene. The villain in these satires is the gentleman or woman who is invested in sensual pleasures beneath the veneer of respectability, and it is the genre's task to unmask the elite and punish them for their moral and physical debauchery. I discuss this both later in the Introduction and in Chapter 1.

[53] Ghosh, *Power in Print*, 119.

Introduction 19

the urban and rural reader alike in their easy-to-read, portable form. As books, their production value stood in contrast to that of collectibles such as a copy of Krittibas' *Rāmāyana* or an illustrated edition of "*Vidyāsundar*"; the satires were akin to ephemera, meant to be read and not preserved. As in form so also in content, most *prahaśan* had no literary pretensions. They were formulaic, usually telling the story of simple folk unmasking the moral and physical debauchery of the *bhadralōk* or genteel class with the latter getting justly punished and the former receiving praise for their virtuous conduct. Authors, named and anonymous, paid little attention to language, choosing provocation and sensationalism over grammar and polish. Their frequent use of vulgarity and insults not only sent the message that the morally virtuous masses were always watching their betters, but just as importantly, used Bengali outside the confines of elite- and middle-class respectability. The popularity enjoyed by *battalā* satires elicited condemnation from both colonial and Bengali elites alike who saw these texts as a sign of the lower class's vulgar tastes and an impediment in Bengali literature's development, but this disapproval did little to dent the rate at which the genre was produced and consumed.[54]

A rung below satires were the *pathapustak* or the *hetochorā*, literally translated as "street books" and "low rhymes," respectively. As their names suggest, these were products aimed at entertaining the workaday reader who lacked the pedigree of elite- or even middle-class tastes. These readers, accustomed to a diet of mostly oral folk genres, and often newly urbanized in search of a livelihood, sought in the *pathapustak* a representation of their points of view. Titles such as "*Ekei bale pole*" ("Now that's what I call a bridge," referring to a floating bridge in Howrah, 1874), "*Bāhabā cōddō āiyin*" ("Kudos to the fourteen laws," referring to the 1867 Contagious Diseases Act which aimed at curbing prostitution), or "*Drain-er pāncālī*" ("Song of the drain," 1874) reveal the concerns of the common person navigating the streets of Kolkata. Like the satires, *pathapustaks*, too, found a ready market not only because issues spoke to topical concerns, but also because publishers managed to keep prices competitive, often by compromising on the quality of paper and ink, and by paying compositors the lowest possible wages.[55]

---

[54] In this, the elites call to mind Wilkie Collins' essay "The Unknown Public" (1858) in which Collins bemoans the popularity of the penny dreadfuls in corrupting readerly tastes. The relationship of these satires to print is similar to that shared by the penny dreadfuls in that they are both designed for mass consumption, cheaply produced, and perceived to be vulgar in content. However, *battalā* satires are far more concentrated in their subject matter, and mostly stick to social commentary.

[55] Sripantha's resource-rich and lyrical books, *Battalā* (1997) and *Jakhan chāpākhānā elō* (1977) give us an insight into the varied registers of print in nineteenth-century Bengal.

20   *The Novel in Nineteenth-Century Bengal*

The success of these satires and of the pre-print religious texts is a testament to the Bengali reader's ability—and desire—to read under the rubric of various reading practices. Merely glancing at the number of copies published and the extensive list of titles would suggest a far greater rate of literacy in nineteenth-century Bengal than was the reality. If one is to reconcile contemporary data about the low rates of literacy[56] with the flourishing *battalā* book market, one has to take into account the variety of way in which Bengalis read, and how the act of reading cannot be imagined solely as the individual silently consuming a printed book. Thus, while a genre exclusive to print, such as the satire, does roaring business, so does a genre such as the *pāncālī* which depends largely on a single reader performing the text out loud to a group of listeners. Often, a text is positioned within conflicting practices of reading, as in the case of a satire such as "*Nobhel nāyikā*" in which the anonymous satirist depicts the heroine Rukmini as both reading a novel silently and reading it collectively with her friends as they perform songs from their favorite novels. *Battalā* texts are collectively able to satisfy the demands of print and oral literate readers, and also serve as a bridge between the two groups. Thus, for example, readers new to print literacy can recognize in the conversational nature of the satires clear references to folk forms such as *kabi* performances and *jātrā*,[57] and their appreciation of the jokes is enhanced by the colloquial language. Minimal plots would also be attractive for those readers who would approach print in much the same way they did pre-print manuscripts—as texts to be read out loud to a community of listeners.[58] For others, the act of reading would be secondary to the actual ownership of a book, and for them *battalā* had beautifully illustrated copies of sacred and secular texts.[59] Those wishing to fully embrace print modernity could read silently, cramming in a newly released satire during a busy workday or reading Vidya and Sundar's

---

[56] Bankim's essay "*Bānglār pāthak parānō brata*" (1880), for example, estimates 5 percent Bengalis to be literate (434). The 1881 Census records 48 out of 1,000 to be literate, and further breaks down the number as 90 literate males for every 1,000, and 4 literate females for every 1,000. The 1891 Census records a marginal rise at 56 literate individuals for every 1,000, with 104 literate males and 5 literate females for every 1,000 of each category. Bearing in mind that these are British India-wide numbers, and that the Bengal Presidency was likely to have a higher literacy rate given that it included the capital, Kolkata, still leaves us with a literacy rate of between 4.8 and 5.6 percent (*Census of India 1881*, IOR/V/15/18-32, British Library, *General Report on the Census of India 1891*, chapter 6).

[57] A form of popular folk theater from Bengal.

[58] For more on this form of reading see my discussion of Rassundari in the Conclusion.

[59] Bhabanicharan Bhattacharya's *Kalikātā kamalālay* (1823) satirizes this very species of urban babu. See Chapter 1.

Introduction   21

love story in the privacy of her/his home.[60] Add to this the various available registers of Bengali, and what emerges is a network of reading practices whose nodal point is the *battalā* book market.

IV. The Pitfalls of Reading

If the *battalā* helped democratize reading by bringing texts to the everyday Bengali reader, it also made visible the consequences of such access. As the largest book market in the region, *battalā* provides us with a window into what the nineteenth-century Bengali reader was reading, and into some of the practices of reading performed by this reader. However, it also highlights the moral consequences of bringing print to the masses, and the social cost of reading novels. The market puts into relief the following questions—what happens when everyday individuals are not only taught to read, but also given the ability to buy and consume texts? If we take the sale of Bengali language textbooks and primers as our index, it becomes apparent that in terms of supply and demand, *battalā* presses emphatically said yes to teaching the masses how to read. The material realities of this market—an abundance of textbooks, Bengali language primers, easy-to-read stories, and moral stories for children—demonstrate that both adult and children started to learn Bengali formally from the middle of the nineteenth century onwards. For example, while there was only one primer published between 1835 and 1840,[61] over 120 new and 100 reprinted textbooks and primers were published between 1870 and 1880. During this golden age of primers, 1880 was especially productive with fifty new and reprinted textbooks being published in that year alone.[62] Even though most of these books were originally published either by the Calcutta School Book Society[63] sponsored by the Government, or by highbrow vernacular presses such as Vidyasagar's

---

[60] The prevalence of this becomes apparent against the backdrop of the Bengali intelligentsia's crusade against obscene literature. Bankim takes the lead in lambasting the Bengali reader for her/his love for vulgar literature, and Bharatchandra and Iswar Gupta are presented as metonymic of this tendency. Others such as Chandranath Basu and Akshay Dutta echo Bankim in calling for a purging of Bengali literature of its fascination with the obscene.

[61] *Banga barnamālā* published in 1835 from Tamohar Press in Serampore for 1 anna.

[62] Ashish Khastagir, *Bānglā primer sangraha (1816–1855)*, 14, 16–17 (2000).

[63] Of the numerous textbooks and primers published by the Calcutta School Book Society, the notable Bengali language one is titled *Barnamālā*, published in two volumes between 1853 and 1854.

Sanskrit Press[64] and the Tatwaboōdhinī Press,[65] the *battalā* presses also did quick business by bringing out newer editions of existing titles.[66] As with most other *battalā* wares, textbooks, too, were priced such that they were an attractive option for various classes of buyers. The ninety-page *Śiśubōdhak*, published in Ahiritola by N.L. Shil's press, for example, cost one anna and two pais,[67] and its popularity meant that at least two editions were printed annually.[68] It contained, like many other primers of the period, an amalgamation of introduction to the Bengali and English alphabets, grammar rules, spelling, letter and receipt writing manuals, and basic mathematics. Similarly, Bhubanchandra Basak's Gyanratnākar Press republished two volumes of *Śiśusebadhi Barnamālā* in 1855, building on the success of the primer which is originally designed to be a series of primers and readers for children enrolled in Hindu College's *pāthśālā*.[69]

Embedded in these numbers is a sense of social aspiration. With the English Education Act of 1835, Persian was permanently replaced by English as the language of commerce, administration, and social mobility. However, the Act's requirement that government funds be directed away from vernacular education was challenged by both colonial and Bengali education reformers. As a practical response to the Education Act, more schools were established in Bengal to teach the language, and textbooks and primers were written to aid such a pedagogical approach.[70] At a more abstract level, this shift toward Bengali caused a surge in the number of people who now wanted to, or found it socially or professionally advantageous to, learn Bengali. Thanks to the print market's investment in textbooks—while their titles usually contain a reference to *śiśu* or child, they were used in children and adult education alike—Bengalis from various walks of life could now afford to formally learn the language. This not only provides us with an important caveat to the claim that the *battalā* presses mostly produced lowbrow and vulgar texts, but more importantly creates a more

---

[64] *Barnaparicay* is published from this press in 1855.

[65] This press brings out two volumes of a primer also named *Barnamālā*, the first in 1840 and the second in 1844. Akshaykumar Dutt was instrumental in composing both volumes.

[66] Occasionally this meant flouting the copyright Act of 1857 which provided protection to books published in British India.

[67] One pai being a quarter of an anna.

[68] Sripantha, *Battalā*, 21–2.

[69] Ashish Khastagir, *Bānglā primer sangraha (1816–1855)*, 14.

[70] I provide here only the briefest of sketches of a complex problem as I take up the question at length in Chapter 1. There, I approach the problem of vernacular education to create what I call a reading map of Bengal, identifying the various stakeholders in debates around reading and the process of democratizing the act.

Introduction 23

complete image of the world into which the Bengali novel makes an entrance.[71] People who traditionally had little to no means of becoming literate owing to their caste, financial position, gender, or age now potentially had access to at least basic literacy with the help of *battalā* publications.

This access, however, had moral ramifications. Most social commentators, from the elite and the working classes alike, agreed that with the expansion of the print market, there were now fewer means of controlling who had access to what kinds of texts. The novel in particular drew the ire of these conversations as it was perceived to be one of the most visible threats to the moral purity of Bengali women. With calls for women's education gaining ground, the reality that there were literate women choosing to read novels for pleasure created a moral panic among Bengalis. As I discuss elsewhere in this book, prose was a relative newcomer to the history of Bengali literature, with some of the first prose length narratives being written only at the start of the nineteenth century.[72] The early days of Bengali prose saw experiments in genres such as the *charit* or life narratives with Ramram Basu's *Pratāpādityacaritra* (1801) chronicling the life of Raja Pratapaditya of Jessore, and Rajiblochan Mukhopadhyay's *Mahārāj Kriśnacandra Rāyasya Caritram* (*The Life of Maharaja Krishnachandra Ray*, 1805). Iswarchandra Vidyasagar's *Caritābali* (*Collection of Lives*, 1856) redirected *carit* as a tool for children's education, while Nilmani Basak's *Nabanāri nay nārir jības carit* (*Lives of Nine Women*, 1852) historicized the lives of nine exemplary women, including Sita, Draupadi, and Ahalyabai. Hagiographic texts such as *Caitanya bhagabat* (*The Life of Chaitanya*, 1535) reenter circulation via the print medium, adding to the growing body of Bengali prose writing.[73] Bankim himself composes one of the more famous hagiographic texts of the nineteenth

---

[71] This argument is so much a part of the discourse surrounding Bengali literature and the print industry that to list all its proponents would create several book length studies. Bankim and his coterie of litterateurs, for example, positioned their work, both implicitly and explicitly, against such an understanding of the divide between *battalā* and "good" literature.

[72] What follows in this brief paragraph is meant to provide only the briefest of glimpses into the history and lineage of modern Bengali prose. For more on this see Sukumar Sen's chapter on Bengali prose in his masterful *Bānglā sāhityer itihās* (*The History of Bengali Literature*, 1965), Sripantha's *Battalā*, Priya Joshi's *In Another Country*, Tithi Bhattacharya's *Sentinels of Culture* (2005), Supriya Chaudhuri's "Beginnings: Rajmohan's Wife and the Novel in India" (2015), and Chandrani Chatterjee's *Translation Reconsidered* (2010). Where possible, I have also indicated further titles to consider with reference to particular generic and social concerns. I have not included references to proto-novelistic texts such as Peary Chand Mitra's *Ālāler gharer dulāl* (*The Spoilt Son*, 1857), or later historical fiction such as historical tales such as Bhudeb Mukhopadhyay's *Swapnalabdha bhāratbarśer itihās* (*The History of India as Received in a Dream*, 1895) since I examine them elsewhere in this book.

[73] This text and the role it plays in how women read are the subject of the Conclusion. There I look at *Caitanya bhagabat* against the backdrop of Rassundari Debi's autobiography.

century—*Kriśna caritra* (*The Life of Krishna*, 1886)—seeking to historicize Krishna so as to blur the division between myth and reality in Hinduism.[74] The didactic impetus of the *carit* is accentuated in the various advice manuals that become increasingly popular throughout the nineteenth century. Ramram Basu's *Lipimālā* (*Collection of Letters*, 1802), Nazir Ahmad's *Mirat-al-arus* (*The Mirror of the Bride*, 1869), Ashraf Ali Thanawi's *Bihisti zewar* (*Heavenly Ornaments*, 1905), Benimadhav Shil's "*grihinir guide*" in his *panjikās* or almanacs all instructed nineteenth-century Bengali readers on different aspects of their lives from letter writing, to running a home, to being pious.[75] The parodic, too, added to the development of Bengali prose in the form of the *naksās*. *Naksās* or sketches became popular as Kolkata developed a pronounced urban identity, and the genre became a ready tool for articulating social critique in a comic or parodic manner. Bhabanicharan Bandopadhyay inaugurates the genre with *Kalikātā kamalālay* (1823), followed by *Nababābu bilās* (1825), *Duti bilās* (1825), and finally *Nababibi bilās* (1831). In each of these, he pokes fun at the *bābu* and *bibi*—the newly urbanized gentleman and woman—and their extravagant and capricious lifestyle. *Hutom pyancār naksā* (*Sketches by Hutom the Owl*) by Kaliprasanna Singha documents life in the city and its strange quirks, and is the next important milestone in the history of *naksās*. While neither Bhabanicharan nor Kaliprasanna are *battalā* authors, the popularity of their books prompts an array of *naksās* for the masses. Sripantha notes that even though most of these titles have not been discovered by scholars, we still know of works such as Kshetramohan Ghosh's *Kākbhuśundir kāhinī* (1865) and Narayan Chattaraj Gunanidhi's *Kalikutuhal* (1856) that captured readers' imaginations as *battalā* took the lead in publishing *naksās*.[76]

For a variety of reasons, none of these genres elicited the same cautionary response as the novel. If women were encouraged to read, they were generally guided toward the hagiographic and didactic as a means of bettering themselves, while satires and *naksās* were generally thought to be too lowbrow for women to consume with any consistency.[77] The image of the woman reading novels in

---

[74] For more on the *carit*, see Nandini Bhattacharya's "Ecce Homo—Behold the Human! Reading Life Narratives in Times of Colonial Modernity" (2020) and Ipsita Chanda's *Tracing Charit as a Genre: An Exploration in Comparative Literature Methodology* (2003).

[75] For more on Nazir Ahmad and al Thanawi, see Chapter 4.

[76] Sripantha, *Battalā*, 25.

[77] Sumanta Banerjee's *The Parlour and the Streets* (2018) and Anindita Ghosh's *Power in Print* provide an insightful reading of the presence of the lowbrow and the vulgar in intimate domestic spaces.

Introduction 25

the seclusion of her own room, however, became a staple of caricatures and condemnations for *battalā* and *bhadralōk* publications. Radhabinod Halder's "*Pās karā māg*" ("Educated Woman," 1902), for example, narrates the tragedy of Kironshoshi who destroys her life after reading too many novels and desiring a novelized life. In a slightly different take, Bireshwar Pare's *Adbhut swapna bā strī purusher dwanda* (*A Strange Dream or a Battle between the Sexes*, 1888) positions the female reader as gullible enough to take everything she reads too literally thus causing her to lose her sense of marital, and by induction social, propriety. The novel's popularity even leads to the establishment of anti-novels as a category by themselves in which the author uses the form of the novel to critique the act of reading them. Anti-novels such as Jogindrachandra Basu's *Model bhaginī* (*Model Sister*, 1886–7) and *Cinibās caritāmrita* (1886) and Indranath Bandopadhyay's *Kalpataru* (1874) all set their sights on the educated Bramho woman, parodying her for her liberal values and depraved tastes in literature. In each of these cases, the reader is assumed to read in a multitude of ways—literally, metaphorically, closely, and broadly—but always, badly, either because they read things that are not meant for them, or the things they read are in themselves flawed.

V. Reading Practice or How to Read a Novel

Few readers in nineteenth-century Bengal actively record their own reading practices, leaving the scholar with the unenviable task of culling such records from policy documents, letters, reviews, subscription lists of periodicals, and the occasional memoir, to complement the evidence to be found in the novels themselves. What emerges are traces left by our *dramatis personae*—the novelists, their readers, publishers, and reviewers—as they utilize available structural and aesthetic frameworks to comprehend *what* the Bengali novel is at its moment of inception. Spanning the first four decades of this genre's life, from the 1860s to the 1890s, this book theorizes this complex network as reading practice. In discussions from the period, reading is seen as the relationship between the author and the reader, with the latter being either malleable and open to ideological instruction from the former,[78] or as possessing radical agency in choosing how

---

[78] This is a fairly common position in nineteenth-century Bengal espoused by Bankim and a number of his most influential reviewers, including Purnachandra Chattopadhyay and Chandranath Basu, all of whom wish to educate the reader into correct ways of reading novels; when reading the plays of Harachandra Ghosh such as *Bhānumati Cittabilās* (1853) and *Cārumukhcittaharā* (1864), one

they read.[79] Contemporary scholarship on nineteenth-century readers and on book history—both in the context of Bengal and Britain—accords the reader a more participatory role, suggesting that they read in ways hardly expected by authors and reviewers. However, even here reading is largely construed as the relationship between the author and the reader, with the former establishing expectations which are followed, disregarded, and otherwise engaged with by the latter.[80] My point here is not to suggest ideological or theoretical similarities between theorists of reading from the nineteenth century, and those theorizing reading in the nineteenth century from the vantage point of late twentieth and early twenty-first centuries. Rather, I wish to draw attention to the persistence of the idea that reading as an act consists of either the reader being told how to read, or the reader exerting agency in choosing how they read, or a combination of these two positions.

Against this, I contend that in nineteenth-century Bengal reading as a practice is the holding in tension both these possibilities in a constellation of readers, authors, reviewers, printers, publishers, distributors, policymakers, and

---

notices a similar impulse as the playwright Indianizes Shakespeare in an effort to inculcate in the reader a love for Shakespeare, and good literature, even if they do not know English. Examples of individuals adopting the same position in eighteenth- and nineteenth-century Britain are too numerous to cite in full, but notable among them are Joseph Addison and Richard Steele's discussions around the need to cultivate readerly taste, William Makepeace Thackeray's depiction of bad readers, and George Eliot's polemics on "silly novels."

[79] This is frequently presented in terms of bad readers willfully ignoring authorial dictates. Discussions of readers choosing to read how they will against the better judgment of the author abound in both Bengal and Britain, and more often than not, these conversations are to be found in the same works as mentioned in the previous footnote. Bankim, for example, laments the presence of bad readers who fail to appreciate good literature because they read good work expecting it to provide the same pleasure as vulgar or obscene literature. Similarly, Wilkie Collins berates the unknown reading public for not only preferring the vulgar penny dreadfuls, but worse still, for bringing those same standards into their reading of good literature.

[80] Here I refer to recent scholarship on literary publics in South Asia, and in particular in India, such as Jennifer Dubrow's *Cosmopolitan Dreams* and Maryam Wasif Khan's *Who Is a Muslim* (2021). While both Dubrow and Khan examine Urdu literary culture and the making of a Muslim identity, their work is applicable to print culture in India as a whole in understanding reading as participatory. As Dubrow in particular discusses, the exchange of letters between authors and readers demonstrates a level of intimacy and responsiveness on the part of both parties. The reality of readerly participation in shaping literary genres is equally well documented in the field of book history. For example, Anindita Ghosh's *Power in Print* is a masterful study of *battalā* presses soliciting readers' interest in deciding which texts are made more visible, while *Print Areas* (2004), one of the first volumes on book history in South Asia, edited by Abhijit Gupta and Swapan K. Chakravorty, documents how readers' desires dictate the trajectory of novels in India during the nineteenth century. Nicholas Dames' *The Physiology of the Novel* (2007) and Leah Price's *What We Talk about When We Talk about Books* (2019) both underline just how prevalent physiological and distracted reading is in nineteenth-century Britain. Regardless of gender, class, or social aspirations, Victorian readers read in ways that baffled the arbiters of taste and culture, and they frequently displayed the tendency to read not just bad literature but to read all literature badly.

Introduction 27

available literary and aesthetic structures. Each position limits the other such that reading occurs in the flux between them, and this reading practice is, at its core, a pragmatic approach to a newly emerging genre. As a practice, it is not determined by any one or two players in the book market[81]; its contours become visible only when it is seen as both shaping and being shaped by the market as a whole. The presence of a book and a reader implies an interpretive community and, in the instance of the Bengali novel, included in this community are the readers, authors, reviewers, publishers, distributors, and all those involved in the book trade in nineteenth-century Bengal, across social, religious, and linguistic strata. The novel encounters these individuals and institutions, and each of these encounters separately and collectively creates what it means to read the genre. The Bengali novel is, after all, something entirely new, and everyone involved in reading it uses what tools they have to hand, and by looking at which tools are chosen and which not, one can get a sense of the practice of reading novels.

However, the concept of reading being a practice in which the reader and all those around them have to choose aesthetic tools is absent in all scholarship surrounding the early Bengali novel reader, be that nineteenth-century or contemporary discussions. This is caused in great part by the logic of comparison whereby novel or literary reading is seen as a transmittable act, capable of being learned and performed by any reader. While Bengali novelists are seen as experimenting with form to suit the genre to their particular context, their readers are assumed to be reading much like their Victorian counterparts. The act of reading novels is never under discussion because reading is seen as simply a method of decoding the language on the page; thus for most interested parties, *what* one reads comes to be of far more importance than *how* one reads. Addressing this omission is not merely quibbling with academic literary history. It is an attempt at restoring those alternate ways of reading and the life worlds associated with them which are displaced by the assumption that reading has a singular definition. This definition grounds reading in Enlightenment rationality; it presupposes this practice to be *the* practice of reading. By reorienting ourselves to the possibility that there exist multiple, often competing and mutually unintelligible, practices of reading at any given moment in history, we can approach readers and their

---

[81] I refer to the practice of reading as occurring within a book market or a trade to include all aspects of book production, consumption, and distribution. The idea of a market also highlights the nature of the book as a commodity with exchange and use values, generating actual monetary profits, and this itself is a reason why every entity involved in the book industry is simultaneously involved in producing the practice of reading novels in nineteenth-century Bengal.

practices on their own terms, without necessarily wishing to confine them within the bounds of a practice that foregrounds critical thinking.

In thus taking reading as the site of investigation, I draw on work of scholars such as Michael Allan and Sarah Brouillette for whom the act of reading in particular ways is indexical of the literary and its material and cultural conditions of production. Brouillette, for example, asks what kind of a reader scholars of world literature have in mind when they assert literature's power to counter world-hegemonic forces, thereby shifting the optic from the literary as a seemingly transparent category to practices of reading that challenge such claims to transparency. Even though her subject is the status of the literary as reflected in the relationship between the UNESCO and world literature in the second half of the twentieth century, her approach allows us to give a more robust shape to the concept of reading practice. Referring particularly to the work of the Warwick Research Collective (WReC) and to Pheng Cheah's *What Is a World* (2016), Brouillette notes that for both—and they are clearly emblematic of a larger group in her argument—a celebration "of a critical world-literary mode impl[ies] that literature reaches a substantial audience of uninitiated readers who need to learn what writers want to teach them."[82] Literature's power, for WReC and Cheah,[83] relies on literary reading as an unquestionable good and as a skill that can be learned and practiced by all so as to successfully challenge the power of global capital. I ask along with Brouillette, "To whom is literature's countering force relevant? To what audience of literary readers does it speak?"[84], as I marvel at the longevity of the assumption that literary reading, as a universally humanizing act, is available to and performed by all in the same fashion, regardless of context. That the assumptions about literary reading are located in the contemporary Global South furthers my claim that readers from vast swathes of the world were and continue to be seen as imitators of reading practices originating in the Global North. Despite the celebration of texts featuring "multiple narrative temporalities, disjunctive and dueling worldviews, and irrealisms,"[85] practices of reading native to where these texts come from continue to be almost wholly ignored by academics and market forces alike.

---

[82] Brouillette, *UNESCO*, 3 (2019).

[83] While WReC and Cheah would not see themselves as belonging to the same camp, Brouillette's argument nonetheless is effective because she critiques both as exemplifying the tendency in scholars of world literature to see literature as a political force in and of itself.

[84] Brouillette, *UNESCO*, 3.

[85] Brouillette, *UNESCO*, 3.

Introduction   29

If Brouillette's work affords one way to resist invisibilizing readers and their practices by looking at the intimate relationship between changes in the UNESCO's policy and global economic trends, then Allan invites us to investigate colonial Egypt as another instance where the specificity of the act of reading is replaced by the universalizing tendencies of literary reading. Continuing to work within the frame of world literature, Allan asks what kind of reading practice is "necessary for a text to be recognized as an object of literary analysis" in a context where memorization gives way to analysis, and the former "ceases to be understood as literacy."[86] He uses a range of texts, including the Rosetta Stone, Arabic literary history, and Naguib Mahfouz's *Palace of Desire* (1957), to demonstrate the encroachment of a practice of reading founded on Enlightenment reason in nineteenth- and early-twentieth-century Egypt. To learn to read comes to mean learning to read critically, and this act further implies that the reader has cultivated a particular rational sensibility. What this means in the context of colonial Egypt—and I would argue in the context of colonial Bengal as well—is a rejection of existing reading practices; these can now be conveniently indexed as backward, ignorant, and premodern because they are not founded on critical thinking. The reader thus educated in identifying and consuming the literary thus becomes a confidant participant in modernizing their own culture and aesthetic traditions. I echo Allan's concern that institutionalizing literary or critical reading blots out alternative, preexisting forms of reading leading to the false—but deeply entrenched—perception that reading is the neutral medium that any reader can and should learn so that everyone has the same access to texts, regardless of their particular form of situatedness.

In order to counter the hegemony of literary reading, I turn to the reader sitting with the novel, and ask of this scene, what are the elements that have gone into its production? Who is sitting alongside the reader? In what linguistic and aesthetic traditions is the latter literate? How do those traditions construe meaning, and how did the reader come by this literacy? Who wrote the book, and which press printed in? How did this book reach the reader, and how does the reader come to know of its existence? It is only when one explodes reading through a plethora of questions about production, consumption, and distribution that the concept of a reading practice begins to emerge. This fairly simple scene conceals within it all the above questions whose responses may not

---

[86] Allan, *In the Shadow of World Literature*, 7 (2016).

30   *The Novel in Nineteenth-Century Bengal*

always be in agreement with each other, and no single individual or institution is at the heart of this practice. What emerges as reading practice, then, is relational, with no singular key that can unlock its meaning, and the task of the scholar is to engage with these relationships on their own terms. The process is necessarily messy and jagged, too specific in places while tending toward generalizations in others, but it is only when one grapples with this that the abstract nature of reading practice becomes concrete.

The questions animating this theory of reading rest on the assumption that the practice of reading cannot be affixed to any one of the various poles offered by existing discussions of reading and the reader; neither is the text the focal point, resisting or urging readers to particular readings either at its surface or its depth, nor is the reader entirely free to decide how they will derive meaning from the book they read, nor is the author the invisible hand orchestrating the act of reading. One has to take seriously the presence of the book market as a whole, which means one must consider all the players involved in this market as existing within interdependent relationships, and the practice of reading as existing within this constellation. Thus the practice of reading exists as much in the transaction between the rural landlord and the itinerant bookseller taking his wares from the city to the *muffasil*,[87] as much as it does in the intellectual circle of which the author is a part. The former limits who has access to which texts, and is motivated by the printer/publisher's desire for a profit and the bookseller's desire to maintain a steady customer base. The latter frequently decides what origin stories will be affixed to texts depending on various affiliations shared by members of the intelligentsia who often double up as reviewers, and in both situations, the act of reading is conditional to the participation of different members of the book market.

That this practice of reading exists by holding in tension a number of possibilities and positions becomes evident even in a brief review piece. Mir Mosharraf Hossain's *Ratnabati*, published in 1869, elicits a great deal of interest not only because it is the first Bengali novel by an Islamic author, but also because of the Sanskritic nature of its prose. The reviewer in *Grāmbārtāprakāśikā* comments on Mosharraf Hossain's use of Bengali as confounding the reader who would normally not expect such "*bimugdha bāṅgālā*" or pure Bengali from an Islamic author.[88] The reviewer concludes the twelve-line review by informing

---

[87] Broadly translated as suburban and rural.
[88] *Grāmbārtāprakāśikā*, October 1869.

Introduction   31

readers of where to buy the novel, the kind of press it is printed on, and of its cost. The reviewer saves most of the compliments for the language and its ability to appear in the mold of standard Bengali rather than being inflected with *musalmānī bānglā*. On the surface of it, the review might appear to be reading the novel from the point of view of the Hindu intelligentsia who saw Bengali as predominantly a Sanskritic language, and to be addressing a Hindu reader who would be suitably surprised, or a Muslim reader who would rejoice at Mosharraf Hossain filling in a lack on behalf of the community.

Yet several other elements are present which the twenty-first-century reader might not have immediate access to, and which form the various points within which the reviewer is reading the novel. The first two of these are the venue, *Grāmbārtāprakāśikā*, and the identity of the reviewer,[89] Harinath Majumdar, popularly known as Kangal Harinath, founded *Grāmbārtāprakāśikā* in 1863, first in Kolkata before moving to Kushtia in what is today Bangladesh, to expose the inhumane treatment of indigo farmers. As the periodical's name suggests, Harinath wished to reveal (*"prakāś"*) the news of the villages (*"grāmbārtā"*), and as a former employee of an indigo factory, he had first-hand experience of how British and the landlords exploited the peasantry. *Grāmbārtāprakāśikā*, then, would have had a mixed audience, both rural and urban, spread across the social classes, often sharing conflicting religious and linguistic affiliations. Harinath was also a disciple of Lalon Fakir,[90] and followed a syncretic religion that was neither Muslim nor Hindu but rather one founded on a rejection of violence and a belief in the transformative power of music.[91] To bracket this aspect of Harinath's identity would be to misread the review as coming from mainstream Hindu beliefs. The third point in this constellation of elements is the inclusion of the information about where the novel is printed. This was a standard part of most reviews and it told readers not only where they might buy the text from, but also of the quality of print and paper they could expect. Bengali print fonts were far from stable even in the mid-nineteenth century, and which press the text was printed on told the reader how reliable or consistent the actual marks on the page would be. Given that a significant part of *Grāmbārtāprakāśikā*'s target audience would have lived far from Kolkata, knowing the address of the

---

[89] While the review itself is not signed, knowing what we do of how nineteenth-century periodicals functioned, it is fairly certain that the founder would be the chief editor, and would review received books.

[90] A prominent nineteenth-century Baul mystic and social reformer.

[91] For a detailed discussion of this, see Chapter 4.

press meant that they could either order it directly from the press or know which itinerant bookseller to ask, if they wanted to buy the novel advertised in the periodical. All of this might seem incidental to those of us who have access to texts in a multitude of ways, and for whom very little of this is new. But for the nineteenth-century reader, each of these elements would have contributed to how they read the text, not to mention how they accessed it. Neither the reviewer, nor the publisher, nor the author, nor the reader can take the lead in dictating how the novel is to be read; they each function simultaneously, limiting and being limited by the others, and it is this relational network that I call reading practice.

The practice of reading iterated above is unique neither to nineteenth-century Bengal nor to the novel, but is indispensable to understanding how the Bengali novel becomes such a popular genre almost overnight. To see what I mean, let us turn to another example and take a closer look at three moments in the early life of the first Bengali novel, Bankim's *Durgeśnandinī* (1865), all located within Bengali commercial theater performers, popular presses, and, broadly speaking, within the world of mass entertainment. Each moment manifests this reading practice as it constantly moves between different participants, demonstrating this practice as existing in a flux within the book trade. The first moment looks at Girishchandra Ghosh, playwright, actor, director, and a signal figure in the history of modern commercial Bengali theater, reading and dramatizing the novel; the second focuses on his protégée, Binodini Dasi and fellow actors participating in reading and performing the novel; and finally the third moment describes Durgadas De, a late-nineteenth-century satirist, poking fun at Binodini, Bankim, and the novel through the figure of Miss Bino Bibi.

Following the publication of *Durgeśnandinī*, the Bengali literary response is divided into two camps: the Sanskritists and the Anglicists. These camps, consisting of Sanskrit pundits, public intellectuals, government officials, and authors, become self-appointed adjudicators of generic origins, producing considerable written material to create a non-novelistic discourse surrounding *Durgeśnandinī*.[92] Alongside these debates, the novel acquires a certain kind of popularity never before achieved by a Bengali language text, and it is read by individuals who are creators in their own right. One of these readers, Girishchandra, first comes into prominence writing songs for Michael

---

[92] This is the story I take up in Chapter 2.

Introduction 33

Madhusudan Dutt's first play *Śarmiṣṭhā* (1858). By the time Girishchandra dramatizes *Durgeśnandinī* in 1873, he is bringing to his version of the novel his expertise in devotional plays, in particular, plays based on *pōurānik*[93] plots to an audience that would have been familiar with religious plays or *dhārmic nātak*. The technique Girishchandra relies on in staging religious plays is the audience's familiarity with the plot,[94] which then allows him to focus on producing in the audience the necessary *bhāb* or the emotional essence of the piece, a technique central to the classical Sanskrit treatise on performance, *Nātyaśāstra* by Bharata. Yet, this is not merely a regurgitation of the *Nātyaśāstra* given that Girishchandra is equally invested in modernizing Bengali theater along the lines of the commercial stage in Victorian England. Note now the list of novels by Bankim which he stages, *Durgeśnandinī, Kapalkundalā, Mrinālinī, Biśabriksha*; all bestsellers[95] whose plots at least the audience would have known. Thus Girishchandra as the reader of Bankim's novel is drawing on both his reading of the text, along with his audience's identity as readers who have either read the novels or know of the plot second hand, to ensure that the audience is adequately moved by the play's *bhāb* while simultaneously appreciating the nuances of proscenium theater. The success of the play version of *Durgeśnandinī* relies not so much on the text of the novel but rather a shared knowledge of the plot as it circulates via reading and telling.

Girishchandra's leading heroine, and one of the first women on the Bengali stage, Binodini Dasi provides us with yet another element in this practice of reading in her autobiography *Āmār kathā*. Her description of learning to perform under Girishchandra's tutelage is of particular interest here, and I quote from her at length:

Girish-babu [Girishchandra] taught me with great care the performance of parts. His teaching method was wonderful. First he explained the essence [*bhāb*] of the part. The he would ask us to memorise it. Then when he had the time he would sit in our house, with Amrit Mitra, Amrit-babu (Bhuni-babu) and others, and narrate to us as stories the writings of several British actresses, of great British poets such as Shakespeare, Milton, Byron, Pope. Sometimes he would

---

[93] Stories based on Hindu *puran*s or myths.
[94] Rimli Bhattacharya notes this in her 1998 translation of Binodini Dasi's autobiography *Āmār kathā* (*My Story and My Life as an Actress*).
[95] Jogeshchandra Bagal provides the following information in his preface to the collected novels of Bankim: *Biśabriksh* had eight editions during the author's lifetime, *Mrinālinī* had at least three, *Kapalkundalā* had four editions, while *Durgeśnandinī* had thirteen editions (*Samgra upanyas*, 31–6).

34 *The Novel in Nineteenth-Century Bengal*

read and explain from their books. He would teach various moves and gestures [*hāb-bhaāb*] one by one. Because of his care, I began to learn the work of acting using my knowledge and intelligence.[96]

Note here the amalgamation of Sanskrit *bhāva* (*bhab* in Bengali) with British literary aesthetics, as Binodini transitions from rote memorization to understanding the text she is meant to perform. She does not position herself as the reader, but rather as an actor learning her craft through her teacher reading to her. This act of reading performed by Girishchandra is substantiated by the verb "explain" which allows Binodini to appreciate the meaning of the text rather than its words. Reading, here, appears to mimic the older oral tradition of the *guru* (teacher) and the *shishya* (disciple), but Binodini is at pains to note the presence of the text in this interaction. Binodini's learning is conditional upon Girishchandra explaining his reading of the novel, and her understanding of his reading.

Later in the text, she continues:

I liked only the stories of famous British actors and actresses that Girish-babu narrated, those books that he read aloud. When Mrs. Sidnis [Siddons] left theatre work, and then returned to the stage after spending ten years in the married state, then where in her acting which critic found what flaws, which parts were excellent, which lacking etc., he would read and explain from books. Which actress in Britain practiced her voice alongside the sound of birds in forests, that too he told me. How Elenterry [Ellen Terry] dressed, how Bandman dressed as Hamlet, which outfit of flowers Ophelia wore, Bankim's '*Durgeśnandinī*' was written in the shadow of which book, '*Rajanī*' was inspired by the *bhab* of which English book, so many things of this nature; thanks to the loving care of Girish-babu and other affectionate friends, I cannot recount the number of stories of great English, Greek, French, German etc. authors I heard. I not only listened, but collected the *bhab* from them, ceaselessly thinking about the same.[97]

Binodini continues her self-presentation as the apprentice, but in this she also allows us access to the practice of reading prevalent within the theater community in nineteenth-century Bengal. This reading is imbued with *bhab* or essence, both as an aesthetic concept, and, more importantly, from a pragmatic point of view. To understand this *bhab*, to reflect upon it, while simultaneously being aware of the latest acting techniques coming out of Britain, is to ensure one's success

---

[96] Binodini, *Āmār kathā*, 29, translation mine.
[97] Binodini, 31, translation mine.

Introduction 35

as a heroine in a cutthroat competitive world. Thus Binodini and members of her company learn the *hāb-bha[āb]* of acting and the *bhāb* of these texts so as to better embody these characters, and in turn give sold-out performances. The act of reading is central to her *bildung*, as is the book as an object; she takes her cues from a reader she trusts, Girishchandra, and ruminates upon the text in order to learn her craft, and be more cultivated so as to earn respect.

Binodini and her performance of Girishchandra's plays based on Bankim's novels inspire a range of popular satires later in the nineteenth century that led us to yet another moment in this network within which I situate the practice of reading. Durgadas De's satire *Miss Bino Bibi. B.A. Honour in a Course* narrates the story of its eponymous protagonist, Bino, as it puns on her reluctance to marry an ordinary man (*B.A.* stands for the qualifications Bino desires in her potential groom, but is also a phonic representation of the Bengali word for marriage, *biye*). Bino's behavior is pitched at high melodrama, a mode made famous by her namesake, Binodini, as she recounts the uselessness of all men who are not like heroes such as Bankim's Jagatsingha. Here, then, we see yet another iteration of the reading of Bengali novels, this time routed through their stage performances. The satire's content is about the morally devastating effects of women reading *bankimī* novels, while its form is based on Girishchandra's and Binodini's reading of these texts. *Miss Bino Bibi* draws on a complex system of textual distribution in which each individual entity—Bankim, Girishchandra, Binodini, reviewers of all three, Bengali readers, and theater-goers—reads with, against, and tangential to each other.

It is this system within which Girishchandra, Binodini, and Durgadas read, and within which Mosharraf Hossain's *Ratnābati* is reviewed that I term reading practice. During the first three decades of the Bengali novel's life, the newness of the genre requires readers, publishers, and distributors to bring to the text their knowledge of other kinds of texts, be they printed, handwritten, or oral. They carry as well their own religious, aesthetic, and linguistic allegiances, creating an intricate network of reference points. The authors desiring popularity and literary fame both introduce their own frames of meaning and adapt these frames depending on the response of the readers. The text itself is a dynamic object, shaped by the material realities of quality of paper, stability of font, and the provenance of the ink. Finally, where the text is located and how the reader accesses it—whether they own it, or borrow it from an acquaintance, or a library or a book society—each of these become elements of this constellation of individuals and institutions. Taken together, this is a fluid network, with entities

frequently changing places,[98] falling in and out of favor,[99] and in general being buoyed by a sense of possibility when it comes to the novel as a genre. What I propose as reading practice is not a mere celebration of difference or multiplicity that further exoticizes the inscrutable orient, but rather one that acknowledges the lived reality of the book trade, and of readers as existing within that trade. Reading practice occurs not in a teleological or developmental manner whereby a set of readers experiment, and that is passed on to another set who build on the previous group's efforts; neither is it Darwinian in that authors and publishers gauge what sells well and jettison the rest in favor of that which is popular. Rather, to comprehend this practice of reading, one must take seriously the fleeting nature of reading, catch glimpses of it at various available sites, and map these moments into an interrelated network. An image appears of those involved in the book market engaged in a practice of reading that is organic to nineteenth-century Bengal, with each entity making possible the others' reading while simultaneously limiting that reading.

VI. An Overview

In examining reading practice, I situate my arguments at the juncture of Sanskrit and Perso-Arabic aesthetics, British colonial pedagogy, and the production and distribution system sustaining the growth in the Bengali novel's popularity. The following four chapters navigate a path through the network created by the interaction of the above elements in an attempt to understand both the nature of these interactions and the contours of the network itself. I draw on debates in comparative literature, postcolonial studies, and global Anglophone studies on the one hand, and on recent scholarship on reading and book history on the other, to reimagine reading as a dynamic practice. The overarching argument of this book posits that there did not exist in nineteenth-century Bengal a singular normative method of reading novels as mandated by any authority position, be they British or Bengali. Neither was there a certain inevitability of imitation on the part of Bengali novelists or their readers. We have grown accustomed to approaching the postcolonial novel and its readers in terms of a secondariness

---

[98] For example, when a reviewer becomes the author's patron, as in Harinath and Mosharraf Hossain's relationship.

[99] As is the case with Binodini's rise to fame and then fall from it.

Introduction   37

born of a historically conditioned lack, and in tracing this hierarchy to the rise of print culture and a subsequent mushrooming of Indian versions of genres imported from Europe. Yet as these chapters demonstrate, in Bengal alone the novel reader had before them at least three available practices of reading— Sanskritist (deriving from the Hindu-oriented texts), Perso-Arabic (deriving from Islamic-oriented texts), and Anglicist (deriving from Western/Victorian-inspired texts). Of these, the Sanskritist practice of reading dominated novel production and consumption during the nineteenth century, while the Perso-Arabic practice of reading formed a secondary alternative. The Anglicist reading practice was merely a possible third option and overshadowed the others only at the start of the twentieth century.

As I began thinking about this book, I was struck by the narrative of radical rupture surrounding nineteenth-century India in general, and Bengal in particular. The scholarly consensus in postcolonial studies, comparative literature, and Anglophone literature was that the gradual decline of Sanskrit and Persian as languages of power[100] coupled with the expansion of British colonial presence led to a massive epistemological shift in the nineteenth century.[101] Coming out in the early 2000s, this body of work built on the first wave of postcolonial scholarship as it sought to provide a more rigorous material and cultural explanation for what had been earlier posited as multiplicity or difference. This cognitive change rested on a linguistic one—Sanskrit and the Persianate languages gave way to English as the language of power which led to a conceptual reordering of the world.[102] The argument that sometime during the first half of the nineteenth century there occurred in Bengal a move toward English, and consequently toward the epistemology of the Enlightenment, was a compelling one for me. It was what I had been trained in during my undergraduate and graduate career, and there appeared to be ample evidence suggesting that post the introduction of print modernity and colonial pedagogy, the past became irrevocably severed from the present. Following this line, I was inclined to claim that the "tangled

---

[100] See Sheldon Pollock's "The Death of Sanskrit" (2001) and *The Language of the Gods in the World of Men* (2006) for Sanskrit, and Jennifer Dubrow's *Cosmopolitan Dreams* and Pramod K. Nayar's *Colonial Education in India 1781–1945* (2020) for Persian.

[101] The list here can be endless, but of note are Sudipta Kaviraj's "The Sudden Death of Sanskrit Knowledge" (2005), Gayatri Chakraborty Spivak's *An Aesthetic Education in the Era of Globalization* (2013), Anindita Ghosh's *Power in Print*, Priya Joshi's *In Another Country* (2002), Tithi Bhattacharya's *Sentinels of Culture* (2005), and Ulka Anjaria's *Realism in the Twentieth Century Indian Novel* (2012).

[102] I am indebted to Kaviraj's formulation here.

genealogy"[103] of the postcolonial novel in India revealed aesthetic experiments with the form but was ultimately secondary to the material conditions of its production and consumption. I wanted to see nineteenth-century Bengali novelists and their readers as radically removed from their past because of the insertion of this wedge of Enlightenment epistemology.

However, this argument, despite all its nuances, assumes a total dissemination of a singular knowledge system, percolating down to every segment of nineteenth-century Bengali society. It posits a conceptual change that affects everyone, regardless of their proximity to the English language and the worldview associated with it, and a simultaneous dislocation of existing structures of knowing. A question naturally arises—could this, or was this, truly be the case, and would it be more productive to think of this radical rupture as a potentiality rather than an actuality, albeit a potential that comes to fruition by the end of the nineteenth century? Two elements provoked this question for me during the early stages of research, and both are related to Bankim and *Durgeśnandinī*. The first of these is the sheer popularity of this novel—*Durgeśnandinī* ran into thirteen editions during Bankim's lifetime alone[104]—suggestive of a number of readers across social and gender categories, not all of whom would have had access to this cognitive shift. The second, related to the first, is the popularity of *bankimī* Bengali which is heavily inflected by Sanskrit not merely in content but also in grammatical structure. These readers demanding so many editions must have been comfortable reading a form of Bengali that was about as far removed from the Anglicized world as was possible. Even such a superficial glance at readers and their practices of reading, then, suggests the need to revise this history of radical rupture, and take seriously the possibility that during the better part of the nineteenth century the past and the present existed in a continuum stable enough to resist the pressures of this epistemological shift.

As these chapters demonstrate, theorizing reading poses challenges peculiar to itself, not least because despite the long-sustained interest in novels and the history of the book, the act of reading remains under-theorized. Existent scholarship on reading, in the context of nineteenth-century Bengal, approaches reading primarily via book history, and the impact of the printed book in making visible colonial readers in Bengal cannot be overemphasized. However, because this conversation takes as its point of departure the book rather than its

---

[103] I draw this phrasing from Meenakshi Mukherjee's 2006 essay, "Epic and Novel in India."
[104] Jogeshchandra Bagal, *Bankim Racanābalī*, preface, 31.

Introduction 39

readers, the latter is discussed mostly as a necessary consequence of the arrival of print modernity to colonial India.[105] A more recent body of work on reading publics and the development of a literary cosmopolis identifies reading as an ideological tool, but here too, the act of reading, when examined, is in the service of answering a set of questions not related to reading.[106] If one turns to Victorian Britain, there emerges more sustained discussions of reading as an act in and of itself, whether one is considering contemporary readers consuming nineteenth-century texts,[107] or physiological[108] and distracted readings[109] performed by Victorian themselves. Yet even here, the paucity of scholarship is noticeable, suggesting that there exists a major lacuna when it comes to studying reading practice, whether in colonial Bengal or its British counterpart. Even if one leaves behind the nineteenth century, reading practice remains oddly invisible in the world of theoretical interventions into the literary.[110] Take, for instance, world literature and the close engagement with the postcolonial text as a site for reimagining both the text and its relationship to the reader, in which, despite the

[105] Given that this is a dominant strain in scholarship on book history in South Asia, it would be beyond the scope of a single note to account for all the works. The reader is almost always present in these studies, and frequently as an active participant in the forming of the physical, conceptual, and cultural aspects of the book trade. The practice of reading, however, is never accorded the same attention, and reading is discussed as either a way of socializing the text (e.g., Abhijit Gupta's 2012 essay "Popular Printing and Intellectual Property in Colonial Bengal") or in terms of developing high and low literary cultures (e.g., Priya Joshi's *In Another Country* and Anindita Ghosh's *Power in Print*).

[106] Discussions of literary publics marked the start of the 2010s, and have predominantly focused on Islamic literary cultures in South Asia, as seen in works by Ronit Ricci, Jennifer Dubrow, Maryam Wasif Khan, and Francesca Orsini. The scholarship here is particularly useful in understanding the split between Urdu and Hindi—and the concomitant divide between Muslim and Hindu reading publics—as a product of mid- to late-nineteenth-century India, and the role played by readers in imagining national polities.

[107] I am thinking particularly of Sharon Marcus' *Between Women* (2007) in which outlines the seminal theory of just reading as a method of comprehending the centrality of female friendships in producing and sustaining heterosexual marriages in Victorian novels. Marcus deftly navigates the novelistic text as one of the repositories of subversive gender practices, but her discussion of reading these texts is firmly rooted in the twenty-first century; Marcus is interested in the contemporary reader and her practices, not in the Victorian reader.

[108] Nicholas Dames' *Physiology of the Novel* is a pivotal text in this instance. His theory of physiological reading is one of the first, and till date one of the only, sustained engagement with the question of how Victorians actually *read*. By looking at novels, reviews, and journals for discussions of good and bad reading, Dames is one of the first to suggest what an archive for a scholar of reading practice might look like.

[109] Leah Price's most recent work, *What We Talk about When We Talk about Books*, suggests that contrary to scholarly and popular belief, Victorians readers were not a disciplined lot. They read much like us, distracted by their environment, losing their place in the book, and defying chapter chronology when it suited them.

[110] Even though one finds it recurring in the world of neuroscience which is interested in how the human brain cognitively processes words. For more, see the work of Nadine Gabb at Harvard Medical School, or David Dodell-Feder's work on reading fiction and empathy.

attention to textual difference, the reader and their practices remain remarkably consistent.[111] Paradoxically, symptomatic reading has continued to fall out of fashion over the last two decades, despite being perhaps the most-theorized reading practice in the Anglo-American world today. Its emphasis on unmasking the text's ideological aspirations has come under scrutiny in the form of paranoid reading,[112] close reading,[113] just reading,[114] and critical reading,[115] to name only four, all of which resist the surface-depth model espoused by symptomatic reading. Yet in all their nuances of thought, these conversations around reading remain restricted to the West, and more frequently, to the Anglo-American academia. They, like the other approaches mentioned in this section, have little, if anything, to say about *how* those readers in nineteenth-century Bengal encountering a new genre for the first time *actually* read. Thus in the chapters that follow, I place these above discussions in the background, looking instead for a theory of reading practice attentive to the particular context of production, distribution, and consumption of novels in nineteenth-century Bengal.

To that end, each chapter in this work examines parts of this network of producers, consumers, distributors, and reviewers. Thus the narrative arc of this book begins with authors and colonial policymakers establishing literacy and determining taste, before looking at the ways in which authors and readers create three distinct practices of reading at the moment of the Bengali novel's inception. I move then to examining the dominant reading practice, Sanskritist, and the twice marginalized one, Perso-Arabic, before concluding by briefly looking at the ever-fleeting female reader.

It is important to note here that these three practices of reading that I examine are not intended to segregate readers along a neat overlap between linguistic affinities and socio-religious categories. As the above sections demonstrate, languages such as English, Sanskrit, Persian, Arabic, and Urdu were not read exclusively by insulated communities; rather, it was the porous boundaries between these languages and identity categories of their readers that allowed

---

[111] Pheng Cheah takes world literature to task for not adequately theorizing the reader—note, his focus is the reader, rather than reading, but in this he is consistent with a significant number of scholars on reading—in *What Is a World?*, but the only theory of reading Cheah provides is eerily reminiscent of the good, interpretive close reading practiced in the Anglo-American graduate classroom.

[112] Eve Kosofsky Sedgwick, "Paranoid Reading and Reparative Reading, or, You're So Paranoid, You Probably Think This Essay Is about You" (1997).

[113] Heather Love, "Close Reading, Thin Description" (2013).

[114] Marcus and Best.

[115] Warner, "Uncritical Reading" (2004).

Introduction   41

for the plurality of reading practices. In other words, my argument is not that only Bengali Hindus followed the Sanskritist practice, or that only Muslims the Perso-Arabic. Rather, I contend that these were two of the many available modes of reading which the Bengali reader had before her/him. Which they chose to practice depended on their social, religious, cultural, and linguistic communities, and to read the relationship between readers and the kinds of readings they practiced as deterministic would be to miss the plurality of their socio-historical contexts. Of these practices, I restrict myself to three—Sanskritist, Anglicist, and Perso-Arabic—for both the practical question of scope and their ability to gesture toward other practices of reading. Thus, for example, pulling on the threads of the Sanskritist practice reveals that the majority of the readers of *Durgeśnandinī* would have had a quotidian familiarity with, rather than a scholarly knowledge of, Sanskrit literary aesthetics. As they read the novel, they would have noticed echoes of other genres and languages—such as the *mangal kābya*,[116] the Bengali of domestic spaces,[117] or the Vaishnava poems of Vidyāpati—through which Sanskrit had become a part of their lived reality. Each of these signals a different mode of reading, and while examining all of them is beyond the scope of any single work, it is their presence that creates the varied landscape of reading that is nineteenth-century Bengal.

The first chapter takes up the narrative created both by Bengali intellectuals such as Bankim and Mosharraf Hossain and by the colonial government, and asks why, despite the volume of texts produced and consumed in Bengali during roughly the second half of the nineteenth century, do all parties perceive a critical lack of sophisticated readers? In this chapter I examine the debates over print literacy in colonial Bengal to create a reading map identifying the primary stakeholders in these debates. I provide a historical overview of each of the three reading practices, the Sanskritist, the Anglicist, and the Perso-Arabic, and document their articulations of the relationship between the individual and the text, such that the individual can be deemed a competent reader. I look at colonial education documents such as William Adam's *Reports on the State of Education in Bengal and Behar*, published between 1835 and 1838, and James Long's commentary on the same, to chart the failure of trickle-down educational policies, and answer the chapter's opening question from the perspective of

---

[116] Early modern Bengali religious poems celebrating the indigenous deities of rural Bengal, such as Manasa, Chandi, and Dharmathakur, and their assimilation into Vedic mythology.

[117] In the conversations between Bimala and Diggaj Pandit in particular.

the British government. However, the contentious history of Persian slowly losing ground as a language of prestige, and the concomitant rise of a Hindu intelligentsia demonstrates that there exists in Bengal a far more complex relationship between readers and literature than can be explained either by a top-down model of literacy, or by an analysis of the burgeoning book market. They both present only a part of the picture, which is completed by this chapter when it introduces into this network the conjoined problems of basic literacy and reading competency vis-à-vis the common Bengali reader.

One of the most vocal critics of trickle-down literacy, Bankim, is the subject of Chapter 2 which begins with an examination of the non-novelistic discourse surrounding his novels, with a particular focus on *Durgeśnandinī*. The chapter's argument crystalizes around an anecdotal moment in Bengali literary history; in 1864, a few months before the publication of *Durgeśnandinī*, Bankim performs a reading of the novel's manuscript version before a select audience—an act which he never repeats for his other sixteen novels—in an effort to indicate both an absence of and a desire to inaugurate a practice of reading novels. Reviews and personal essays published by readers respond by performing either a Sanskritist or an Anglicist reading of the novel, thus creating a trend of reading Bankim's novels as guided by either Sanskrit aesthetic, grammatical, and literary frames, or the Enlightenment principles of British and European novels. The narrow focus on *Durgeśnandinī*, and reviews and essays related to this novel in particular allows me to both pinpoint the start of the Anglicist/Sanskritist debate and demonstrate the effect *Durgeśnandinī* has on practices of novel reading till the end of the nineteenth century. The non-novelistic texts are of further significance because they reveal the stakes of this divide—each reading practice strives to become *the* definitive practice of reading for the modern Bengali reader.

If the previous chapter charts the emergence and importance both the Anglicist and the Sanskritist reading practices, then this chapter documents the brief but powerful life of the latter. While the Sanskritist practice of reading definitively disappears with the rise of Rabindranath Tagore's prose experiments at the turn of the twentieth century, the primacy of this reading practice during Bankim's lifetime is indisputable. This chapter, then, examines the novels of Bankim in light of classical Sanskrit literature and the *rasa* theory, and argues that practices of Sanskrit *kāvya* literature are as dominant in the structural and aesthetic elements of the Bengali novel as Western forms of novel production. The arguments are located in the reader to suggest that Bankim's novels train her to read the Sanskrit past as encoded in the text, and coexisting with the

Introduction 43

westernized colonial present, albeit in a difficult relationship. The chapter pays particular attention to the novelist's adaptation of two forms of Sanskrit prose, the *kathā* and the *ākhyāyikā*, and his exploration of the *śṛngāra* (erotic) *rasa*. I read three novels—*Durgeśnandinī* (1865), *Biśabriksha* (1873), and *Ānandamath* (1882)—from three different moments in Bankim's career as a novelist, and show not only his, but also his readers' sustained investment in the Sanskritist reading practice. The chapter reinforces this book's core argument that while the Bengali novel emerges after the introduction of its Victorian counterpart, the former is a product of engagement with tensions foreign to the British novel. Exploring this alternative reading practice provides an opportunity to understand how Bengali and Sanskrit—in terms of literature and culture—are part of the lived experience of both Bankim and his nineteenth-century reader, and the aesthetic and ethical foundation of the early Bengali novel.

The fourth and final chapter moves away from the Hindu Bengali novels to study texts written by the first Muslim Bengali author, Mir Mosharraf Hossain, focusing in particular on his second novel *Biśād Sindhu* published between 1885 and 1891. The novel is an instantiation of the Perso-Arabic reading practice which relies simultaneously on the Islamic ethico-aesthetic concept of *adab*, and on a folk performance unique to Bengal, *jārigān*. The performative nature of this reading practice becomes central to the Bengali Muslim reader's experience of the novel genre. The chapter highlights the twin pressures of the global and the local faced by nineteenth-century Bengali Muslims, as they are marginalized both by the loss of the Mughal empire and by the predominance of Hindus in Bengal's social, political, and literary life. Through the arguments of this chapter, *The Novel in Nineteenth-Century Bengal* effectively dismantles the image of nineteenth-century Bengal as parochial and inward looking. As one delineates the Perso-Arabic reading practice, one discovers that section of nineteenth-century Bengali novel readers who claim allegiance to an extra-national, global community through the shared performance of *adab*, while never losing touch with intensely local aesthetic forms such as *jārigān*. In telling the story of the Perso-Arabic reading practice, the chapter also demonstrates its deliberate alienation by both the Sanskritist and the Anglicist camps. The sheer paucity of mainstream Islamic authors writing in Bengali, and of literary publications in Islamic Bengali suggests the dual erasure of the Perso-Arabic reading practice by the Hindus and the British. This chapter takes on the task of excavating this rich practice of reading, and revealing the extent of its viability during the second half of the nineteenth century.

While in the rest of the book I leave the reader largely ungendered, I take up the question—and the problem—of women readers in the conclusion. This chapter is neither corrective in its relation to the other chapters, nor is it exhaustive in terms of documenting women who read in the nineteenth century. Rather, I stage two sites of reading using Rassundari Debi's autobiography *Āmār jīban* and Nawab Faizunnesa's narrative text *Rupjālāl*, both published in 1876, to demonstrate the private and intimate nature of reading practiced by these two authors. Both texts are temporally located within the literary world of Bankim and Mosharraf Hossain, and yet they are curiously removed from the public nature of that world. Neither Rassundari nor Faizunnesa is concerned with becoming the modern reader, or even with reading novels; for them, the act of reading is itself novel and one that can be performed within the private space of the home. The idea of reading for the sake of reading is foundational here, as is the practice of women transmitting texts by reading them to their community. My claim in this chapter is that the colonial book market should be understood in relation to the domestic sphere within which women read, cook, and share with their confidantes stories of heartbreak. The act of reading enters this space via stolen pages and supernatural experiences because they alone can give women the opportunity to read, albeit in a limited fashion within a patriarchal context.

At stake in the conclusion—and in *The Novel in Nineteenth-Century Bengal* as a whole—is the desire to comprehend the aspirational nature of these practices of reading. Whether the reader performing the Sanskritist, Perso-Arabic, or the Anglicist practice views their particular approach as *the* definitive one, or women readers view their practice as the only one available to them, Bengali readers seek to transmit their practice of reading to future readers. They aim to define the contours of the Bengali reading public which they, rightly, perceives as being in flux during the second half of the nineteenth century. There is no inevitability in the shape the Bengali novel and its readers will assume in the twentieth and twenty-first century, and the great possibilities of the nineteenth century are revealed in the struggle over defining what reading practice means to each entity within the life of the Bengali book. That the Anglicist practice emerges victorious at the cost of making obsolete the Sanskritist and making alien the Perso-Arabic stands testimony to the enduring power of colonial violence, but as this book demonstrates, the second half of the century presents a brief but creative window to a world in which all three practices are viable, and actively imagining their futures.

1

Breaking the Cycle of Bad Readers: Battala Literature, Colonial Pedagogy, and the Idea of Education

I. Mapping the Terrain: Debates over Literacy and Reading

In 1823, Bhabanicharan Bandopadhyay published *Kalikātā kamalālay*, a work satirizing the habits of the urban *bābu*.[1] The text is in the form of a dialogue between a naïve villager who asks a person living in Kolkata a series of questions in the hopes of trying to understand the latter's ways, and eventually be a competent urbanite himself. The villager is suitably awed by the wealth he has seen in the city, but he also knows that in order to make it in the city, he must grasp the nature of both wealth and learning. He remarks to the city dweller, "Sir, here in Kolkata, there are some people from my country [village] who are employed in the homes of some well to do people. I have learned from them that wonderful books of various kinds in Persian, English, Arabic are bought and beautifully displayed in glass fronted almirahs."[2] But the babu, he continues, cannot even imagine that these books would ever be touched, let alone read. This confuses him to no end—he knows he is merely a simple villager, but even in his village, he has seen *punthis* or manuscripts be read rather than displayed. The villager wonders if books are like idols in a temple, meant only to be displayed and worshipped rather than actually touched. The babu is visibly annoyed by this question, and berates the villager for failing to understand why books are produced. A wealthy man, the babu says, takes care of all his possessions but doesn't always use every one of these objects. He has already paid good money to buy these books, so why should he be obliged to read them? Since his livelihood

---

[1] An urban or urbanized gentleman.
[2] Bandopadhyay, sixty-seven, translation mine.

46   *The Novel in Nineteenth-Century Bengal*

doesn't depend on using books, he feels no desire to use these objects. After all, what one does with books is not written in stone.

This fluid and indeterminate relationship with the print text is one that Bhabanicharan knows well, and uses to his advantage. As one of the first Bengali print entrepreneurs and print authors, he bases the satire on his knowledge of the emergent book market in Bengal, and in his conscious choice to associate books with the verb *byabahār* or "to use" rather than *parā* or "to read" he draws attention to the value books have in this market as objects rather than as reading material. For some, these objects are to be revered, for others, a symbol of wealth, and for yet others, objects to be deciphered through reading. As a bookseller catering to both the urban and the rural audience, Bhabanicharan is well placed to represent the villager's seemingly innocuous question, and to thus poke fun at the urban "reader" who is usually deemed educated enough if he knows how to maintain his own accounts.[3] Reading, as the babu suggests, is something that is workaday, and only someone who needs to make a living from books needs to read. For the babu, the printed book is a collectible indicating social status, a curiosity, and far from being a marker of literacy. The distinction between using and reading books is an important one to note; one can use a book in various ways, and frequently this use is to display one's ability to buy a book, to make an investment in the book, and thereby constrain Lakshmi or the goddess of wealth to remain at one's home.[4] Unlike Bhabanicharan's babu, the *khudra nabab* or the little nawab of the anonymously composed *Young Bengal Khudra Nabab* does read books, but as the narrator remarks, even he doesn't really know how to read. Published forty years after *Kalikātā kamalālay*, *Young Bengal* satirizes the upstart, Anglicized Bengali man who despises everything Bengali just to be seen as cultured and civilized. The narrative voice tells us that the *khudra nabab* is a fool for rejecting his Bengali heritage in exchange for the worn hand me downs given to him by the British, and he learns a smattering of English in his efforts to fashion himself as an Anglophile. He cares little for the "nasty Bengali language" or for Bengali books, all of which are utter rubbish.[5] However, for all his posturing, the little nawab doesn't actually know how to read the books of his masters; for him, reading is limited to mindless aping which is not founded on any understanding. He knows the stock phrases

---

[3] Bhabanicharan, p. 66.
[4] The idea here is that wealth is representative of not just Lakshmi's blessings, but a manifestation of the goddess herself. So the more expensive objects one can store in one's home, the more the goddess is compelled to remain, bound as she is to these objects.
[5] *Young Bengal Khudra Nabab*, 299 (in *Bat talār boi* Part 1), translation mine.

when it comes to denigrating Bengali books and newspapers, and celebrating those written in English, but his education stops at memorizing commonplaces. What he calls reading is him identifying these stock phrases in the pages of the print text, and even that is possible because he has memorized these phrases.

Nineteenth-century Bengali literature is full of such scenes of comically bad readers misreading texts and failing to understand what books mean. As scholars of book history suggest, this is a result of the gradual process of socializing the book,[6] but this explanation fails to account for texts such as *Young Bengal Khudra Nabab* or *Kerāni purān* published well into the nineteenth century, by which time the book is a familiar object. What I argue in this chapter is that these instances of bad reading, rather than revealing a society becoming accustomed to print culture, suggest instead the lack of a singular, stable definition of the relationship between books and readers. These are not examples of readers not knowing how to read but something more fundamental—for these readers, what it means to read a print text is far from a given. The relationship between the reader and the text is a fluid one given not just the novelty of the print medium, but also its inaccessibility for the vast majority of Bengalis. What does one do with the book as an object, and how does one approach it? What does it mean to *read* a book, and who is the authority deciding the meaning of this verb "to read"? These are questions occupying not just the babu and the villager in *Kalikātā kamalālay* in the 1820s, but also the Hindu intelligentsia in the 1860s, the Muslim intelligentsia a few years later, and the lower-class satirists, both Hindu and Muslim, in the 1880s. Running parallel to this is the colonial government's engagement with the same problem—how might reading be best defined and disseminated such that first the Company and then the Crown derive the most benefit? Through the course of the nineteenth century—and certainly during the first half of the century—those involved in the book market and in knowledge production identify reading as the ground they need to control so as to capitalize on what is an increasingly lucrative industry. Thus indigenous booksellers and publishers such as Bhabanicharan and Gangakishore Bhattacharya encourage their readers to think of reading print versions of sacred texts as no different than reading traditional *punthi* or manuscript versions,[7] while Baptist missionaries promote

---

[6] Abhijit Gupta for example discusses this at length in "Popular Printing and Intellectual Property in Colonial Bengal" (2012).

[7] Gangakishore advertises that copies of the *Bhagavad Gita* published by him are printed using ink mixed with the holy water of the Ganges, and that the texts are blessed by Hindu priests, thereby ensuring that the printed version of the *Gita* is as ritually pure as the handwritten manuscript.

the book as an object worth possessing as much for itself as for the knowledge it contains. Both Indian and English social reformists gauge the extent to which what is done in indigenous schools can be properly called reading, and at the same time, Hindu parents resist sending their children to Missionary schools for fear that they would be ensnared by the printed book and converted upon learning to read the word *Jesus* in print.[8] Each of these entities seeks to define reading so as to stabilize the relationship between books and readers, and in the process make available multiple practices of reading. That reading is a practice that is far from being stably defined in the nineteenth century is the foundational argument of this book, and as the next three chapters demonstrate, there are at the very least three dominant practices in circulation with respect to the Bengali novel alone—the Sanskritist, the Anglicist, and the Perso-Arabic.

In this first chapter I create a reading map of Bengal, identifying the primary stake holders in the book market and their various, often conflicting, motives. What connects each of these entities is the common desire to first demarcate reading as an unchartered and unclaimed territory, and then provide a normative definition of reading so as to definitively occupy this space. This chapter outlines the elements of the three reading practices mentioned above, and provides an aerial view of the ways in which they congeal. These, then, are our *dramatis personae*—the British education reformers, members of the Hindu and Muslim intelligentsia, and the authors and publishers of the popular *battalā* presses—and as we examine their articulations of what reading should mean, it becomes obvious that they are all trying to define a particular relationship between the individual and the text such that it positions this individual as a competent reader. What competency consists of, of course, is the substance of these discussions. This relationship between the text and the Bengali is in turn made dependent on the language, content, and quality of the text, all of which make authors, policymakers, civil servants, publishers, and book sellers a part of the act of reading, thus creating what I have been calling a practice of reading.

As one turns from the debates over reading staged by the Hindu intelligentsia and British reformers, it becomes increasingly evident that the Muslim community is by and large marginalized by both of the other two groups. The history of this marginalization can be traced back to the Battle of Plassey when the British defeat Siraj ud Daulah, the Nawab of Bengal, and gain monopoly over trade in the region. As I discuss at length in the introduction to this

---

[8] Long, preface to Adam's *Report*, 4 (1868).

work, part of the process of consolidating power in Bengal assumes the form of systematically dismantling the primacy of Persian as the administrative language, and of favoring upper- and middle-class Hindus over their Muslim compatriots. From 1829 onwards, the policy of the colonial government begins to gradually phase out Persian as the administrative language of the region. The English Education Act of 1835 formalizes this transition, permanently replacing Persian with English as first the language of colonial education, and then as the official language. English goes from being the language of the foreign rulers to a necessary tool required for getting any government job, and Persian falls out of favor, both officially and socially, thus entering a phase of decline from which it never recovers in India. As a result of British educational and linguistic policies, Bengal of the 1830s comes to be a very different place compared to a century prior when even a major Bengali Hindu poet like Bharatchandra Ray (1712–60) was chastised by his family for choosing to learn Sanskrit over Persian. He had to learn Persian to ensure that he could get a job or any form of official recognition in the Mughal state. To add to the primacy of English, the efforts of Fort William College and the Mission Press had crafted Bengali as *the* vernacular of the region, leaving no room for the development of Persian or Arabic.[9] This effected the language of textbooks and school curricula, both of which favored either English or Bengali.

This transition to English and Bengali suited aspirational Hindus more than Muslims as for the former the move away from Persian is an easier one for two reasons. The first was that the attention paid toward developing Bengali meant that they could learn English while still having Bengali as a cultural and domestic language. The second reason lay in the nature of their allegiance to Persian or English—neither of these two languages defined their social, religious, or cultural identity. The educated Hindu of the early nineteenth century was literate in Persian because that was the social norm, but for the educated Muslim, the picture was considerably different. Persian and Arabic were not merely administrative or classical languages for the Muslim, but were intrinsically tied to being a Muslim. In Bengal Arabic was never the language of communication; it was the language of the sacred Qur'an, the language of prayer, and the language connecting the Muslim community to the larger Islamic *ummā*.[10] Knowing

---

[9] However, interestingly, the College had begun by teaching Persian and Arabic, and Bengali was a later inclusion. For more, see the Introduction to this work.

[10] From the Arabic *ummāt-al-Islam* or the Islamic community superseding local, national, or geographical allegiances.

Persian, however, was necessary to be a socially, culturally, and professionally successful Muslim. Thus by removing Persian from the administrative sphere, the British effected the destruction of a significant aspect of Bengali Muslim identity, leaving the latter to negotiate not just the loss of a language, but that of a way of being in the world.

A consequence of this intimate relationship with Persian, and a deliberate undermining of the privilege granted to Muslims by the Mughal rule meant that even for upper- and middle-class Muslims making the transition to this new Bengal of English and Bengali was considerably difficult. While English was taught at several *madrasās*,[11] including Calcutta Madrasa (established in 1781 by Warren Hastings), Nizamat College in Murshidabad, and Mohsin College in Hooghly, few students could afford to attend these classes.[12] With the Act of 1835, the government withdrew financial support from schools of traditional learning to encourage an English language curriculum, and while this move was later challenged and altered by subsequent colonial administrators, *madrasās*, *maktabs*[13] never received much funding after this moment, and depended substantially on private donations. Most Muslim students were forced to drop out as they found either their educational institutions closing down because of a lack of funds, or because the curriculum adopted by English and Bengali language school left no room for learning what their family would have considered fundamental. The question of money is an acute one at this point since as a community, the Muslims had struggled to gain financial security following the Permanent Settlement of Bengal (1793). The Settlement was an agreement between the East India Company and Bengali landlords which forced the latter to hand over the bulk of the revenue generated by taxing the peasants, and the amount to be given to the Company kept increasing. This affected both Hindu and Muslim landlords, most of whom declared bankruptcy within a few years. However, Muslim landlords were hit disproportionately hard because under Mughal rule, most of the profitable land in Bengal—though by no means all—was owned by Muslims. Those Hindus who lost their land, or lost their jobs as a result of the landowner losing their land, saw in the Company new job opportunities and trained themselves in English to secure these positions.

---

[11] A school of Islamic learning, training students in Islamic law, the Qur'an, Arabic, and Persian.

[12] As Anisujjaman notes, the perception that most Muslims refused to engage with an English education owing to religious fundamentalism or a deep resentment toward those who had defeated the Mughals has little historical basis till at least the 1880s (*Muslim-manas o bangla sahitya*, 2012).

[13] Islamic primary schools.

Breaking the Cycle of Bad Readers   51

The Muslims, having lost their social status, were faced with the realization that they no longer had any claim to ruling the region. Their process of recovery and reinstatement in Bengali social life was slow, and, for most, impossible, given the predominance of Hindu presence in Bengal.

What this historical detour reveals is that looking for the views of the Muslim intelligentsia on reading or writing texts in Bengali resembles an archeological dig, requiring the scholar to brush away layers of Bengali Hindu texts before revealing a slim body of work. By the time one has discovered this body, one is already into the 1870s, and even here the majority of the discussion revolves around works written in imitation of Sanskritic Bengali.[14] However what this limited archive should not suggest is that the Muslims were not producing or consuming literature through the course of the nineteenth century; judging by subscription data on Bengali periodicals, they were certainly reading in Bengali. As the work of scholars such as Jennifer Dubrow and Maryam Wasif Khan suggests, Muslim Bengalis were part of a vibrant pan-Indian community writing and reading in Urdu, and occasionally in Persian. When it comes to writing in Bengali, the Muslim intelligentsia appears to share some of the same concerns as its Hindu counterpart—this writing should be attentive to the social and moral needs of the Muslim reader. There is, however, a communal aspect that colors most available discussions of reading within this community. That the reader needs morally sound texts is undeniable, but that these texts should be produced by Muslims as they are the ones who know the reader's needs best is equally evident. Thus this practice of reading still uses the same markers as the Hindu texts—quality of paper and font, location of press, and literary respectability— but these are now filtered through the lens of Islam, and more importantly, the text's identity as part of a Bengali Muslim literary culture. What is also worth noting here is that despite this reader's proficiency in Urdu and Persian, and in literary traditions expanding outside Bengal, most discussions still present as

---

[14] Part of the reason why the 1860s and 1870s are significant in making visible Muslim thought in colonial Bengal has to do with calls for a systematic reform of Islam in the region. Reformist leaders such as Titu Mir, those of the Tariqa-e-Muhammadiya, and of the Faraidis seek to purge Islam of its non-Islamic elements, which these leaders feel have seeped into the religion via the close relationship between Islam, Hinduism, and a number of syncretist folk beliefs. Reformers sought social, religious, and linguistic change, combatting colonial power on the one hand, and Sufi pirs on the other. They focused particularly on ameliorating the conditions of the Muslim peasantry whom they identified as suffering from the combined pressures of the colonial state and religious confusion. This reformist push led to an increased need felt by Bengali Muslims to articulate their identity as either Bengali or Muslim, given the Hindu undertones associated with the Bengali regional identity. Rafiuddin Ahmad's *The Bengal Muslims* and Anisujjaman's *Muslim-manas o bangla sahitya* examine at length the peculiar position of Bengali Muslims during the second half of the nineteenth century.

fluid the reader's relationship with Bengali works. The awareness that Bengali as a language is near exclusively a Hindu one permeates the Muslim imagination, and it leads to a need to educate the Bengali Muslim in reading Bengali in ways devised by those in their community, rather than accepting the relationship between the text and the reader as agreed upon by Hindus or the British.

In what follows, I divide the debates over reading and education into three sections. The first investigates colonial pedagogical policies with particular reference to William Adam's *Reports on Vernacular Education in Bengal and Bihar* and the material appended to this text by James Long. Here it becomes apparent that first the East India Company and then the British government prioritize utility over taste when it comes to educating the masses, and that their primary concern was not providing Indians with an English language education but rather a transmission of English ideals through suitably bolstered vernaculars. The debate over languages of instruction is as detailed as that over curricula, and juxtaposing these two lines of thought—what language to use and what material to teach—creates an intriguing literacy map of colonial Bengal. The idea of trickle-down education is dismissed by most British educators and civil servants owing to the cost of implementing the method, and the colonial policymakers are far more concerned with giving the masses basic literacy than with creating a "class of persons Indian in blood and colour, but English in tastes."[15] The masses, or the *shādhāran* (average) Bengali, is also the subject of much discussion within the Hindu intelligentsia invested in cultivating a literary market. It is worth noting here that while a number of these discussions do not directly discuss Bengal or are experiments in reading conducted far outside the region in places such as the Agra Prison and the north-western provinces,[16] they all have an impact on the ways in which reading is imagined and taught by colonial and colonial-adjacent schools. The discussion curated here demonstrates the various axes along which reading was being imagined and implemented in the curricula by the British in colonial India. The second section of this chapter looks at the Hindu intelligentsia—largely, though not exclusively, identified as the *bhadralōk* (gentleman)—and their efforts to secure the allegiance of the *shādhāran* reader, and define the idea of the literate reader. The dominant rhetoric in this conversation is that of obscenity or vulgarity, and

---

[15] Macaulay, "Minute on Indian Education" (1835).

[16] An administrative region in British India, covering the area of what is today northern India, including Delhi, Punjab, and later Uttar Pradesh.

of the need to rid Bengali of its unsightly appetite for popular or low literature. The final section turns to the debate over reading within Muslim readers, and here one notes that the real threat comes from the predominance of Hindu writers and readers, and from a book market that all but invisibilizes the Muslim community.

II. Bad Readers and the Debate over Education

In the Preface to the first issue of *Bangadarśan*, one of the most important literary periodicals of its time, the editor remarks on the shortcomings of the "filter down" policy of education. The editor, Bankimchandra Chattopadhyay, questions why those at the top of the social ladder should be the first to receive comprehensive schooling, given that this system appears to benefit only the colonial government and places the burden of educating the vast majority of Bengalis on the colonized elite. Bankim's seemingly facetious description of the policy conceals within it a deep distrust of the British pedagogical approach:

> Currently, there is talk of the "filter down" of education. What this means is that it is enough to educate the upper classes, without feeling the need to separately educate those belonging to the lower classes; they will become educated by the by. Like a sponge requires moisture only on the upper surface for its lowest strata to become wet, the educational waters can moisten the commonest classes of the sponge that is the Bengali race, by being applied only to the topmost layer.[17]

The elaborate metaphor speaks to the colonial administration's inability to comprehend social realities—Bengal is far from being a singular, uniform sponge with each stratum in some form of contact with the others—and the sheer amount of time it would take such a process of knowledge transfer to occur, were it even a possibility. For Bankim, the fallacy of this plan is evident in the distance between educated natives and the impoverished masses, and in the presence of the huge population of bad readers who remain morally and intellectually untouched by the waters of education.

Bankim is far from alone in questioning the efficacy of trickle-down education. William Adam, a missionary and education reformist tasked with examining existing schooling systems in Bengal, argues elaborately against what

---

[17] Bankim, "Preface," *Bangadarśan*, vol. 1, 1872, 3, translation mine.

he terms "descending" education.[18] In 1835, Adam is employed by the General Committee on Public Instruction (formed in 1823) on the recommendation of William Cavendish Bentinck, the governor general of Bengal, to conduct a census of Bengal and Bihar's schools, teachers, and pupils, and he submits three reports in 1835, 1836, and 1838. In these reports—formally titled *Report on Vernacular Education in Bengal and Bihar*—Adam argues for measures which would provide some form of state-supervised vernacular education to the masses. Adam notes that to expect education to merely descend would be a fallacy on the General Committee's part since it fails to account for two significant elements—simply educating the upper classes in urban centers will not ensure that students are attracted to the rural schools to form the mass to whom education can then descend to, and neither will this method be cost effective since it will not be able to take advantage of preexisting infrastructure and have to start every school from scratch. Instead, Adam suggests basing education on "native institutions" and on improving the vernacular languages to create a large body of students possessing basic literacy, some of whom can then be given further training in an English education. In his *Report*, he notes that though most districts in Bengal and Bihar have native schools, these are ill-equipped, riddled with caste and religious prejudice, and while Bengalis are becoming more open to the idea of attending or sending their children to the Vernacular and Normal schools established by the British Raj, attendance is still fairly low.

The practice of reading Adam recommends is based on the principle of utility—the masses should be taught to read such that they possess basic useful knowledge, and they should be taught in vernacular languages rather than English because that will be the most efficient method of communication. In order to extend the benefits of European knowledge to the greatest number of people possible, Adam proposes to begin teaching rudimentary reading and writing skills at the village level rather than creating a more elaborate curriculum for the elite few. The emphasis on practical knowledge is framed so as to rectify a "mechanical effect upon the intellect of their [the ignorant teachers] pupils which is worked upon and chiseled out, and that in a very rough style, but which remains nearly passive in their hands, and is seldom taught or encouraged to put forth its self-acting and self-judging capacities."[19] This particular remark is

---

[18] Adam, *Report*, 257–8 ("The fallacy of education merely descending").
[19] Adam, *Report*, 94.

Breaking the Cycle of Bad Readers 55

based on Adam's observation of Bengali Hindu schools or *pāthśālās* in Natore[20] but its sentiments are echoed throughout the report; the education provided in native schools is mechanically transmitted (presumably referring to the Sanskrit practice of *śruti* or aurality), and even if students learn anything, that knowledge does not inspire the intellect. Even when Adam investigates *madrasās*[21] he appears to find a very similar situation wherein the *maulvi* or teacher is as inept as the *pandit* or the *guru mahāśay*.[22] If anything, he finds the Muslim population to be far less amenable to education owing primarily to their poverty and marginal status in what he notes are predominantly Hindu areas. The *Report* also suggests that the little education that is imparted to these students—be they Hindu or Muslim—fails to be of any practical use because the instructors lack both a sense of vocation and, in most cases, any familiarity with the printed book. Thus both parties are compelled to be at the mercy of whatever little knowledge possessed by the teacher, and on the unreliable *punthis*, manuscripts, almanacs, and the "stray missionary tract."[23]

The absence of print texts brings Adam to one of his most significant recommendations—the need to disseminate standardized textbooks. Adam believes that for knowledge to be useful it must be based in texts that are consistent and verifiable. To that end, he dedicates a considerable portion of his *Report* to determining the nature and number of books available to native teachers and students, and he finds them to be virtually absent. The *Report* notes that barring the very young who merely repeat sounds without understanding their meaning, "native school-boys learn every thing that they do learn not merely by reading but by writing it."[24] And yet, it is only when by looking closely at the material that they are reading can Adam understand why, despite the seeming investment in reading and writing, the "native school-boy" emerges as abysmally undereducated. To his dismay, he discovers that what these students call reading is restricted to texts such as "*Saraswati Bandana*, or salutation to the Goddess of Leaning" whose samples he compares to find that "they are quite different from each other [...] and both are doggerels of the lowest description even among Bengali compositions."[25] Not only, then, is the scant reading

---

[20] A district now in northern Bangladesh.
[21] Islamic schools.
[22] Teachers in *pāthśālās*.
[23] *Report* 97.
[24] Ibid., 100.
[25] Ibid., 97.

material poor in quality and inconsistent, but the students aren't even engaged in actually reading them. Adam continues in the same vein as he describes what he calls the "four different stages in a course of Bengali [Hindu] instruction"[26]; to write means to make marks on the ground and then on palm leaves (neither of which he finds suitable surfaces), and to read means to recite by memorizing in some capacity.

Having surveyed the length and breadth of Bengal, and even parts of Bihar, Adam returns to his recommendation—Bengalis must be introduced to real, useful learning, and if using the existing social infrastructure means that they will be gradually wooed into the English system of education rather than rejecting outright a foreign imposition, then that must be adopted as the most efficient course. He proposes a four-part series of vernacular school books for this improved method of instruction so as to negate the possibility of native school teachers having the freedom to define essential skills such as reading according to barbaric principles. As one reads through the detailed description of what will be covered by each book in the series, it becomes evident the kind of reading he wishes to implement. The first book of the series, meant to allay the fears of those natives apprehensive of European encroachment into religion and culture, will present in print form the methods of reading and writing in use in native schools. Thus this book will give teachers and students "instruction in writing on the ground, on the palm-leaf, on the plantain or sal-leaf, *and on paper*; in reading *both written and printed* composition."[27] Adam suggests teaching students not only how to read print and write on paper, but he wishes to commit to print the ephemeral and the intangible, and to reintroduce to the Bengali material that is already familiar to them but through the defamiliarized form of print text books. Through learning to read this first textbook, the Bengali student can learn to read known practices, but this time from the perspective of the outsiders who has deemed it necessary that these be seen as the first step toward acquiring real, practical knowledge. Adam also recommends translating Sanskrit into Bengali for this textbook, and uses it to teach the student how to read all of the basic elements of the entire course of education taught at Hindu schools. The descriptions of the rest of these books make for fascinating study, but suffice it to say that each book in the series moves from one area of practical knowledge to another—starting with agriculture, to law and civic science, to a

[26] Ibid., 98.
[27] *Report*, 271.

working knowledge of geography and astronomy. Given Adam's insistence that both teachers and pupils be regularly tested and pitted in friendly competition against each other to see which school is doing the best, it becomes apparent that reading in his world is the process of imbibing information and repeating it when required. One is reminded of his own critique of native schools for being too mechanical, but this new system, for Adam, is one that employs the "reading, memorizing, repeating" formula to provide the Bengali the benefits of a practical education.

Despite all his efforts, Adam's textbooks never come to fruition as the General Committee rejects his proposal deeming it impractical and, ironically, too expensive. The rejection, however, has less to do with the recommendations themselves and more to do with the internal disputes between the Orientalists and the Occidentalists, with the former wanting colonial education to include texts in classical Indian languages such as Sanskrit and Arabic, and the latter urging for a curricula based exclusively in English. The intricacies of this debate over education are not this work's focus and have been discussed at length by scholars such as Gauri Viswanathan,[28] Pramod Nayar,[29] and Parimala Rao.[30] What is of interest to me here is the popularity of Adam's suggestions among education reformers in colonial India, and the extent to which that interest is tied to the medium of instruction which, paradoxically, is one of the main reasons behind the *Report*'s dismissal. Adam provides one of the strongest arguments in favor of promoting European education using vernacular medium, and it is because of his emphasis on using languages known to the masses that he can successfully articulate a pedagogical system that begins at the village school level and moves up to urban schools and ultimately to the level of the university. In his *Report*, he is able to sidestep the Orientalist/Occidentalist debate entirely by presenting the vernacular as the linguistic medium that can be developed to convey English thought while being simultaneously imbued with the literary merits of Sanskrit or Arabic. The language of instruction as envisioned by Adam would thus encourage the colonized Indian to read texts in a familiar language with a seemingly natural affinity for literary productions in classical Indian languages, but in reality be a means for introducing this reader to the true knowledge contained within English.

---

[28] *Masks of Conquest* (1989).
[29] *Colonial Education and India* (2020).
[30] *Beyond Macaulay: Education in India* (2020).

58   *The Novel in Nineteenth-Century Bengal*

He frames this linguistic approach in terms of how textbooks might avoid inciting religious controversy, but if one takes a closer look at the section of the *Report*, the larger implications of such a move become apparent. It is worth quoting at length here:

> Perhaps, the best way in which this [religious neutrality] might be effected would be, without employing any direct forms of religious inculcation, to cause the spirit of religion—its philanthropic principles and devotional feelings— to pervade the whole body of instruction on other subjects. On these other subjects, physical science, moral truths, and the arts and philosophy of civil and social life, the aim should be, not to translate European works into the words and idioms of the native languages, nor to adopt native works without the infusion of European knowledge, but so to combine the substance of European knowledge with native forms of thought and sentiment, and with the precepts, examples, maxims, and illustrations of native literature as shall render the school-books both useful and attractive. For this purpose the union of European and Native agency would be necessary, European agency aided by the best works that have been framed in Europe and America for the use of schools, and Native agency of a higher order of qualification to command readily the resources and appliances of native learning.[31]

Adam eschews both the translation of European works into vernacular languages, and the adoption of unfiltered Indian texts in his method. His focus instead is on combining and creating a union between European thought and Indian languages such that what is produced is Indian in form and European in spirit. This practice, which I have called a hollowing out of the vernacular elsewhere in this work, relies on retaining enough of "native forms of thought and sentiment" to draw the native speaker of the vernacular into believing that what is being communicated is known and familiar. Having worked as first a Baptist and then a Unitarian missionary, Adam has first-hand knowledge of the barrier posed to communicating foreign thought in a foreign language. Similarly, as an associate of Baptist missionaries such as William Carey and John Clark Marshman, Adam knows that translating European knowledge into vernacular languages such as Bengali and Hindi produces at best incomprehension on the part of the colonized, and at worst, laughter and derision.[32] The alternative he proposes

---

[31] *Report*, 272.

[32] Carey's nephew, Eustace Carey, notes in his *Memoir of William Carey* (1836) the numerous sessions Carey had with Indians when he believed he had successfully communicated teachings from the Bible in Bengali only to be flabbergasted on realizing that his Bengali sermon was all but unintelligible to his audience.

is thus born of practical experience with the inhabitants of rural Bengal, and he argues for using the vernacular to provide the explanatory mechanisms—such as examples, illustrations, and maxims—needed to transmit the spirit of European thought. In this section, we see as a reliance on native informants who, having received the benefits of an Anglicized education, now possesses the higher qualifications necessary to recast tried and tested schoolbooks into the mold of "native learning."

This bringing together of Indians teaching each other with the idea of an improved vernacular finds numerous takers across nineteenth-century colonial India, and in places as far afield as the north-western provinces and its capital Agra, and Manipur, we see Adam's suggestions being implemented in teaching Indians the basic tenets of literacy. For example, James Thomason, the lieutenant-governor of the north-western provinces from 1843 till his death in 1853, established a system of village schools to promote popular education, and strongly advocated for this education to be in the vernaculars of the region. In Thomason's promulgations we see the continued emphasis on training Indians to teach themselves while being "aided by the distribution of books" written in an improved vernacular.[33] He sent to his Collectors statistics drawn up by Adam to encourage them to implement this pedagogical structure, and this notice to the Collectors also delineates the curriculum to be followed. Thomason includes with the notice six "Indigenous Books on spelling, arithmetic, mensuration" to impart "to the peasantry certain plain practical everyday knowledge."[34] That the rural population is the specific target of Thomason's efforts becomes evident from his desire to educate "the peasantry" as he finds institutions of higher education teaching in classical Indian languages, already in existence in urban centers, supported both ideologically, and more importantly, financially, by wealthy Indians themselves.[35] For the masses, Thomason devices a pedagogical policy that crucially equates vernacular with elementary education. As his biographer, Richard Temple notes, Thomason's educational efforts stemmed from the latter's interest in reforming land and property rights in northern India. According to Temple, "[Thomason] thought, that unless the peasant proprietors should learn to read the entries regarding their own lands, they could never be fully sure that

[33] As quoted in vol. 63 of *The Calcutta Review* (1876), 129.
[34] As quoted in Long's Preface to Adam's *Report*.
[35] Thomason terms this the "Hulkabandi system of education," referring to teaching clusters of *hulqs* or groups of villages. Parimala Rao's *Beyond Macaulay: Education in India, 1780–1860* explores Thomason's work at length.

60   *The Novel in Nineteenth-Century Bengal*

the record, with the changes occurring from year to year, was fully kept up."[36] Reading, then, was to be taught as an essential skill to ensure regularity in record keeping, which helps us further understand the nature of a practically useful education. The reason behind the reading material provided to these soon-to-be educated students in the six "Indigenous Books" becomes apparent— mensuration to ensure that the peasant farmer knows how to measure their land and its produce, and spelling and arithmetic to guarantee that this same farmer can then keep an accurate, updated record. Adam's four-part textbook series may not have seen the light of day, but in Thomason's six books, written in the vernacular, they find an articulation.

I want to conclude this section with one other example of colonial Indians being taught to read as means of acquiring practical knowledge. One of the most notable instances of the same is Dr. Walker's experiments, first conducted in the Manipur Jail, and then more successfully in the Agra Prison in 1851. The superintendent of the Agra Prison, Dr. Walker, introduced a system whereby prisoners were taught basic vernacular alphabets and arithmetic, and they in turn instructed other inmates. The method was seen as so successful that Frederic J. Mouat, secretary to the Calcutta Council of Education, commended its ability to turn the prisoners themselves into "chief agents in their own amelioration."[37] A number of Walker's recommendations are interesting for the way they echo the prevailing attitudes in favor of mass vernacular education, and both Walker and Mouat receive the full support of the Governor-General of India, Lord Dalhousie. A glance at Walker's prescribed syllabus helps explain why it is so desirable for the colonial government, and why it is partially at the root of Bankim's lament that the Bengali individual is improperly educated:

"Before a prisoner can pass the first examination, he must be able—

I.—To read the Surajpur kahani, (a Village Tale).
II.—To repeat the Multiplication Table up to 16×16.
III.—To repeat the Multiplication of Fractions up to 6 1/2×25."[38]

The following examinations required prisoners to repeat the first examination, and be tested on additional texts such as *Patra Mālikā* (*Letter Writer*), *The Kisām Opdesh* (*A Brief Explanation of the Revenue System and Village Accounts*), *The Shudhi-Darpan* (*A Popular Treatise on Hygiene*), *The Gyān Cālish Biburn* (*Forty*

---

[36] Temple, 171 (1893).
[37] As quoted in Long's *Adam's Report*, 16.
[38] Ibid., 15.

Moral Maxims In Verse with Explanations and Deductions), alongside subjects such as simple and compound arithmetic, and geography.[39] With the exception of *The Gyān Cālish Biburn*, the concept of critically explaining a text does not feature in this syllabus, and even with this work, the focus is on memorizing the maxims. The idea of learning by rote or repetition is deeply engrained in this system of education—a practice which continues to inform much of school and higher education pedagogy in India even today—and academic success is gauged by the student's ability to retain information, rather than analyze the same. In valuing repetition over analysis, Walker and his contemporaries are merely following the most innovative pedagogical techniques of their day, which encouraged the memorization of facts, and following the teacher or the class leader in repeating phrases or multiplication tables. The other point to note in this syllabus is the attention it pays to the needs of the agricultural community; the *Kisām Opdesh* is supplemented by information pertaining to land revenue, measurement of agricultural land, and the basics of bookkeeping. However, the most telling factor of this syllabus, and of the system of education it represents, is the impetus on vernacular languages as the medium of instruction. As the Education Despatches of 1854 and 1859 reveal, there is a growing demand for educating the colonized in their own languages so as to ensure maximum reach of ideas at minimum cost to the government.

The success of Walker's method along with the successes in the north-western provinces under Thomason create a strong case for the reintroduction of ascending vernacular education in Bengal, despite the initial rejection of the plan. Following Thomason's death, Lord Dalhousie issues a Minute in October 1853, urging the Court of Directors of the East India Company to continue to implement Thomason's Vernacular Education scheme in Bengal, despite its initial failure, because it is "the plan best suited for the mass of the people of Bengal and Behar."[40] Dalhousie's Minute, Thomason's Vernacular Education plan, and later Charles Wood's Despatches of 1863 and 1864 ensure that the Bengali masses are seen as fit subjects to be educated according to syllabi closely matching Walker's experimental Agra Prison syllabus. The notion of trickle-down education is emphatically rejected, with Wood going so far as to suggest that the government sponsor only the education of the general populace, and ask those belonging to the upper classes to pay for their own education. The argument Wood and his

[39] Ibid.
[40] Lord Dalhousie's "Minutes on Vernacular Education," as quoted in Long's *Adam's Report*, 17.

62   *The Novel in Nineteenth-Century Bengal*

colleagues propose is that following the establishment of the universities in the Presidency towns, the government will have done as much as possible to place the benefits of Western education before the elite classes.

As this overview of the British pedagogical policies in colonial India demonstrates, the Bengali individual educated by this system would have learned to approach reading as an entirely practical skill. Such a reader would possess basic literacy, and even as they made their way through the system, the primacy of useful knowledge in a hollowed-out Bengali language would have been reiterated at each level. Reading thus defined—through the lens of Thomason's "Indigenous Books," Adam's introductory textbooks, and Walker's prison curriculum—would appear to be pragmatic, use-driven, and with little literary or aesthetic aspirations. Those Bengalis lucky enough to attend an institution of higher education such as Hindu College or Sanskrit College would certainly have had a very different approach to reading, but as the statistics in each of these educational Despatches show, they would have formed a near invisible minority. However, these very Bengalis, belonging as they did to the upper classes, sought to challenge the British stranglehold on skills such as reading, and their efforts to define the practice of reading is what I take up in the next section.

III. The Hindu Intelligentsia's Critique—Consequences of Basic Literacy and the Obscenity Debate

When James Long conducts the first wide-scale census of the Bengali print market between 1851 and 1860, he discovers there are at least forty-six native- and British-run presses in operation in Kolkata alone.[41] Long is able to catalogue over 1,400 titles in Bengali, English, Persian, Arabic, Urdu, Assamese, Sanskrit, and Burmese, 19 Bengali newspapers and periodicals, as well as list the names of 515 "Persons Connected with Bengali Literature, Either as Authors or Translators of Printed Works."[42] Using the *Returns* and his *Descriptive Catalogue of Bengali Works*, one is able to form a fairly detailed picture of what the Bengali

---

[41] Long performs three separate censuses between 1851 and 1860, with the 1833–4 year showing the sharpest rise in the number of presses. For a detailed analysis of Long's census, and for a more complete list of presses operating in Bengal for the period 1801–67, see Abhijit Gupta's Bengali bibliography system and location register of Bengali books 1801–67. Available at: www.compcon-asso.in/projects/biblio/welcome.php?redirect¼/projects/biblio/index.php.

[42] Long, *Returns Relating to Native Printing Presses and Publications in Bengal*, 89.

reader would have been reading during the first half of the nineteenth century. The range of print texts available to this reader is impressive—from books on arithmetic and geometry, to Hindu myths and Muslim folk tales, to translations of English plays and novels, to the origin stories of cities in Bengal such as Burdwan, to sketches of popular life. There is even a cookbook, *Pākrājeśwar*, a Bengali translation of recipes in Sanskrit approved by the *śāstras*, published by the Bhaskar press which sold over 400 copies. This suggests that readers read widely, whether to entertain themselves or reacquaint their household with the correct way of preparing meals. Long includes as part of his *Returns* the location of these presses, and that reveals that a number of them are *battalā* (lit. under a banyan tree) or cheap presses catering to the average Bengali reader by pricing their books and pamphlets for one or two annas each.[43] The *battalā* forms its own book industry—often consciously setting itself apart from books and periodicals produced by the upper classes and the intelligentsia—providing Bengalis with farces, folktales, *pāncālīs*,[44] scandalous tales, and true crime reports. While Long's surveys only record the printed matter produced in Kolkata, we can gather from other sources such as memoirs and letters that a significant portion of these texts make their way into the *mufassil* or the rural hinterland. Added to this are major centers of print production in cities such as Dhaka, Medinipur, Rajshahi, Burdwan, and Nadia, to name only a handful. That the printed book is able to overcome entrenched barriers of caste and religion is largely the effort of print entrepreneurs such as Bhabanicharan and Gangakishore, but the readers, too, display considerable interest in consuming these texts in a variety of ways. As Long's catalogue of titles and the number of copies sold demonstrate, nineteenth-century Bengal had readers with pronounced tastes, and they were curious and sophisticated, reading for both entertainment and information.

However, this vibrant scene all but disappears when seen from the point of view of the Bengali *bhadralōk* or the upper and middle class, predominantly Hindu, Bengali. These are individuals who identify themselves as urban, and while they take Kolkata as their intellectual center, they know rural and semi-urban Bengal as spaces they have left behind in search of culture and development. Led by literary celebrities such as Iswarchandra Vidyasagar and Bankim, the Bengali *bhadralōk* imagines the vast majority of his compatriots to be constrained within

---

[43] A currency unit used in British India. One anna equaled 1/16th of 1 rupee.
[44] Ballads, often narrating the folk version of Hindu myths, and origin stories of gods and goddesses along with the method of worshipping them.

a world where reading means a memorized sing song oration of Hindu epics such as the *Mahabharat* and the *Ramayana* translated into Bengali, or the barely literate *pāthśālā* pundit dispersing what little education he has to his inattentive pupils. That the rural, agricultural, poor, or working-class Bengali is caricatured as backward in strikingly similar ways by the Hindu intelligentsia and the British is no coincidence. The Hindu intelligentsia as a class is trained in British-inspired institutions of higher education such as the Hindu College and the Sanskrit College, and they play a signal role in shaping British educational policy. This group is thus not only familiar with the debates over reading as espoused by Adam, Thomason, and Trevelyan, but is also vocal in articulating its opinions vis-à-vis language, content, and method of educating the Bengali people.[45] While the *bhadralōk* class is far from unanimous in how it thinks the masses should be taught to read, there is remarkable homogeneity in their condemnation of how— if at all—the vast majority of Bengalis read. The *bhadralōks* have spirited debates over whether or not Bengalis should be taught in English, or whether the lower classes should receive as much state-sponsored attention as the upper classes, but they agree that the Bengali individual must be taught to read properly. They echo British assertions that the vast majority of Bengalis do not know how to read, and existing practices of reading reveal merely an ingrained apathy toward literary merit. Despite the volume of texts produced and consumed, the Hindu elites see the Bengali masses as somnolent, often possessing no more than basic literacy. If anything, this unchecked quantity of texts is blamed for having an ill-effect on these rudimentary readers by glutting them with reading material that is at best of questionable quality and at worst, vulgar and obscene.

However, unlike their colonial masters, the intelligentsia's need to create a reading practice is not mercantile but ideological; it is rooted in a desire to rid Bengal of its common, vulgar past and replace it with an urbane, eloquent, and developed version of culture. As a leading social commentator, Bankim provides us with some of the most articulate explorations of the relationship between reading and culture, and in his essays, we find distilled the approach adopted by the Hindu intelligentsia in constructing what they hope will be *the* reading

---

[45] As it is not the intention of this book to engage substantially with the educational debates, I will keep my remarks brief, but even a cursory look at the speeches and letters of the Bengali intelligentsia reveals the extent to which it was involved in both advocating for and resisting British educational policies. They took sides on the question of English or vernacular as the medium of instruction, on the question of ascending or descending educational systems, and on grant-in-aid or taxes as the method of actually paying for this education. For more on this see the rich body of work produced by Gauri Viswanathan, Poromesh Acharya, and Nandini Bhattacharya.

practice for Bengal. On the one hand, popular Bengali literature is branded as obscene, and thus underdeveloped, which creates the illusion that there is a need for more refined texts written in a Sanskritized version of Bengali, and on the other, there is an increased attention paid to crafting this particular kind of Bengali. What emerges is frequently referred to as the Bengal Renaissance, and is marked as a period of incredible literary productivity which goes a long way toward fashioning Bengal's identity as a site of cultural progress. That this is also the moment when the Bengali reader receives the most attention, both within the texts they read and in the discourse surrounding these texts, is very rarely commented on[46] as the focus remains on either literary and linguistic innovations,[47] the shape of the print market,[48] or the political implications of this period. By conceptualizing the efforts of the Bengali *bhadralōk* in terms of a reading practice—which involves a complex interplay of high and lowbrow presses, allegiance to old and new Bengali literature, and the process of the periodical becoming a quotidian object—reveals the extent to which this class is invested in defining the relationship between the ordinary Bengali and the printed text as good or proper reading. Seen from this perspective, the question of inculcating readerly taste is not merely a matter of teaching the reader how to read, but of ensuring that how the reader reads is circumscribed by what texts they have access to, by the kind of Bengali that text is written in, and by the aspirations this reader should have while reading the text.

We turn to Akshaychandra Sarkar's autobiography "*Pitā-putra*" ("Father-Son") for one of the many articulations of this process of circumscribing. As an editor of well-known literary periodicals such as *Sādhāraṇī* (1874) and *Nabaīiban* (1884–9), and as a close associate of Bankim, Akshaychandra was a familiar face in Bengali literary circles. He positioned himself as a champion of the Bengali language, and I examine his reviews of Bankim's novel in the second chapter of this book. Here, however, I am more interested in how he narrativizes the act of reading in his autobiography which is styled as a *bildungsroman*, charting Akshaychandra's growth as an author and an editor. As Gautam Bhadra notes in his essay "*Bāṅgāli pāṭhak ō tār bāṅglā boi parā*," the

---

[46] One notable exception is Gautam Bhadra whose work on the *battalā* presses provides a detailed commentary on the centrality of the reader and how they read, but this is a text known exclusively to scholars who read Bengali as it has not been translated.

[47] The work of postcolonial scholars such as Tanika Sarkar, Sumit Sarkar, Partha Chatterjee, Dipesh Chakraborty, Gayatri Spivak, Rosinka Chaudhuri, to name only a few, is noteworthy here.

[48] This has been the particular domain of scholarship on book history in South Asia.

66   *The Novel in Nineteenth-Century Bengal*

autobiography reads as a manual for reading Bengali books in the nineteenth century. Akshaychandra starts not with himself but with his father, Gangacharan Sarkar Bahadur's childhood, so the narrative takes us to the Chinsurah of the 1830s when Gangacharan begins to attend the *pāthśālā*, and the author notes that this is also when Adam is conducting his survey of schools in Bengal.[49] The text makes evident the conflict between Bengali and English that follows on the heels of colonial reformists, suggesting that Bengali initially suffered because it lacked both mature prose and printed versions of the same. Akshaychandra then marshals the curriculum his father studied at the "College of Mahammad Mashin"[50] to demonstrate how authors such as Mrityunjay Tarkalankar rose to the challenge of providing Bengali with good prose in the form of *"Prabadh candrikā"* and *"Puruś parikkhā."*[51] Using his father's biography as a narrative pretext, Akshaychandra proceeds to insert a brief history of Bengali prose to remind his reader of the remarkable growth experienced by Bengali literature during the first part of the nineteenth century.

Having thus established his allegiance to Bengali, Akshaychandra describes the literary atmosphere within which he grew up:

> In this peaceful gathering [at his paternal home] special emphasis was placed on discussions of Bengali literature alongside that of pure music. That was when [Iswarchandra] Vidyasagar's *Betāl pachisi*, *Jībancarit* was published. He published Bharatchandra's *Annadāmangal* "based on the original Krishnanagar manuscript." Tarashankar's *Kādambari* was published. All these books and other books of the time—printed in good font, good editions, as they were published, father would buy a volume; and in these evening gatherings, they would be read, discussed, cause a fervor (*āndōlita*). From that revolution, a fountain of joy would run.[52]

I draw your attention here to the texts being celebrated, causing a "literary revolution"—each of these texts represent a watershed moment in Bengali literary history. The Sanskrit Press, run by Vidyasagar, brought out an edition of Bharatchandra's *Annadāmangal* (1853) which was the first to identify a manuscript version as the original, spend considerable time and effort collecting the manuscript from the Krishnanagar Palace, and then base the print version on

---

[49] *"Pitā-putra,"* 470 (1904).
[50] Hooghly Mohsin College.
[51] The latter was translated from Sanskrit.
[52] *"Pitā-putra,"* 482.

this original. Bharatchandra Ray wrote *Annadāmangal* in 1752–3, but there were several manuscripts of this work, and while Gangakishore had published the first print version of *Annadāmangal* in 1816. However, Vidyasagar's version of the text, along with *Betāl pachisi*, was able to make a claim for authenticity because it emphasized the originality of the manuscript on which it was based, and because Vidyasagar was able to add his considerable literary fame to the edition.[53] For someone like Akshyachandra or Gangacharan, this editorial history was what set apart Vidyasagar's *Annadāmangal* from other available versions, and by reading it as monumental achievements, they became willing participants in creating a new literary history for Bengal. This history, as Akshaychandra is at pains to emphasize, placed modern Bengal in a continuum with its past, but cleansed the past of what was deemed vulgar and obscene. Thus *"Pitā-putra"* does not mention here how popular a section of *Annadāmangal* was, and continued to be, independent of Vidyasagar's editorial interventions. This segment, which formed the second part of the three-part *Annadāmangal*, is popularly referred to as *Vidyāsundar* or *Kālikāmangal* and narrates the love story of Vidya and Sundar, but it was deemed by the Bengali *bhadralōk* to be far too erotic to be decent. We will return to this charge of indecency with Bankim, but what is interesting here is that by adding a small detail—Bharatchandra's *Annadāmangal* "based on the original Krishnanagar manuscript"—Akshaychandra is able to show that the good or correct reading takes into account only that version of the text that has been editorially sanitized, and which bears the markers of refinement. Tarashankar Tarkaratna's *Kādambari*, published in 1849, was the first Bengali translation of the seventh-century poet Banabhatta's Sanskrit prose text of the same name. Including this reference allows Akshaychandra to demonstrate that modern Bengali remained in close touch with its Sanskrit past, and even in that past, we can find a form as modern as the romantic prose novel.[54]

But the texts are not the only way that Akshaychandra circumscribes the world of reading. Even in the brief section quoted above, we see the significance of the book as a material object, and to the relationship being established between this object and the individual. These books are prized possession—reminding us of

---

[53] Vidyasagar taught briefly at Fort William College, working alongside others such as Madanmohan Tarkalankar and William Carey, and he derived his notions of originality and the sanctity of the manuscript from there. I discuss the role of the College in shaping Bengali at length in the introduction.

[54] It is also interesting to note that Bankim uses *Kādambari* as one of his literary inspirations in his first novel, *Durgeśnandinī*. For more on this see Chapter 3 of this work.

Bhabanicharan's babu and his collection of books—and the good reader must make note of the font, paper, and edition. The object's provenance is almost as important as the content, which is why Akshaychandra is able to seamlessly incorporate the editorial information about *Annadāmangal*. It is *that* particular edition that his father Gangacharan buys and makes available to the young Akshaychandra. It is *that* particular edition that causes a fervor among its readers as it is being read and celebrated. On the topic of celebrating literature, Akshaychandra has much to say. He vehemently rejects the modern fad[55] of bringing out the "critical knife"[56] the moment one has read a few lines of a text. That, he says, is a bad way to read a text because the entire focus is on dissecting it for the purposes of writing a critical commentary or a review. Good reading should instead assume a worshipful stance toward the text such that "reading *Kādambari* is almost like worshipping Varanasi's *Viśweśwar*."[57,58] This is an act of reading that is reverential, sacred, and embodied. The reader is no mere critic, scanning the text for intellectual purchase alone, but a *bhakt* or a devotee who is overcome with joy when reading a book of high literary merit. The fountain of joy returns as a motif in several parts of the autobiography to describe the sensation of reading, and to establish reading as an act of worshipping literature. The reader is thus able to experience literature as an "object of pleasure" and as an "object of worship."[59] Akshaychandra is able to effect this melding of pleasure and worship because at every moment in his text, he has taken care to demonstrate how this reader is given both physical and emotional access to the printed word. Good reading, as he describes it, can only happen when both forms of access are controlled and guided, and that guidance is precisely what his autobiography is offering the reader.

Akshaychandra's autobiography can, and should, be the subject of an entire work, but guided as we are by reading, we move now to another, less personal, discussion of what constitutes good reading. Bankim, one of Akshaychandra's literary mentors, was a passionate advocate for encouraging Bengalis to read, but he was also equally influential in crafting the image of the average Bengali as a lazy and bad reader who was lulled into somnolence by bad literature. For

---

[55] The narrative has moved forward in time by this section. He is addressing here the late-nineteenth- to early-twentieth-century reader, and contrasting this reader with those of his youth.

[56] "*Pitā-putra*," 483.

[57] Another name for Shiva here referred to as the form worshipped in the ancient Hindu city of Benaras or Varanasi.

[58] "*Pitā-putra*," 483.

[59] Ibid.

Breaking the Cycle of Bad Readers   69

most social commentators in the nineteenth century, the existence of basic literacy among a significant portion of the Bengali population is an accepted fact. Bankim, writing in 1880 in the *Māgh* issue of *Bangadarśan*,[60] suggests that despite obstacles such as the tortures of a *pāṭhśālā*, a considerable number of people in Bengal are literate enough to count as rudimentary readers:

> How many of the nearly two crore inhabitants of Bengal can read? Twenty lakhs? Or fewer? [...] If forty percent of the boys [in a village] attend the *pathsala*, twenty percent leave before learning the alphabet. Of the remaining twenty percent, ten percent learn the bare minimum, growing up to be able to read printed *punthis* such as the *Ramayan* with some difficulty. The remaining ten percent receive a comparatively better education. If one counts only this final ten percent, there are about twenty lakh people in Bengal who can read [...] Even if someone argues that the number of readers in Bengal cannot be this high, I have no disagreement; I am ready to slash twenty lakh readers to ten lakhs. There can be no doubt that five percent of the population can read.[61]

Bankim here creates a distinction between merely literate individuals and those who "receive a comparatively better education" and are by implication on the path to being trained in literary aesthetics. Most of the readers, however, are those who are merely literate; they can read the printed text, but beyond this basic capacity to read, they lack any form of aesthetic training. Another distinction becomes apparent at this point, that between the supposedly true printed text, one that is designed exclusively for the medium, and the palm-leaf manuscript or *punthi* masquerading in print. The latter, given its origins in a non-literate— in terms of formal Western education—culture inculcate in its reader the same forms of unthinking rote memorization which the recitation of *punthis* is associated with. These ten lakh readers, though literate, cannot distinguish good literature from bad, and lacking proper guidance are thus guilty of consuming all forms of low-quality texts. The problem, Bankim implies, stems from the mistaken assumption that equates literacy with the ability to identify literary merit, and the consequence is a proliferation of substandard works of literature.

Bankim addresses the same problem in the essay "A Popular Literature for Bengal," which he begins by further breaking down the broad category of Bengali readers into their social classes and distance from the metropolitan

---

[60] A Bengali literary periodical founded and edited by Bankim, published from 1872 onwards.
[61] "*Bānglār pāṭhak parana brata*" ("The Vow to Teach the Readers of Bengal"), *Bangadarshan*, vol. 7, no. 82, 433–4, translation mine.

70   *The Novel in Nineteenth-Century Bengal*

center.[62] The "purely Bengali" reader is here identified as belonging mostly to the lower and the lower-middle class, often living in rural Bengal—in the village or the *moffusil*. The "really well-educated classes," belonging to the urban professional upper-middle class or the aristocracy, form one end of the spectrum, and are not a subject of discussion here. Presumably, the really well-educated individual, like Bankim himself, is a trained reader, fluent in both English and Bengali, and, by means of their exposure to the West and to the best of Indic literatures, capable of both appreciating and creating good literature. The common Bengali reader, mostly from the rural parts of the region however, falls far short of this mark and reads indiscriminately, often favoring the entertainment provided by poor-quality literature for the effort required to appreciate good texts. The entertainment is identified by Bankim to be provided in large part by obscene and vulgar literature, popularized in Bengal by eighteenth-century authors such as Bharatchandra and Iswarchandra Gupta,[63] or the early modern erotic poetry from the Vaishnava[64] tradition. As with Akshaychandra, Bankim, too, is keen on creating a distance between the vulgar and the popular on the one hand, and the refined and the literary on the other. If the popular and the quotidian religious can be conflated to appear vulgar and uninspiring, then the readers of the same, often in reality possessing considerable readerly sophistication, can also be jettisoned as the barely literate.

Bankim asserts that the average Bengali reader living in the villages of nineteenth-century Bengal is only capable of basic literacy since they are the primary consumer of obscene literature. The logic supporting this claim is that only a reader lacking aesthetic training would be drawn to obscenity repeatedly. To substantiate this claim, Bankim draws attention to Iswar Gupta, editor of the periodical *Sambad Prabhākar* and a popular Bengali author during the first half of the nineteenth century.[65] Bankim's relationship with Iswar Gupta is worth noting in this instance—the latter was one of his literary mentors, and some of Bankim's earliest work was published in *Sambad Prabhākar*. However, it is Iswar Gupta's poetry that Bankim refers to when discussing the problem of obscene literature in the essay "Bengali Literature."

---

[62] Bankim, *Bankim Racanāvali*, 97.
[63] Popularly known as Iswar Gupta.
[64] Belonging to the Hindu religious sect devoted to the worship of Vishnu.
[65] For a detailed discussion of the role of Iswar Gupta in the formation of modern Bengali poetry, and the problem of obscenity, see Rosinka Chaudhuri's "Cutlets or Fish Curry?: Debating Indian Authenticity in Late Nineteenth-Century Bengal."

Breaking the Cycle of Bad Readers 71

The latter's popularity becomes metonymic for the Bengali readers' lack of taste and the perpetuation of Bengali books that are too obscene to be read in their entirety. While at first glance it may appear that Bankim is objecting to the moral depravity of the reader who popularizes Iswar Gupta, a juxtaposition of the two essays, "A Popular Literature for Bengal" and "Bengali Literature," reveals a very different argument. The Bengali reader, having grown up on a diet of popular Bengali poetry narrating Vaishnavite plots such as the extramarital love of Rādhā and Kṛṣhna, and the crude *kabi*[66] songs of Ram Basu and Haru Thakur, does not know *how* to read the elevated moral sentiments expressed in a better class of literature. If such a reader prefers the crass poetry of Bharatchandra or Iswar Gupta, it is because their literacy is limited to following a narrative plot, and does not encompass the training one requires to appreciate aesthetic—and by induction, moral—finesse.[67] It would also be incorrect to assume that this reader's growth is stunted owing to popular Bengali literature's predilection for poetry; popular prose writers simultaneously reinforce the lack of aesthetic development. Bankim applauds authors such as Tekchand Thakur—the *nom de plume* of Pearychand Mitra— and Kaliprasanna Singha, or Hutam, for bringing Bengali prose to the modern age, but laments that they, too, have failed to adequately train the reader. Both Tekchand Thakur, best known perhaps for his parable-esque novel *Ālāler Gharer Dulāl* (*The Pampered Brat*), and Hutam, made popular by his *Hutam Pyāncār Nakśā* (*Sketches by Hutam, the Owl*), are ineffectual owing to their use of obscene language. While both authors draw attention to the various evils and follies of contemporary Bengali society, they fall prey to "racy vigorous language, not seldom disfigured by obscenity," thereby contributing little, if anything, to the education of the Bengali reader.[68]

---

[66] A form of Bengali folk performance in which the emphasis is on a contest between performers who can compose and sing taunts and responses on the fly.

[67] It is worth noting here that the concerted efforts of Bankim and his ilk do little to dampen the popularity of Iswar Gupta or *Vidyāsundar*. The sheer number of print editions of *Vidyāsundar* published by the *battalā* presses stands testament to the Bengali readers' ability and desire to read unconstrained by the moral or aesthetic notions of the *bhadralōk* class. I discuss *Vidyāsundar* at length in the Introduction. Iswar Gupta's influence on Bengali literature, particularly poetry, should not be understated either. He represents the tradition of literature that takes seriously the average Bengali and their language as lived entities. The comfort and familiarity of his verse are attested to by Akshaychandra who compares Iswar Gupta's writing to homemade fish curry—no fanfare, no foreign influence, and perhaps a tad common, but in this commonness lies its attraction (*Kabi Hemcandra*, 1911). Rosinka Chaudhuri's "Cutlets or Fish Curry" provides an excellent reading of Iswar Gupta's role in Bengali literary history.

[68] Bankim, "Bengali Literature," *Bankim Racanāvali*, 112.

72   *The Novel in Nineteenth-Century Bengal*

However modern Bengali literature can only avoid the trap of obscenity if it is able to reform itself as a language. That language is central to Bankim's project of creating a Bengali reading public is evident given his role in standardizing modern Bengali, but it becomes even more observable in his advice to the editors of Bengali newspapers and periodicals in particular, and to writers in general. To return to *"Bānglār pāthak parāna brata,"* part of the need for good periodical literature for the Bengali reader is the cultivation of a simplified Bengali language unencumbered by the academese of both Sanskrit and English.[69] This language should be "simple, beautiful," capturing the way the average Bengali thinks, and effortlessly leading him/her toward intellectual development.[70] The language Bankim chooses to denounce in this particular essay is that used by the learned because, though it contains within itself only the illusion of learning, its very nature alienates the popular reader. It reinforces the policies of "filter down" education by privileging the elite, and restricting the reading public to just a handful of well-educated readers.

The goal of the alternative language should be to ensure that it can be read and comprehended by the masses, and convey information which the readers can align themselves with. The specific emotion to be aroused by texts written in this simplified form of Bengali is *sahānubhūti*, a word of Sanskrit origin, literally translated as sympathy. Yet in this instance, *sahānubhūti* implies not merely the sympathetic reader, but rather one who is accepting of the content, and this feeling of acceptance can only be encouraged if the language is accessible and inclusive. Bankim argues "why should the Bengali be accepting of newspapers which provide them with news of German politics" in language comprehensible only to the learned?[71] To accept, then, the moral and intellectual guidance provided by periodicals and good works of literature, the reader must be addressed in an accessible language. The literal

---

[69] On the face of it, this might appear to be a somewhat contradictory position for Bankim to occupy given the persistent view that his Bengali is far too inflected with Sanskrit to be the language of the common reader. However, it must be noted that till Rabindranath Tagore's prose achieves popularity at the turn of the twentieth century, Bankim's Bengali is that standard for formal prose writing. The speed at which Bankim's prose becomes archaic, following his death in 1894, is itself worth further exploration, but beyond the scope of this chapter. In the mid-to-late nineteenth century, however, the Bengali of *Bangadarśan* is supposed to set the standard Bankim wants other periodicals to emulate.

[70] Bankim, *"Bānglār pāthak parāna brata,"* 438, translation mine.

[71] "Je sangbādpatra āche, tāhāte jarmmān desher rājnīti [...] likhita thāke, tāhāte bāngālir sahānabhūti kena janmibe." *"Bānglār Pāthak Parana Brata,"* 437, translation mine.

meaning of *sahānubhūti*, sympathy, is no less important given that Bankim perceives the average Bengali reader to be an emotional subject, moved by the Bengali language. As he says in "A Popular Literature for Bengal," "[t]o me it seems that a single great idea, communicated to the people of Bengal in their own language, circulated among them in the language that alone touches their hearts, vivifying and permeating the conception of all ranks, will work out grander results than all that our English speeches and preachings will ever be able to achieve."[72]

This particular essay, while ostensibly examining traditions of popular Bengali literature, draws attention to the language best suited for instigating in the average reader a desire for, and an appreciation of, good literature. The allusion to language sparking life in the reader is not an incidental one as it establishes a contrast central to Bankim's project of creating the modern Bengali language. The language becomes the site where he reclaims the racial stereotype of the colonial Bengali subject; like its users, the Bengali language is cast as more emotional and sensuous than the hard alien rationality of English. It is not a language intended for preaching and haranguing, but is rather the medium for creating literature which can be appreciated by the modern Bengali subject. However, it is also important for Bankim to distance this emergent form of Bengali from that used by the early Bengali poets such as Jayadeva[73] and Vidyapati,[74] and establish the moral superiority of the new language. The older kind of Bengali substantiates the colonizer's perception of the Bengali as an ineffectual race because by reading works in that language—such as *Gītagōvinda* and *Vidyāsundar*—the Bengali reader became a race lacking "manly feeling," being instead "grossly sensual," "inactive," and "incapable of comprehending any other class of conceptions [than love songs]!"[75] The obscene and constrictive language of popular Bengali literature pulled the reader into the morass of "his hookah and his love-songs" and prevented him/her from seeing beyond the binds of tradition.[76] Unlike the Bengali of Jayadeva and Vidyapati, the Bengali championed by Bankim permits

---

[72] Bankim, "A Popular Literature for Bengal," 97, *Bankim Racanābalī.*
[73] A twelfth-century Sanskrit poet, most famous for the epic poem *Gītagōvinda*, describes Kṛiṣṇa's love for Rādhā, while placing the latter as more important than Kṛiṣṇa. For Bankim, this poem is emblematic of the effeminacy engendered in the Bengali reader.
[74] A fourteenth-century Sanskrit poet, also known for his corpus of love songs, praises the love between Rādhā and Kṛiṣṇa.
[75] Bankim, "A Popular Literature for Bengal," 98.
[76] Ibid., 99.

its reader to align him/herself with the finer expressions of sentiment in the form of aesthetically pleasing literature.

Yet if Bankim must distance himself from the crass Bengali of popular literature, he needs to do the same with English. To that end, he decries the absurd Anglicization of the middle- and upper-class Bengali in "The Confessions of a Young Bengal."[77] Here his point of contention is their over-reliance on English as the adopted language of the Bengali individual. The talented writers of the Young Bengal movement are not inclined to write in Bengali because it is "degrading for the dashing young Bengali who writes and talks English like an Englishman, to be caught writing a Bengali book."[78] The Bengali language, and by extension the common Bengali reader, is perceived as vulgar and thus beneath the social standing of the Anglicized Bengali. In charging the English-like Bengali of neglecting their mother tongue, Bankim once again draws attention to the colonial stereotype symbolized by the Bengali language. It is a vulgar language because it is so intimately wrapped up in the very Hindu orthodoxies rejected by rational, Western science, and because it is used by the common shopkeeper and the village *zamindar* with no aspirations toward greatness. The Bengali fashioned by Bankim needs to compete with the fashionable library of the Anglicized gentleman, and be capable of producing literature as morally edifying as Tom Paine's *Age of Reason* and as aesthetically sound as the *Complete Poetical Works* of Lord Byron. Even when a member of Young Bengal writes in Bengali, Bankim argues, his sense of shame prevents him from associating his name with the work, and so "many of [Bengal's] best books are anonymous."[79]

Another interesting site on which the debate over linguistic superiority plays out is the Bengali primer, and in particular one such primer written by Bankim for the exclusive use of those Bengalis ill-trained in the art of writing in the language. *Sahaj Racanāśikkhā* (*An Easy Guide to Composition*) is one of two primers Bankim writes in a bid to train the Bengali author, and the Advertisement to the text reveals the extent of Bankim's concerns regarding an accessible Bengali language. While the primer itself is written in Bengali, relying

---

[77] The group known as the Young Bengal were mostly followers of Henry Louis Vivian Derozio, who rebelled against orthodox Hindu traditions while embracing European Enlightenment thought as the more rational and modern mode of being. A number of Young Bengal members later contributed to what is commonly known as the Bengali Renaissance, and despite Bankim's apparent critiques, these same people produced some of the earliest forms of Bengali literature Bankim was to endorse.

[78] Bankim, "A Popular Literature for Bengal," 100.

[79] Ibid.

upon "no English model," the Advertisement is in English, ostensibly to attract even those students with very little experience in Bengali:

> It is a standing reproach against the educated Bengali that he cannot write in his mother tongue. The reproach has perhaps an application still more forcible in the case of those who receive only an elementary education in the Vernacular schools than in the case of their more educated brethren turned out of the colleges ... In the second chapter he [the writer, Bankim] has explained the existing practice of the best writers under three heads, (1) Correctness, (2) Precision, and (3) Perspicuity.[80]

The student of the vernacular schools is as important to the project as college-educated Bengalis, because it is the former who is the common Bengali reader for whom Bankim wishes to create a better class of literature. This student, unlike their "more educated brethren," would have received the kind of elementary education advocated by Adam's *Report on Education* and Walker's experiments in Agra Prison. By addressing the reader as a potential author, Bankim further narrows the gap introduced by the colonial state's educational policies, while simultaneously encouraging the reader to understand the so-called behind-the-scenes of producing good literature. This second task becomes evident from the description of the second chapter, alerting the reader/writer to the hallmarks of good writing—not only must the language be grammatically correct, it must also be precise and clear. Bankim demands the same qualities from editors of newspapers and periodicals, and from authors writing in Bengali because, for him, only by constructing itself as such can the Bengali language rid itself of the vulgarity of popular Bengali, the fake learning of the Sanskrit pundits and the foreign ways of the Anglicized Bengali.

IV. The Muslim Reader

In his untitled autobiography, Muhammad Reazuddin Ahmad laments that "they [the Hindus] have plenty of newspapers. We [Muslims] have this one alone,"[81] and so the latter must protect this newspaper at all costs. The newspaper in question, *Sudhākar* began publication from 1889, and served as the mouthpiece

---

[80] Bankim, "Advertisement," *Sahaj Racanāśikkhā*.
[81] From Reazuddin's untitled autobiography as published in *Sambad-sāmayikpatre unish śataker bāngāli musalmān samāj*, 655.

76   *The Novel in Nineteenth-Century Bengal*

of those Bengali Muslims who felt their faith to be under threat from Christian missionaries and Hindus seeking to convert poor, rural Muslim communities. It also provided a space for Bengali Muslim readers where they found themselves to be the primary audience. It is difficult to capture the pathos expressed by Reazuddin, the editor of *Sudhakar* and a prominent late-nineteenth-century journalist, in English; the phrase "*ei ekkhāni mātra*" ("this one alone") reveals a sense of desperation when coupled with the construction "*tāhāder tōh anek kāgaj āche*" (they have plenty of newspapers). The word "*tōh*" emphasizes the difference in the number of Hindu- and Muslim-run newspapers in Bengali, suggesting not merely a numeric disparity but an unequal social situation whereby the Muslims have to struggle to become a part of the Bengali literary scene. While by the last two decades of the nineteenth century—the period Reazuddin is referring to—Bengali Hindus not only have numerous newspapers but have also incorporated printed periodicals as part of their quotidian life, the Muslims continue to remain on the periphery of the literary scene with few Bengali language publications, and an even more tenuous relationship with printed texts in that language.

I emphasize the language of these publications because Bengali Muslims are far from being novice print readers; they are part of a pan-Indian publishing industry printing mostly Urdu and Persian texts, and occasionally Arabic ones as well. From 1859 onwards, they publish letters and articles in Urdu in the wildly popular *Avadh Punch* coming out of Lucknow and write fan letters to Ratan Nath Sharashar in response to his Urdu novel *Fasana-e Azad*. The *Avad Punch* based itself on a London weekly named *Punch*, and encouraged its subscribers to actively rethink modes of social interaction via the medium of satirical pieces. Meanwhile, we find Persian weeklies such as *Aina-e-Sikander*, edited by Moulvi Sirajuddin Ahmed and published from Kolkata, often carrying advertisements for new works of poetry in Urdu and Persian. These newspapers were part of a developed reading practice serving as vehicles not just of news and opinion pieces, but also a means to advertise new texts being published in Urdu and Persian. For example, in the late 1820s, *Aina-e-Sikander* advertised Mirza Asadullah Baig Khan's, better known by his penname Mirza Ghalib, *Gul-e-Raana*, a book of poetry supposedly curated by the poet at the personal request of Sirajuddin Ahmed.[82] Bengali Muslims were equally interested in political drama; the Urdu

---

[82] For more on the Urdu print world in the nineteenth century, see Jennifer Dubrow's *Cosmopolitan Dreams* where she identifies a body of Urdu readers, both Hindu and Muslim, making up what she terms a "Urdu cosmopolis" (2018).

newspaper *Sultan ul Akhbar*, also published from Kolkata and edited by Rajab Ali, reported on the trial of Shamsuddin Khan, the Nawab of Loharu, in 1835, openly accusing the British government of framing Shamsuddin for the murder of the British agent in Delhi, William Fraser. When the First War of Indian Independence broke out in 1857, *Sultan ul Akhbar* published letters from its readers in Bengal supporting Bahadur Shah's claim as the last Mughal emperor of India.[83] The "Gagging Act" passed by Charles Canning, the governor-general of Bengal, in 1857 suppressed a number of these publications because not only were they now required to obtain an official license but also forced to publish nothing that would impugn the government. By the time the Vernacular Press Act is passed in 1878, Persian and Urdu publications, as with other vernacular publications, have the choice to either convert to English (as *Amritbazar Patrika* does) or be severely limited in the content they can publish. Regardless of these restrictions, there continue to be numerous periodicals in Persian and Urdu throughout the nineteenth century in Bengal, supplementing a huge body of literary texts in these languages.

The examples mentioned above touch only the tip of the well-established network of periodicals and literary texts being published in Urdu and Persian from Kolkata and other parts of British India from the early 1820s onwards.[84] They also suggest that Bengali Muslims were avid readers in the nineteenth century, who actively shaped the literary scene, had well-developed aesthetic and political tastes, and read a wide variety of material, including subscription-based periodicals. How then do we understand Reazuddin's next comment, a few lines down from the first one in his autobiography, blaming this same reader for not knowing how to be a participant in a print economy? Following the initial financial struggles of the journal, Reazuddin hands the rights to *Sudhākar* over to Nawab Sirajul Islam, but within six months of this, the magazine goes under. Reazuddin claims this closure happens because the new owner stopped the system of using agents to promote subscription numbers and collect dues. The owner, says Reazuddin, "forgot that Muslims are new travellers on this road [of becoming readers and subscribers], they needed to be forced into becoming

---

[83] The history of Persian and Urdu newspapers is a complex and fascinating one, draws as it does on the tradition of *akhbar navees* or news reporter from the Mughal court. While this history is unfortunately beyond the scope of this chapter, it is a subject dealt with at length by scholars such as Dubrow, Maryam Wasif Khan in her *Who Is a Muslim* (2021), and Margrit Perneau's "The *Delhi Urdu Akhbar*" (2003).

[84] That Bengali Hindus read the Persian texts as well is evident from the first Persian periodical, *Mirat ul Akhbar*, founded in Kolkata by Raja Rammohan Roy in 1822.

78   *The Novel in Nineteenth-Century Bengal*

subscribers."[85] From his autobiography—and indeed from the remarks of other Bengali Muslim thinkers of the late nineteenth century such as Syed Nawab Ali Chowdhury and Mearajuddin Ahmed—we find a very different picture of the reader when compared to the reader of Urdu and Persian. When it comes to Bengali, Muslim readers appear to be novices in every way; they do not know the importance of subscribing so as to keep a periodical alive, they have very few options when it comes to reading material in Bengali generated by their community, and seem to not really know how to read. In fact, Nawab Ali Chowdhury feels the Bengali Muslim to be backward enough as a reader to need a separate literary society, Bangiya Sāhitya Bisayinī Mussalmān Samitī (Muslim Society on the Subject of Bengali Literature), where they can be trained to read and discuss Bengali literature. This society, founded in 1899, is eventually merged with the better-known Bangiya Mussalmān Sāhitya Samitī (Bengali Muslim Literary Society) a decade later in 1911, but even then, the tenor of discussions remains similar to those voiced by Reazuddin, nearly twenty years prior.[86]

Thus, if the Hindus feel the need to define reading as a means of moving away from the popular and the vulgar, and the British seek to restrict reading to a means of acquiring basic literacy, Muslims aim to place on reading the burden of clearing a space for themselves in a literary scene that is explicitly Hindu and actively exclusionist. For the Muslim intelligentsia, learning to read and write in Bengali, then, is a new activity fashioned as being uninformed by their fluency in foreign languages such as Urdu or Persian. They approach the Muslim reader as the *tabula rasa* on which they can imprint a familiarity with and a preference for Bengali such that by reading Bengali, this reader can insert themselves into a Bengali identity. That this identity is either overtly Muslim or at the very least rid of its Hindu underpinnings becomes evident in a range of texts, including periodicals such as *Islām Pracārak*, also edited by Reazuddin, and *Hitakarī*, edited by Mir Mosharraf Hossain, and in the first Bengali Muslim novels by Hossain. As a conclusion to this chapter, I would like to examine a few examples from *Islām Pracārak*, *Sudhākar*, and *Hitakarī* to understand how the Muslim intelligentsia seeks to cultivate Muslim readers of Bengali. It is worth stating here that Reazuddin—and thus the two periodicals edited by him—is politically

---

[85] *Sangbad-samayikpatre Unish Shataker Bangali Muslim Samaj*, 655.

[86] The very first issue of the Samiti's journal, *Bangiya Mussalman Sahitya Patrika*, for example, begins by noting the lack of literature being produced by Muslim authors, and sets itself up to rectify this problem.

Breaking the Cycle of Bad Readers   79

at odds with Mosharraf Hossain's *Hitakarī*. I allude to this difference briefly in the following discussion, and take it up more fully in Chapter 4.

Founded in 1891, *Islām Pracārak* billed itself as a journal contributing to progress in the fields of Islamic religious and social norms, history, and literature.[87] The name of the publication translates to "The Announcer of Islam," thereby underscoring its identity as a venue for and by Muslims. The journal had to stop publication in 1893 owing to a lack of funds, and when it restarted in 1899, the editor Reazuddin saw fit to preface the first of the new issues with a warning to potential readers. The first iteration of *Islām Pracārak*, Reazuddin claims, ran aground partly because of the faults of the owners and managers, but mostly because of a lack of indulgence on the part of the subscribers. He thus pleads with potential readers to pay their subscription fees in advance and stop misbehaving as readers.[88] The *"durbyabahār"* or bad behavior of readers/subscribers does not stop at non-payment of fees; those belonging to the upper classes (*"bara lōk"*) are negligent enough to give their employees the money and never follow up to check where the money has been spent, while others are swayed by these same employees who urge them to spend their money elsewhere. The middle-class intelligentsia suffer either from an aversion to Bengali newspapers (if they are Anglophiles) or, if they do read in Bengali, they would rather spend their time debating which periodical is better than the other, rather than actually reading the publications. Reazuddin continues to list the ways in which Bengali Muslims are incompetent readers, sometimes dividing them up according to class, sometimes according to linguistic preference, and sometimes according to a preference for Hindu newspapers, but always as individuals who only know how to read superficially. The result of these bad reading habits is the creation of a group who cannot separate literary productions from other commodities, and are thus stuck in a cycle of trying to achieve petty gains by cheating newspaper editors of subscription fees.[89]

The preface continues to berate the Bengali Muslim for being bad readers even as it weds good reading habits with correct Islamic behavior. In this it moves away from Hindu Bengali or British examples of reading as a way to cultivate morality as both couch the ethical position in secular rhetoric. *Islām Pracārak*, however, is explicit in urging its readers to be good readers *so as to be*

---

[87] The journal's subheading provides this description, which also serves as its mission statement.
[88] *"Atma-nibedan," Islām Pracārak*, July 21, 1899.
[89] Ibid.

good Muslims—bad reading practices indicate a failure to perform the tenets of the faith, good ones suggest that one is a good Muslim in every sphere of life. Seen from this perspective, the refusal to pay fees or be negligent in checking whether or not they have been paid is un-Islamic:

> Such cheating is a deeply unpleasant act for Muslims. Remember how ghastly the consequences are according to the *shastras* (here referring to the teachings of Islam). Is it a matter of little contempt and shame to come under the sway of petty greed and perform such unfair acts? ... As it is, the condition of our society is deplorable, on top of it if the avenues of such cheating and embezzlement are thus widened, the foundation of society will be totally loosened, and everyone should remember this.[90]

The emotionally heightened register used by Reazuddin works in this context precisely because it is adopting the tone of a sermon, thereby converting proper reading into a moral act sanctioned by religion. The author's missionary zeal places on the reader the responsibility of holding together the social fabric, and of ensuring that Muslim society does not sink any further into ignomiy. The very few who are both educated and socially conscious are called on to not only read and write in Bengali—so as to set an example for the others—but also to convince these delinquents in a simple manner (*"saral bhābe"*) and return them to the path of righteousness (*"sōjā pathe"*).[91]

Toward the end of the preface, however, one notes a curious return to the idea of a pan-Indian reading community which draws on the practices engendered by Persian and Urdu. Thus far in the text there is no mention of either language, or an awareness that Bengali Muslims might be readers, competent or otherwise, of other literary traditions. The last page and a half initially moves toward a community outside Bengal by suggesting first that "inhabitants of Europe and America" have succeeded in progressing through their own efforts, and Muslims will be able to do the same as well.[92] In order to accomplish this task, *Islām Pracārak* promises to publish not only religious works but include a wide range of texts from travel narratives to lives of great people, reminding us of the periodical's mission statement. Having reiterated the publication's goals, Reazuddin asserts that this course of action will ensure the magazine has at least 10,000 readers in "wider Bengal, Assam, Odisha, Chotanagpur (Jharkhand and

---

[90] *"Atma-nibedan,"* *Islām Pracārak*, July 21, 1899, translation mine.
[91] Ibid.
[92] Ibid.

Bihar) and Bramha Desh (Myanmar)."[93] The locations he identifies are not the major sites within a Urdu-Persian literary community, but the gesture is based on the understanding that Bengali Muslims are part of discursive networks that extend far beyond Bengal.[94] The implicit acknowledgment that this group of readers have traditionally been readers of other language traditions allows Reazuddin to remind his readers that they do know how to read, perhaps just not in Bengali. What is equally interesting about the places he names is that this region has historically been identified as part of a greater Bengal, an affiliation which in modern Indian history has been one of violence, with Bengal being the aggressor. So Reazuddin effects a merger of two seemingly contradictory entities—an Indian aesthetic and intellectual network driven by Islam and founded on Persian and Urdu, with an idea of a greater Bengal united by a common Sanskritic language mutually intelligible to inhabitants of eastern India.[95] Bengali Muslims are thus given access to both these worlds, and encouraged to believe that they can draw on their experience of reading in the Persianate world so as to develop a practice unique to them in Bengal. As one continues to flip through the title page of issue after issue of *Islām Pracārak*, one finds this principle of combining both worlds guiding the contents. The larger Islamic realm appears in the form of Muslims of Liverpool and China, Shibli Nomani's travel through what is today the Middle East, and translations in Bengali of Persian and Urdu texts, while greater Bengal returns through essays such as *"Banga o Bihār biśay"* ("On the Subject of Bengal and Bihar") and *"Banga o Bihār bijay"* ("Conquering Bengal and Bihar").

While Reazuddin's *Islām Pracārak* draws on the Bengali Muslim reader's familiarity with reading as part of a trans-regional group, Mosharraf Hossain's *Hitakarī* adopts the opposite approach by making his journal intensely local. In *Hitakarī* we find reports from various parts of rural Bengal including the districts of Nadia, Tangail, and Krishnanagar, with a particular focus on the villages within *mahakumā*[96] Kushtia, where the journal is based. When the periodical

---

[93] Ibid.

[94] In texts by Bengali Hindu, there are frequent references to regions outside Bengal within similar contexts, but there the tendency is to see other places not a site containing Bengali readers but as part of a world that will gradually come to know Bengal. Bankim's letters to Shambucharan Mukherjee, the editor of *Mukherjee's Magazine*, is a prominent example of this, as are several essays in the collected works of Aurobindo Ghosh. A similar note is struck by Bhudeb Mukhopadhay's historical works, and the list can be proliferated *ad infinitum*.

[95] Sudipta Kaviraj provides an eloquent discussion of this linguistic tradition in several works, including "Perfumed by the Past."

[96] An administrative subdivision within a district.

is launched in 1890, it is backed by Mosharraf Hossain's considerable literary fame as the first Bengali Muslim novelist, and he re-serializes his most popular novel *Biśād Sindhu* in *Hitakarī* to boost its sales, but the editorial focus remains on rural news. Thus, each issue contains reports on the effect of weather on crops, on criminal and civil cases heard by the local courts, and on the tensions between landlords and peasants. Literate peasants and those belonging to rural lower classes are the publication's target audience, with occasional references to concerned middle-class citizens who would be interested in the former group as their *hitakarī* or well-wisher. Regardless of whether the reader is an agricultural worker suffering from the effects of a drought and negligent landlords, or a well-wisher, they are part of a tightly knit rural community. To emphasize this sense of kinship, reports frequently refer not just to specific villages by name, but to individual villagers affected by events. Thus we hear of Macchlib Sabaj Ali and Rajchandra Saha from the village of Balla in Tangail district who lost their homes to a cyclone in late May 1890,[97] and of Sabdal Sekh from near Kushtia who is being tried at the Sessions court[98] for killing his wife but the man might be mad.[99] Recounting events from everyday life with such attention to details while simultaneously not sensationalizing them turns reading into a quotidian act; even if one does not know the people named personally, they are presented as members of the reader's community, coming from the same locales as the reader and inhabiting the same conditions. Even when such harbingers of distance as trains are mentioned, the context is local; for example, the editor reports of having received news from Madanpur Station, belonging to Eastern Bengal Railways, that had there not been intense rains in 1889, the region would have produced ample jute and rice.[100] The train is instrumental in bringing the news to the reader, but the reader is reassured that this news is about a context intensely familiar.

Mosharraf Hossain includes both Hindus and Muslims as his readers, by sometimes including news and opinion pieces explicitly addressing the plight of peasants of both communities, and at other times by judiciously choosing whose names to mention in the reports, as evidenced by the cyclone story mentioned above. However, that this is a journal meant for Bengali Muslims

---

[97] *Hitakarī*, July 13, 1890, p. 39.
[98] The highest criminal court in a district.
[99] "*Sthāniya sangbād ō mantabya*" ("Local news and comments"), *Hitakarī*, July 30, 1890, p. 59.
[100] *Hitakarī*, July 13, 1890, p. 39.

becomes evident from the very first issue when the "Editor's Remarks" includes two pieces of significance. The first is a report on the number of Muslim students who cleared 1789 Entrance Exam vis-à-vis the number of Hindu students. This exam which allowed students entry into the final years of school leading to presumably a college had become a requirement by the end of the nineteenth century for most educated middle-class Bengalis as it offered the promise of social and financial stability. As Mosharraf Hossain notes, however, that out of a total of 2,642 students who cleared the Entrance, only 174 are Muslims, even though there are nearly as many Muslims in the region as Hindus. The brief report continues to lament the Bengali Muslim's lack of ambition and education in a tone that includes the reader as part of the Muslim community, and perhaps even one of these students who are not realizing how they are harming their own interests. The second text alerting us to the identity of the journal's intended audience comes in the form of a response to a letter to the editor. This letter written anonymously by a "*janaik Musalmān*" or "a Muslim person"—also included in the same issue—calls out the Hindu periodical *Bangabhāsi* for referring to Muslims as "*mlechha*" (lit. non-Hindu but used as a slur to demean someone whose practices are unclean). Mosharraf Hossain gladly welcomes (*ādare grahan*) this letter, arguing on its behalf because Muslims are not the true unclean or *mleccha*. The term should be used for those who are truly unclean, he continues, the "*Kōl, Bhīl, Cōwār, Bunō, Bāgdī,*"[101] but not the Muslims are part of a united Hindustan (India).[102]

What is notable in the inclusion of these texts, and in reinforcing the status of the local in the journal is Mosharraf Hossain's positioning of the Bengali Muslim reader as someone who is a concerned citizen, capable of both bemoaning the fate of their community and defending its honor against Hindu onslaughts. This is a reader who wishes to be informed of local news and, unlike Reazuddin's reader, is already a competent reader who is part of a reading practice spanning Kushtia's tiny villages and Kolkata's bustling Kolutala neighborhood. This familiarity with the local community, when coupled with the reader's knowledge of Kolkata-based weeklies such as *Bangadarśan*, creates

---

[101] Each of these terms refers to specific indigenous communities within Bengal. Mosharraf Hossain placing them together, almost indiscriminately, as examples of the truly unclean refers to the prejudices held by caste Hindus and upper-class Muslims.

[102] "*Sampādakiya mantabya*" ("Editor's notes"), *Hitakari*, June 28, 1890, pp. 24–5, translation mine.

84   *The Novel in Nineteenth-Century Bengal*

the image of someone who is already a part of Bengal and can thus claim a natural affinity with the Bengali Hindu reader and their practices of reading. While Mosharraf Hossain's Bengali Muslim reader reads in Urdu and uses that language in conjunction with Bengali,[103] they are equally comfortable reading detailed discussions of Sanskritized Bengali grammar.[104] Thus in *Hitakarī* we see less a need to claim a special practice of reading for Bengali Muslims and more an assertion that as Bengalis, these readers already know how to read. They are drawn toward the plight of their community which is acknowledged as being marginalized, but even this emotional affiliation does not take away from their overarching affiliation with Bengal as a whole. The Bengali Muslim's knowledge of Urdu is proclaimed as a part of their communal identity, but even here, a kinship relation between Bengali and Urdu is asserted, with the former being the Bengali's *mātribhāṣā* or mother tongue and the latter being a *bhrātribhāṣā* or brother tongue.[105] This insertion of the reader into the fold of the average or *sādhāran* Bengali accords the reader all of the reading knowledge already acquired by the Bengali (Hindu), removing the need to cultivate a different way of teaching this reader to read.

The push and pull between the local and the global, and reading properly in order to be a good Muslim, are all concerns made explicit in Mosharraf Hossain's novel *Biṣād Sindhu.*[106] What they demonstrate is the struggle faced by the Bengali Muslim in recasting the Bengali language—and by induction, the literature written in it—as one that can belong to both Hindus and Muslims. Thus it is not enough that authors such as Mosharraf Hossain and Reazuddin describe the relationship between the text and the Muslim individual, but that they do so while resisting the conflation of Bengali with Hindu. The Hindu nature of standard Bengali becomes evident when one notes the indignance of readers of *Hitakarī* at the inclusion of "*musalmānī kathā*" in otherwise chaste Bengali, and this reveals the ways in which Bengali Muslims are systematically deemed alien to their own language. In a larger sense, this equating of Bengali

---

[103] I refer here to Mosharraf Hossain's response to a letter to the editor from the July 2, 1891, issue in which the journal is accused of allowing "*Musalmānī kathā*" or "Muslim words" (Urdu, Arabic) in articles and news reports. I discuss the question in detail in Chapter 4.

[104] Notable examples are the review of Chandrakumar Lahiri's textbook of Sanskrit grammar, *Byakaran klahār* (November 1890), and several discussions of the state of India and the relationship between Hindus and Muslims.

[105] Refer to Chapter 4.

[106] A topic I take up in Chapter 4 as well.

with Hindu leads to the secularization of Hinduism whereby Hindu Bengali becomes "Bengali" with Hindu being the unspoken, neutral norm. It is only when one traces the various ways in which the act of reading is conceived in nineteenth-century Bengal that the contours of this secularization become visible. In looking at the Bengali Muslim's relationship with the text one finds, then, the need to control not just what reading means, but to define what being Bengali means.

2

Becoming a Reader: Letters, Reviews, and Memories of Reading

I. Claiming *Durgeśnandinī*: The Anglicists and the Sanskritists

In a remarkable passage in his essay *"Bankimcandra o Dinabandhu"* ("Bankimchandra and Dinabandhu"), Purnachandra Chattopadhyay writes of the first time *Durgeśnandinī* was presented before an audience. As the first Bengali novel, *Durgeśnandinī* occupies a near-mythic position in the history of Bengali literature, with Purnachandra's account contributing actively to the project of eulogizing the novel and its author, Bankimchandra Chattopadhyay. The event occurs toward the end of 1864, when Bankim gathers in his Kanthalpara home friends, fellow intellectuals, and Sanskrit pundits from Bhatpara,[1] and reads to them from the manuscript of his first novel. The story is part of Purnachandra's attempts at mythologizing Bankim as the literary center of nineteenth-century Bengali intellectual life, as the former narrates the latter's prowess in both Sanskrit *alamkāra śāstras*[2] and English literature.[3] The reading lasts two days, and such is its mesmeric power that members of the audience addicted to tobacco forget to call for their hourly dose of the hookah. For Purnachandra, the narrative serves to establish his own literary credentials as an insider to the social circles within which the Bengali novel was being born, and it also allows him to bolster the figure of Bankim as a founder of modern Bengal's cultural and intellectual milieu. The anecdotal quality of the account peels back the curtain as it were, giving us a peek into an intimate social scene, led by Bankim the celebrity novelist who had doubts initially about his own merits as an author,

---

[1] Locality in Bengal known for being a seat of Sanskrit learning.
[2] Treatises and rules on literary aesthetics.
[3] *"Bankimcandra o Dinabandhu,"* 44 (1922), translation mine.

but whose doubts were quelled by the unanimous and vociferous praise received from this first, and only, reading from his manuscript.[4]

My interest in the event, however, has little to do with either the ins and outs of nineteenth-century Bengali literary society, or the self-aggrandizing narrative of this intelligentsia. Rather, I wish to focus on two things that Purnachandra glosses over somewhat briefly—Bankim performs a *reading* of the novel, and this is the only time he ever conducts such a performance, or allows readers access to his manuscripts. Purnachandra, as a member of this audience, confesses that he so engrossed by the *path* (oral performance of reading) that he fails to notice whether the Sanskrit pundits opened their snuff boxes or not. Similarly, an elderly gentleman in the audience cannot help loudly exclaim his appreciation of Bankim's prowess as a speaker. Such is the power of Bankim reading from the manuscript that both literate and illiterate members of the audience are held spellbound for the entire duration of the performance; thus those able to read, and those accustomed to hearing texts being read out loud both feel included in this event.[5] The sitting room of Bankim's ancestral home hosts what can only be called an inauspicious beginning for the Bengali novel reader, as the reader is turned into an audience before they can perform the act of novel reading; not only are some of them incapable of reading a text, but all of them are positioned as *srōtā* (listeners) rather than as *pāthak* (readers) as Bankim reads *to* them. Purnachandra explains the event as a novice author desiring to know everyone's opinion because "perhaps at that time, he had not yet developed the confidence in his own ability to write."[6]

But what if we move away from the cult of celebrity authors and Purnachandra's obsessive focus on his talented brother? What if we jettison this obsession which later scholars of both Bankim and the Bengali novel share with Purnachandra? Doing so, we find, allows us to return *Durgeśnandinī* to the practices of readings shaped by a network of individuals and institutions including readers, reviewers, publishers, distributors, and periodicals. The Bengali novel was not born and championed by Bankim singlehandedly, as Purnachandra would have us believe, but rather the author was one part of the practice of reading that ensured *Durgeśnandinī*'s financial and literary success. The history of the Bengali novel

---

[4] Purnachandra is at pains to remind us that Bankim never lets readers see a manuscript version of his novels after *Durgeśnandinī*, let alone read out from it "*Bankimcandra o Dinabandhu*," 41–2.

[5] "Bankim o Dinabandhu," *Bankim Prasanga*, 43.

[6] Ibid.

Becoming a Reader 89

can thus be repositioned from the perspective of its readers, and the genre be wrested from the mythic influences of a founding figure. My reading of the anecdote has less to do with Bankim's anxieties as a new novelist, and more with the practice of reading novels. What Bankim performs is an absence of a reading practice, and through this performance, a desire to inaugurate the same. The genre at its moment of inception has neither an identifiable practice of reading nor readers; no one knows *how* to read a Bengali novel because *Durgeśnandinī* is the first of its kind. Purnachandra's story makes available for us that unique moment in Bengali literary history when an absence is made visible, but this absence is a site of rich possibilities, and a site which Bankim attempts to define by sending out in the world the novel and his literal reading of the text. This performance, as with any oral performance, lends a cadence to the text that provides (burdens?) his audience-readers with an additional layer of meaning— one which would have been absent had they been merely given the manuscript or the print version of the novel. This point is worth stressing particularly because of the composition of the audience attending this initial reading. A large portion of them are Sanskrit pundits, specifically trained in orality and the arts of *shruti* and *smriti*, of listening and memorization, for whom how the text is read out loud is a significant interpretive tool. Bankim, then, can be seen as assuming the role of the *pāthśālā guru* (teacher at a traditional Hindu school) imparting to his pupils a method of reading the text. *Durgeśnandinī* is thus sent out into the world carrying not only the weight of being the first of its kind, but also of having to usher into existence a novel practice of reading.

That Bankim is conscious of the kind of reading he is performing—and thereby sanctioning—becomes evident when at the end of the reading, he asks some of the Bhatpara pundits, including Madhusudhan Smritiratna and Chandranath Bidyaratna, whether they noticed the grammatical flaws in the novel's language, to which they both reply that the narrative's mesmerizing powers cover any linguistic flaws.[7] Contained in this brief exchange are the seeds of what I call a Sanskritist reading practice, a practice seeking to align Bankim's linguistic and thematic choices with classical Sanskrit aesthetic traditions. However, soon after *Durgeśnandinī* is published, Bankim earns the sobriquet of the "Scott of Bengal" which suggests that not all readers shared the practices of the Sanskrit pundits, and that there existed alongside the Sanskritist yet another practice of reading, which here I term Anglicist owing to its affinity for European aesthetic

---

[7] Ibid.

90   *The Novel in Nineteenth-Century Bengal*

models.[8] As the reviews of the novel reveal, the readers in Bengal carved for themselves two distinct identities based on the reading practice they affiliated themselves with, and both remained as robust, viable avenues till the first few years of the twentieth century at which point the Anglicist practice becomes *the* dominant—and perhaps only available—practice of reading, given the violence of colonial modernity. What is interesting, then, about the first four decades of the Bengali novel's life are the negotiations between reviewers, readers, politico-cultural institutions such as periodicals and official policies, and Bhatpara or England as centers of learning. The Sanskritist and the Anglicist reading practices occur in the flux between these entities as each practice wants to claim the novel and its future for itself.

For the Anglicists, reading *Durgeśnandinī* and subsequent Bengali novels in the mold of the English version of the genre is both an appropriative and an aspirational act. They wish to claim the philosophical and aesthetic principles of the Enlightenment for Bengali and texts produced in that language. More often than not, the Anglicist reading practice rejects any easy association with the English language—in fact, if one looks at Aurobindo Ghosh's response to the Bengali novel, the term Anglicist is to be abjured simply because it represents an uncritical Anglophilia—choosing to focus instead on Bengali as a language capable of imbibing the civilizational qualities embodied by English. These readers harbor a reformist attitude toward Bengali and frequently praise Bankim for experimenting with the same. As they read in *Durgeśnandinī* the presence of European influences, they admire the novelist's ability to shear Bengali of its conservative and vulgar Sanskrit past, and raise it to the level of a modern world (read, Western) language. The similarities in plot between *Durgeśnandinī* and Walter Scott's *Ivanhoe*—the source of Bankim's literary epithet—become symptomatic of Bankim's talents, and of the reader's ability to appreciate that talent and recognize its source in the West. It is this recognition that I call aspirational; the reader aspires to recognize the novel written in the new Bengali language as a worthy counterpart to its English/European (the distinction is frequently dissolved) version, and at the same time the reader aspires to be seen as someone who can confidently make this connection. This recognition, on

---

[8] While there are obvious casteist and classist implications to these terms—and indeed implications that some of Bankim's readers adhere to—I use these terms to refer to the literary and aesthetic paradigms within which readers read these novels, rather than suggesting an identity for the readers themselves. In other words, to read as a Sanskritist, in this argument, does not necessitate that the reader be a caste Hindu but rather that they read within the framework made available by Sanskrit literary traditions.

which the Anglicist reading practice is founded, derives from the negotiations among different entities mentioned above. It is nurtured by a desire to situate Bengal and England as civilizational counterparts, and manifested in English language periodicals such as *The Hindu Intelligencer* edited by Kashiprasad Ghosh, and cultural institutions such as the Vernacular Literature Society. If the journal allows the Bengali *bhadralōk*[9] to imagine himself as part of a literary tradition that extended from Europe to India, the literary society supports that same imagination by inserting railway timetables alongside images of Hindu gods and goddesses in almanacs. The Anglicist reading practice, born amidst these entities, thus places East and West in a continuum, even as this lineage is sometimes a matter of comfort and pride and at others a source of considerable anxiety for the Anglicist reader.

As against this, there exists the Sanskritist practice, which too perceives Bengal as part of a literary and civilizational tradition, but in this instance that heritage is classical Sanskrit and a Hindu past, rather than England and the Enlightenment. For the Sanskritist reader, the practice of reading hinges simultaneously on Bengali's ability to form itself into a modern language within the limits of Sanskrit grammar, and on the reader's lived knowledge of Sanskrit.[10] The latter is worth stressing as the Sanskritist reading practice consciously distances itself from the conservatism and narrow pedanticism of Sanskrit pundits.[11] The gatekeeping and rule-bound nature of Sanskrit pundits is seen as stifling the natural exuberance of Bengali and inhibiting the language's progress. The Sanskrit that is desired, then, is something of a paradox—it is the ideal, classical version of the language, untainted by the pettiness of grammarians, but it is also the Sanskrit made familiar by everyday use in mantras and epics. As Akshaychandra Sarkar[12] remarks, the Bengali of Bankim touches the reader's heart because it jettisons the pretentions of rigid Sanskrit while affiliating itself with a more effortless, lived version of the language that is evident in the works of only the best Sanskrit poets such as Kalidas. However, if the Sanskritist

---

[9] Middleclass gentleman.

[10] It is also worth noting here that the Sanskritist reading practice would also be more familiar with the manuscript or the *punthi* form of the text. However, owing to the growth of the print industry in Bengal, particularly of the *battalā* book market, the printed text would have become more common than the *punthi* for the average reader. In many cases, the print text would have mimicked the form of the *punthi*, including layout and font, to attract readers. For more on this see the Introduction.

[11] I base my reading here on Purnachandra's comments regarding the distinction between the more liberal Sanskritists and the more conservative pundits.

[12] Nineteenth-century Bengali literary critic and editor.

reader needs to keep the narrow-minded pundit at bay, the same must be done to those authors propagating a vulgar iteration of the vernacular. The price of wresting the language away from the clutches of the grammarians is protecting it from its natural tendency to devolve into the obscene and the erotic, a tendency born of the lack of good literature in Bengali. This simultaneous affiliation with an idealized high Sanskrit and a rejection of low, vulgar uses of Bengali functions under the larger umbrella of resisting the appropriation of Bengali by those wishing to Anglicize the language. This linguistic push and pull through which the newly emerging genre of the novel is perceived is the Sanskritist reading practice performed by readers such as Akshaychandra and Jogendranath Bidyabhushan.[13] This reading practice is formed at the confluence of colonial policymakers and educationists such as Charles Treveleyan and William Adam,[14] the Bramho Samaj,[15] and its various affiliate bodies such as the *Tatwabodhinī Patrikā*, and the Sanskrit pundits of established seats of learning such as Bhatpara, Nabadwip, Harinavi, and Rajpur.[16] Bound up in this Sanskritist reading practice is also a desire to reform Hinduism such that it can return to its true roots, long obscured by pedants, but also rid itself of those aspects of the religion deemed oppressive and superstitious by the reformists. That a single genre and its readers can carry such ideological weight is remarkable but such is the reach and flexibility of a reading practice that is able to accommodate all of the elements engaged in articulating this Bengali Hindu identity.

The ideological power of the novel and the surrounding non-novelistic discourse is perhaps the most addressed subject in the context of nineteenth-century Bengali literary history. This chapter—as indeed this book—is not an addition to that body of scholarship. Rather, at stake for this chapter is to isolate the moment when two competing reading practices become viable avenues for the Bengali novel reader, and in thus pinpointing the start of the Anglicist/Sanskritist debate to lay bare their various moving parts. An interesting consequence of this approach is that it simultaneously reveals those elements of a reading practice which later congeal into an ideologically charged narrative and which perceive the Bengali novel as its most creative articulation. The particular narrative I refer to here is that of nation building and the mythos

---

[13] Editor of *Aryadarśan*, a Bengali periodical aligned with Bramho ideals.
[14] I discuss Treveleyan later in this chapter while Adam is discussed at length in Chapter 1 of this work.
[15] A Hindu reformist movement founded by Rammohan Roy.
[16] For a detailed examination of areas of Sanskrit learning in early colonial Bengal, see Trina Das' "Sanskrit Learning in Bengal under Foreign Invasion and British Rule" (2018).

of the novel reader as entering into subjecthood through the act of reading. Bankim and *Durgeśnandinī*, and later most of the novelist's other works, have been traditionally read as central to the project of imagining the new Indian nation, and to say that this is a dominant line in Bankim scholarship would be an understatement. This attention to Bankim and the subsequent influence exerted by his novels on the history of the novel in India have led most English language scholarship on nineteenth- and early-twentieth-century Indian novels to see the genre as principally associated with nationalist discourses. Alongside this, it is undeniable that each of the individuals studied in this chapter is a significant contributor to the idea of the nation, and thus it is not surprising that the Bengali novel and its readers and critics are absorbed into a nationalist vision. What is unfortunate is the pervasiveness of the narrative of nationhood, both in early-twentieth-century thinkers and in later postcolonial scholars, such that it overshadows other interests and agendas present in practices of novel reading in nineteenth-century Bengal. That the Bengali novel is part of several robust reading practices most of which concern themselves with matters entirely unrelated to constructing the Indian nation becomes evident when looking at the literary history of *Durgeśnandinī*. The Sanskritist and the Anglicist reading practice strives to become *the* definitive practice of reading for the modern Bengali reader, but as the following sections demonstrate, their desire to do so ranges from ensuring global visibility for the Bengali language to bolstering Bankim's superstar status to demonstrating one's love for a Sanskritized Bengali despite its many grammatical anomalies. I take seriously the idea that readers, reviewers, journal editors, British civil servants, social reformers, and Bengali novels engage with each other in multifaceted, often messy, ways, and to reduce this to any singular interpretive frame is to lose sight of the various meanings held by the Bengali novel during the first few decades of its life.

One final note before embarking on an examination of these two reading practices: I base my argument on two related sets of documents—published reviews of Bankim's novels (primarily of *Durgeśnandinī* though by no means exclusively) and first-hand recollections of reading and encountering these novels written and published by Bankim's contemporaries. The second group of essays, written over a period of about ten years after Bankim's death in 1894, couch their reviews of his novels in predominantly eulogistic prose, but are the more interesting of the two sets because of the way they draw authority for their readings from their authors' personal relationships with Bankim. The figure of the novelist prescribing a specific kind of reading appears frequently in the

recollections, and as such, becomes the counterpoint to the readings performed by the essays themselves, Purnachandra's anecdotal narrative, with which I begin this chapter being a case in point. The following section analyzes the reviews and essays to examine the Anglicist reading practice, while the final section addresses its Sanskritist counterpart.

II. Reading Bankim as the "Scott of Bengal"

One of the earliest epithets Bankim earns is the "Scott of Bengal," owing to the uncanny resemblances his readers notice between *Durgeśnandinī* and Walter Scott's *Ivanhoe*. The moniker long outlives both the novelist and the popularity gained by his novels, and marks a peculiar strand in Bankim scholarship—that of proving or disproving the validity of the claims made by some of his earliest readers that *Ivanhoe* is indeed the source text being imitated by *Durgeśnandinī*. As one of the first examples of the novel in Bengali, *Durgeśnandinī* marks the moment when the genre becomes available to Bengali readers in English and in Bengali, thus widening its reach in the region. The story of the genre's importation into Bengal is by now a well-rehearsed one, thanks to the herculean effort of book historians such as Priya Joshi and Anindita Ghosh, to name only two. The "British novel of 'serious standards'" is initially introduced in nineteenth-century India by the Imperial government "as a means of propagating and legitimating Englishness in the colony,"[17] but the genre comes to be the figurehead of more than the British civilizing mission. It contains within itself an aspiration toward what is represented by an English identity, and this aspirational nature leads newly imported novels to be read well outside the educational frame mandated by the Imperial state.

As lending library records and trade figures of book imports show, by the second half of the nineteenth century the novel outstrips all other forms of fictional and non-fictional texts in English.[18] The bulk of the novels made their way to the two Presidency[19] towns of Kolkata and Mumbai which seem to be the obvious choice given their proximity to colonial rule and, as a consequence, openness to Anglicization.[20] Kolkata as the site of some of the earliest experiments

[17] Priya Joshi, *In Another Country: Colonialism, Culture, and the English Novel in India*, 4 (2002).
[18] Joshi, 38–41.
[19] Administrative division in British India referring to the three major metropolitan areas, Calcutta, Madras, and Bombay.
[20] See Introduction and Chapter 1 of this work.

in Anglophone education had sufficient numbers of English language readers to
see a sharp rise in the number of public and private libraries stocking novels.
Lending libraries such as the Calcutta Public Library (later renamed the Imperial
Library, and then the National Library of India post-Independence) supplied
the growing demand for popular fiction, and in their catalogues we see names
of now-forgotten Victorian novelists such as George W. M. Reynolds, Rider
Haggard, and Marie Corelli.[21] Reading societies proliferated to complement the
increase in lending libraries, documenting the existence of English language
readers with access to, and a taste for, Victorian novels. While Kolkata was
the landing site for these texts, they were by no means restricted to the urban
readers alone. *Muffasil* or district towns such as Jessore, Khulna, Sundarban,
Baruipur, Baharampur, Maldah, Alipur, Midnapore, Rangpur, Barishal, Hoogly,
Krishnanagar, Uttarpara, and Konnagar all boasted of developed libraries,
often founded by local landlords. For example, the 1865 catalogue of Uttarpara
Joykrishna Library—reputed to be the first free public library in the country—
documents over 12,000 English titles, a significant number of which are novels,
suggesting that the rural reader was as prolific a consumer of English language
novels as urban readers.[22]

This Bengal-wide demand for fiction, however, countermanded the directives
of the British policy of colonial education which insisted on more didactic texts
to create a morally literate subject population.[23] Once again, the records of the
Calcutta Public Library reveal the sharp divide between official policy and
the readers' demands, as the Library decides to cut back on prose fiction in a
bid to compel its readers to form better reading habits. The readers respond
by withdrawing subscription, and moving to competing libraries—such as
the Burra Bazar Family Literary Club—which, unhindered by government
intervention, continue to satisfy an appetite for eighteenth- and nineteenth-
century British novels. The Bengali reader, as Joshi's study and extant records
show, exercises considerable choice; this reader's taste is not governed by the

---

[21] Joshi, National Library website.

[22] Uttapara Joykrishna Library published *Ekti Alokprobaho: Unish theke ekuś śatak* to commemorate
its bicentenary, and part of the volume is dedicated to documenting the sheer variety and number of
titles held by the Library over the years.

[23] William Adam's *Report* documents the emphasis laid first by the East India Company's Board of
Governors and then by the Colonial government post-1857, on the need to provide Indian readers
with practically useful texts, both in the vernaculars and in English. The utilitarian impulse rarely
considers novels as within the reach of the masses, suggesting instead that works of non-fiction be
promoted in the interest of giving the reader useful skills.

desire for self-improvement, but rather a willingness to be entertained. The picture that emerges is that of a sophisticated reader of the British novel, albeit of questionable taste according to colonial and Victorian morality. In this the reader calls to mind Wilkie Collins' "Unknown Public" whose deplorable taste in literature hinders the rise of great authors.[24] Like their Victorian counterpart, the Bengali reader's choice of reading material may not meet the standards set by the literary critic, but both readers appear to be making conscious choices in favoring entertainment over education. Q. D. Leavis, remarking on public tastes and the consumption of novels in Britain nearly half a century after Collins, is more generous and suggests that readers gradually learn to identify codes such as "manly" and "virtue," as "an idiom for common standards of taste and conduct" develops.[25]

However, for the nineteenth-century Bengali reader, the ability to identify the codes of a Victorian novel signifies more than an awareness of common standards—it denotes a familiarity with an alien worldview. To be able to successfully read a novel by G. W. M. Reynolds or Marie Corelli suggests that not only is the reader privileged enough to have received an Anglo-centric education, but is a participant in the version of Western modernity represented by these novels. The reader's participation in this modernity is a result of literature's pedagogical role in the colonies—British literature, and the novel in particular, is taught in the colonies as metonymic of modern Western culture. Yet what becomes evident from the writings of Anglicist readers is the desire to do more than perceive the text as symbolic of the West; as these readers read, they assume the position of the text's implied reader. True, as cultural figureheads, the novels buy their assent of the value systems encoded in them, and thereby educate the readers to view a particular subject position as civilized and morally desirable, but the readers also give their assent because they perceive themselves to *be* in that position. What the readers read in the novels is far from a self-representation—the colonized cannot become the colonizer, the Bengali reader is not encouraged to become Marie Corelli's heroine in *A Romance of Two Worlds*—but a desire for identification contributes to the pleasure of reading.

As the novel reader in nineteenth-century Bengal imagines and identifies with the implied reader of the texts they are consuming, they take on the cultural

---

[24] Wilkie Collins, "The Unknown Public," *Household Words*, August 21, 1858.
[25] Leavis, "The Growth of the Reading Public," *Fiction and the Reading Public*, 123–4, 1939.

specificities of the latter; they make sense of what they read by assuming that despite the racial and social divides between themselves and the text, they can aspire toward the world presented in the text. The reader practices what I suggest is an Anglicist reading because by imagining themselves as a Victorian novel's implied reader, they assent to those values the reader in England (presumably British) would subscribe to. The reader continues to read Victorian novels because they find plausible and attractive the ideological foundations of the narrative. As they buy into the story, they also buy into the value system necessary to identify with the story. By no means is this a wholesale assent—the reader does not become British by proxy. Rather, they place themselves to comprehend—and thus be free to choose from—the cultural systems indigenous to the text. Seen this way, the threat posed by Victorian novels becomes more imminent; if the reader consumes the novels such that they not only learn of the lax morals of the West, but also imagines themselves as a possessor of the same, the text assumes dangerous proportions.

When *Durgeśnandinī* appears in 1865, its form is as alien to Bengal as is its use of the regional language, and it seems only natural that the existing novel reader, being used to a diet of Victorian novels, reads Bankim's novel in terms of the European genre. The plot contributes in some measure toward this endeavor as *Durgeśnandinī* and *Ivanhoe* share a number of remarkable similarities at the level of the plot. Both are historical romances, set in a past that clearly serves as an allegory of the novelists' present, and have a love triangle as the key narrative device. Both novels are narratives of nation formation, allegorized through the romantic fortunes of the warrior hero. The relationships sanctioned by marriage at the end of the novels—Ivanhoe and Rowena in *Ivanhoe*, and Jagatsingha and Tilottama in *Durgeśnandinī*—represent the national identity championed by Scott and Bankim respectively, while the unrequited loves of Rebecca (and the Norman knight, Bois-Guilbert) and Ayesha come to stand for the exclusions necessary for any conceptualization of the nation. Like Ivanhoe, Jagatsingha abides by the rules of chivalry, and though the battle during which the latter is seriously injured is a real one, and not a jousting tournament as is the case in Scott's novel, Jagatsingha too receives his reward in his union with Tilottama. Their marriage symbolizes the consolidation of Mughal power in Bengal—both Jagatsingha and Birendra Singha, Tilottama's father, support the Mughal emperor Akbar, but are on opposing sides at the start of the novel— but importantly, the unification occurs through the marriage of two Hindu individuals.

Initial responses to *Durgeśnandinī*, however, do not identify the theme of nation building as the most remarkable similarity between these two novels; the relationship between the romantic leads, and how these characters are written form the points of comparison. As becomes evident from several essays, *Durgeśnandinī* is seen to work as a novel because it emulates Scott's narrative—both formally and thematically. Writing nearly one hundred and twenty-five years after the publication of *Durgeśnandinī*, Sisir Kumar Das revisits the popularity of Bankim as the "Scott of Bengal" suggesting that the sobriquet is both positive and negative. Bankim earning the title in the first place is a testament to the novel's success, since a great work of art needs to "accommodate the response of the readership," both contemporary to the work, and in the "periods following it."[26] Das, however, notes the persistence of the moniker. For him, this demonstrates a continued interest on the part of Bankim's readers in the author's relationship with the British novel in general and with Scott in particular, but it also points to this comparison as overshadowing Bankim scholarship. The predictability of Bankim being hailed and denigrated as the "Scott of Bengal," according to Das, demonstrates that most readers, try as they might, cannot read *Durgeśnandinī* but as modeled on *Ivanhoe*.

Das is only one in a long line of Bengali critics to note in Bankim's first novel the contours of Scott's text. Rameshchandra Datta, one of Bankim's contemporaries, and the first president of the Bangiya Sahitya Parishat (the Bengal Academy of Literature), is an early proponent of the Anglicist reading practice. In a review published in the journal *Wednesday Review* in August 1905, Datta comments upon the relative merits of European and Asian literature, philosophy, political economy, and religion. The range of subjects discussed in a relatively short essay necessitates several broad generalities, but it is worthwhile looking at two sections of the work:

> Sir Walter Scott was my favourite author forty years ago. I spent days and nights over his novels; I almost lived in those historic scenes and in those medieval times which the enchanter had conjured up. Scott has, in fact, created a world of his own—a somewhat idealized, but a vivid and, on the whole, faithful picture of the medieval world in Europe.[27]

---

[26] Sisir Kumar Das, "Bankimchandra and the Modern Reader," *Essays in Perspective*, 443.
[27] As quoted in J. N. Gupta's *Life and Work of R.C. Dutt*, 383, 1911.

And of Bankim, he writes in the same essay:

> Bankim Chunder is wiser [than Michael Madhusudan Datta] in drawing from nature, and his portraiture of modern Bengal life is as vivid, as powerful, and as true as the creations of the greatest masters in fiction.[28]

Comparing Bankim to the "greatest masters in fiction"—in this case with the obvious reference to Scott—is hardly coincidental; the move allows Rameshchandra to advance the Anglicist reading practice. For Rameshchandra, this kind of reading, though augmented by learning, comes naturally, even to a Bengali like him. A few pages into the essay, he recalls the opening line as he adds Byron to the list of his "favourite poets forty years ago"—he suggests their appeal lies in their style, simple and lucid enough to be "intelligible even to boys."[29] Rameshchandra weaves this thread of texts which are natural and depict life-like characters—adjectives he employs first to describe Scott's novels, and then Bankim's—to create an image of this reading practice as being organic to the Bengali. If one accepts this as the essay's framing narrative, the diversity of subjects mentioned begins to make sense. It is not merely Rameshchandra the England-returned[30] member of the Imperial Civil Service showing off his knowledge, but rather it is the author's attempt to construct the colonized as comfortably inhabiting European texts and ideas. Thus, the exposition on European history is balanced by a discussion on Indian epics, and no distinction is drawn between the Hindu boy who learns of Hindu myths and reads the religion's sacred texts, and the Christian child who reads the Scriptures sacred to his religion. The Anglicist reading practice is not divorced from Indian (read Hindu) thought; rather, it is one which places Europe and India in a continuum. The reasons for establishing this unbroken connection between the two nations as necessary and inevitable have been dealt with masterfully by scholars of the postcolonial condition. What interests me here is the way in which Rameshchandra, as the reader, conceives of both Europe and India as being organic to him. His reading of Byron and Burns, and being moved by them, occupies the same position as his mother telling him Hindu myths in Bengali, and his father and uncle—though not Christian, as he is quick to remind his reader—narrating tales from Christianity in English as soon as he is old enough to know the language. These

---

[28] *Life and Work of R.C. Dutt*, 388.

[29] Ibid., 385.

[30] *Bilet* (broadly referring to Europe, but usually understood to be England) *ferōt* (returned)—a peculiar turn of phrase quintessential to the Bengali notion of associating status with England.

100   *The Novel in Nineteenth-Century Bengal*

experiences construct him as a successful reader possessing taste and the ability to discern good literature from bad, but more importantly as a reader unique to this moment in Bengal's history who has simultaneous access to both cultures.

Rameshchandra's review of *Durgeśnandinī*, when read along with his essay published in the *Wednesday Review*, explains the nineteenth-century Bengali reader's propensity to perceive in Bankim the shadow of the Victorian novel. The review titled *"Bankimcandra ō ādhunik bāṅglā sāhitya"*[31] is ostensibly a eulogistic piece on Bankim, and the author offers his reading of *Durgeśnandinī* merely as an example of the novelist's talent. The structure of the review is a familiar one—Rameshchandra begins with the influence of Hellenic thought on Christianity, and subsequently on Western culture, and argues in favor of such influence. The impact of Scott upon Bankim is not a matter of concern for Rameshchandra since those "who say that these outstanding men are totally free from the influence of their times and derive strength from within, are in error."[32] The inspiration is not a slavish one, but rather a creative process of one culture informing another. This conceptual framework is central to understanding his reading of Bankim as incorporating the alien into the Bengali in a bid to enhance the greatness of the Bengali race. Scott's novel, or as Rameshchandra names it, "foreign sentiments,"[33] is metonymic of Western education, and Bankim's ability to profit from this relationship and raise the Bengali from being "a puny frail people"[34] demonstrates that the education has "not been a futile exercise"[35] for the Bengalis. If *Durgeśnandinī* reads like *Ivanhoe*, he claims, it is because Bankim has imbibed the best of Western education. However, implicit in this claim is Rameshchandra's own position as a reader attuned to the same education he praises Bankim for having utilized well. The reviewer, as the reader who can spot in Bankim the influence of Scott, deserves accolades for his proper reading of *Durgeśnandinī*, unlike the critics who, though they too identify the foreignness of the novel, are unable to rise above censure.

The debate surrounding *Durgeśnandinī* and *Ivanhoe* starts even before the Bengali novel is published, if one is to believe Bankim's junior colleague Kalinath Datta. Kalinath, working under Bankim during the latter's tenure as deputy

---

[31] Translated by Indrani Halder as "Bankimchandra and Modern Bengal," which, interestingly, replaces "Bangla Sahitya" or "Bengali Literature" with simply "Bengal," 1996.

[32] Rameshchandra Datta, "Bankimchandra and Modern Bengal," *Essays in Perspective*, 73, 1996.

[33] Rameshchandra Datta, "Bankimchandra and Modern Bengal," *Essays in Perspective*, 76.

[34] Rameshchandra Datta, "Bankimchandra and Modern Bengal," *Essays in Perspective*, 74.

[35] Rameshchandra Datta, "Bankimchandra and Modern Bengal," *Essays in Perspective*, 75.

Becoming a Reader 101

magistrate in the Baruipur *mahakuma*[36] in 1864—the year before *Durgeśnandinī*
is published—recalls seeing volumes of the *Waverly* novels on the author's study
table as he is composing his novel. His narrative is interesting not only because
he is one of the first readers of *Durgeśnandinī*—though not of the manuscript—
but also since he provides a glimpse into Bankim's insecurities as a relatively
unknown novelist. Writing eleven years after Bankim's death in the Bengali
literary magazine *Pradip*, Kalinath relates his early encounters with the novelist:

> Around the time that he [Bankim] was completing "Durgeśnandinī" or right
> before it was published, I saw a few volumes of Scott's Waverly adorning his desk
> in his study. He may have given a friend the manuscript of "Durgeśnandinī" to
> read, and this friend may have told him of the many similarities between the
> narratives of Ivanhoe and his text. This may have piqued his curiosity, and he
> possibly bought new copies of the Waverly novels from the market. I do not
> have the authority to comment on whether or not he read "Ivanhoe" prior to
> composing Durgeśnandinī. In the interest of truth, I can only narrate exactly
> what I saw. I read "Durgeśnandinī" first, and Ivanhoe much later. In fact,
> I was amazed at the similarities between the two. Not for once could I forget
> Ayesha while reading the character of the Jewess (Rebeca). Other readers
> accept the composition of Durgeśnandinī to be a shadow of "Ivanhoe." That
> "Durgeśnandinī" has not been composed in the image of Ivanhoe is something
> Bankimbabu has himself repeatedly said. Whatever my own opinions may be,
> they have been retired based on my belief in Bankimbabu's words, because
> I believe his honesty to be unimpeachable. In reality, there is no alternative to
> having faith in his words in this matter.[37]

Let me begin by drawing attention to a few interesting phrases Kalinath employs,
the first being a belief in Bankim's honesty to be "unimpeachable." This is the
crux on which the argument, and indeed the whole essay, rests, for Bankim is an
honorable man. To substantiate his claim that despite appearances, Bankim did
not recast Scott's story in a Bengali setting, Kalinath constructs the character of
a friend who may have been lent the manuscript version of *Durgeśnandinī*, and
then may have informed Bankim of the apparent similarities. Bankim himself
is much perturbed by the suggestion of literary borrowing and rejects even the
mere possibility. I am, however, less concerned with either Bankim's character
or claims; the intriguing question is why does Kalinath feel compelled to mount

---

[36] The subdivision of a district; Baruipur is in the 24 Parganas (South) district.
[37] Kalinath Datta, "Bankimchandra," *Bankim Prasanga*, 131–2. Translation mine from Bengali, 1922.

a defense? What is it in his reading of *Durgeśnandinī* that prompts him to create this elaborate construction of an unimpeachable character when his language indicates otherwise?

The answer to this lies in Kalinath noticing the similarities between the two novels almost despite himself. That Rebecca and Ayesha are alike is less a matter of Bankim's composition than the reader being unable to ignore the resemblance. Later in the essay, the author describes reading yet another text by Bankim, *Krishna caritra* (*On the Nature of Krishna*, 1886), and the experience documented is in stark contrast to that of reading *Durgeśnandinī*. The former is a religious treatise examining the figure of Krishna, and Kalinath finds himself on surer ground when discussing it since he considers himself to be well versed in the study of religion—not necessarily as a scholar or an expert, but rather as a practicing Hindu with deeply held beliefs. Yet with *Durgeśnandinī*, Kalinath has no points of reference given the genre's newness in the Bengali language, and the discomfort that becomes evident in his reading of the novel can be understood as a form of disorientation. Written from the vantage point of the early twentieth century, Kalinath's essay provides a unique perspective—there is present the simultaneous belief in Bankim's literary greatness and the desire to read his first novel as representative of that merit, and the problem of having to contend with that same novel being an imitation. As a reader in 1865, even without having read *Ivanhoe*, Kalinath's awareness of the English flavor of Bankim's language demonstrates his familiarity with both the English language and its literature, and this familiarity inflects his practice of reading *Durgeśnandinī*. Unlike Rameshchandra, he is far less comfortable in performing an Anglicist reading of the novel, but he is unable to go beyond it.

Unlike Kalinath, Aurobindo Ghosh—or Sri Aurobindo as he later styles himself—has little hesitation in noting resemblances between Bankim and Victorian novelists. Writing on Bankim's life and place in Bengali literary and cultural history, Aurobindo rejects Scott as a point of comparison, arguing that Scott's "style is never quite sure" and while the novelist may have been able to "paint outlines [...] he could not fill them in."[38] Instead, he offers Henry Fielding as Bankim's counterpoint, suggesting a similarity in form between Bengali and British novels, rather than asserting imitation as a predominant conceptual framework. The question of comparison thus rises above charges of plagiarism or influence and becomes one of creating a level playing field for both the Bengali

---

[38] Aurobindo, "Bankim Chandra Chatterji," *Early Cultural Writings*, 1890–1910.

novelist and reader. If Fielding is creating the British novel, then Bankim is doing the same with the Bengali novel, and both are part of the same world republic of letters. The reader of *Durgeśnandinī* is thus a reader of world literature, equally comfortable in the world of *Shamela* and George Meredith's *The Egoist* as in that of Dante and Boccaccio. To read Bankim, one has to be conversant in Victorian novels and Enlightenment philosophy on the one hand, and in classical Greco-Roman literature on the other, and *Durgeśnandinī* epitomizes Bankim's merits as an author on a global scale. Aurobindo emphasizes this point by juxtaposing Bankim with Michael Madhusudan Datta, the first Bengali poet to compose in free verse as well as the first to write the first epic in modern Bengali.[39] For Aurobindo, both are "builders of the Bengali language,"[40] but despite Michael's considerable talents, Bankim's works continue to be read far outside Bengal while Michael remains little known because the novelist possessed a nature "with plenty of strength in it [...] not intemperate."[41]

The implicit argument in Aurobindo's essay founds itself on this strength of character; the good reader is one who is able to perform sustained readings, who is moved by the grand passions of Michael but who can ultimately return to the stability offered by Bankim. This is a reader who is comfortable enough in his masculinity to counter the criticism that novels are suitable only for women by saying that "[a]ll honour then to the women of Bengal, whose cultured appreciation kept Bengali literature alive!"[42] And most importantly, this is a reader who can see *Durgeśnandinī* as capturing the essence of a new, robust Bengali language shorn of its archaic past. It is worth revisiting Aurobindo's text at length here:

> Of Bankim's style [...] I will remark this only that what marks Bankim above all is his unfailing sense of beauty. This is indeed the note of Bengali literature and the one high thing it has gained from a close acquaintance with European models. The hideous grotesques of old Hindu Art, the monkey-rabble of Rama and the ten heads of Ravana are henceforth impossible to it.[43]

Aurobindo's Anglicism does not derive from an adherence to English—in fact, he vehemently calls out Anglicized Bengalis for turning their noses at Bengali prose—but from an Anglicization of the Bengali language. Bankim's Bengali

---

[39] Dutt, *Meghnād badh kābya*, 1861.
[40] Aurobindo, "Bankim Chandra Chatterji," *Early Cultural Writings*.
[41] Aurobindo, "Bankim Chandra Chatterji," *Early Cultural Writings*.
[42] Ibid.
[43] Aurobindo, "Bankim Chandra Chatterji," *Early Cultural Writings*.

104   *The Novel in Nineteenth-Century Bengal*

as embodied in his novels comes to represent a radical move away from the closed world of Hinduism and classical Sanskrit toward the world of possibilities offered by "European models." The fortitude mentioned above is a direct product of this new Bengali; the good Bengali novel reader can note in *Durgeśnandinī* both an adherence to European aesthetic principles and a rejection of those drawn from orthodox Hinduism. In thus distancing Bankim from a Sanskritic world, Aurobindo enacts a hollowing out of Bengali in which the form of the language is seen as a vehicle for European rather than indigenous aesthetic and philosophical principles. It is this positioning of Bengali as a language born of European influences that allows Aurobindo to apply to Bankim the leveling logic of comparison, and to see himself as a reader capable of directing the Bengali novel away from the world of the Sanskritists.[44]

Paradoxically, this is similar in form to colonial pedagogical policies which perceive Bengali as the more useful language of instruction given its reach when compared to English, given Aurobindo's anticolonial ideologies, but his review of Bankim's novels demonstrates that the idea of Anglicizing Bengali was not in and of itself ideologically predetermined for nineteenth-century readers. As noted in each of these responses to Bankim, there is a profound sense of internal dilemma when it comes to articulating and accepting an allegiance to English. However, for the Anglicist readers, regardless of their own relationship with English, the West still represents a larger world outside the simultaneous oppression of traditional religion and colonial control. This practice represents an embracing of the tenets of the civilizing mission that present England as the representative of aesthetic and philosophical thought worthy of emulation, even as it rejects the supremacy of the West. That this is far from an impossible position to occupy becomes evident with even a cursory glance at the works of intellectuals such as Rabindranath Tagore and from institutions such as the Indian National Congress.[45] The Anglicist reading practice brings together these conflicting perceptions—Europe is a model precisely because Bengal and

---

[44] Much can be said here of Aurobindo's own upbringing—his father sent him to England at the age of seven to ensure that Aurobindu grew up to be more English than Indian—and his subsequent revolutionary political and reformist spiritual philosophies. His academic and professional training together with his commitment to anti-colonial politics informs much of what he says about Bankim and the Bengali language. For more on Aurobindo see his *Early Cultural Writings*.

[45] Tagore, for example, in his essay titled "*Viswa sahitya*" ("World Literature") articulates literature as the site for expressing the human, both of which he perceives as universal, transcending the narrow confines of "*desh-kāl-pātra*," or "country, time, protagonist" (*Rabindra Rachanabali*, 771). The qualities thus present in great literature do not belong to any single nation or age, as each great writer contributes toward the project of building universal literature.

the East are perpetually inferior, and Bengal can emulate Europe to become its equal, thus inaugurating an arena of world literature, and holds them in productive tension. That the Bengali reader finds family resemblance between the early Bengali novels and those being written around the same time in England causes some discomfort, but no apparent surprise because this reader associates the form with more than just the narrative. Reading Bankim's novels comes to stand for reading—and inhabiting—a rational position informed by Western thought. While Bankim himself maintains his distance from Western influence in the context of *Durgeśnandinī*, his early readers perceive in a number of his novels not only the shadow of Scott, but of other Victorian novelists such as Edward Bulwer-Lytton, Henry Fielding, and Wilkie Collins (with reference to *Rajanī*), and of Shakespeare's Miranda in *Kapālkundalā*. As his friend and another nineteenth-century man of letters, Chandranath Basu, recollects, "[o]n perusing *Durgesnandini*, it seemed to me that Bankimbabu had read Scott's *Ivanhoe* before writing it," despite the claim being denied by the author.[46] For these readers, the novels come to symbolize a way of reading distinct from those already existing in nineteenth-century Bengal and driven by predominantly Hindu (Sanskrit) texts and scriptures.

III. "Beautiful, despite the linguistic anomalies"—Bankim and the Sanskrit Pundits

If the Anglicists focus on narrative and character in Bankim's novels, the readers more familiar with Sanskrit rhetoric and prose comment on the novelist's use— and often misuse—of language. Purnachandra's account of Bankim reading *Durgeśnandinī* to an audience perhaps best captures the Sanskritist reader's concerns:

When "Durgeśnandinī" first appeared, the Sanskrit-walas of Kolkata were all up in arms. The English-walas were of course copious in their praise ... From the very beginning Bankimchandra was worried that the language of "Durgeśnandinī" suffered from grammatical flaws ... However, it was only the pundits of Kolkata who ran Bengali newspapers who took offence at the young writer's temerity in linguistic devaluing.[47]

---

[46] Chandranath Basu, *Bankimchandra: Essays in Perspective*, 16.
[47] Purnachandra Chattopadhyay, "*Bankimcandra ō Dinabandhu*" ("Bankimchandra and Dinabandhu"), *Bankim Prasanga*, 42–4, translation mine, 1914.

The author distances the Sanskrit pundits of Bhatpara from those of Kolkata to draw attention to the latter's intolerance of any experimentation with language, but both groups, along with Bankim himself, appear to have similar reservations. In this context, the attention is not so much on the genre as new and alien, but on Bankim's refashioning of the Bengali language. The Bhatpara pundits, of whom Purnachandra writes more generously, are present at this first reading of the novel, and they too are aware of the flaws in the novel's language; only, unlike their urban counterparts, they are supposedly so moved by the narrative that they are prepared to overlook the linguistic anomalies.

Akshaychandra Sarkar, a late-nineteenth-century Bengali poet and the editor of the literary magazine *Sādhāraṇī*, traces the problematic nature of Bankim's prose to one of the first pieces the latter publishes. In a peculiarly passive aggressive review of Bankim's linguistic habits, Akshaychandra draws attention to an 1856 collection of poems published by Bankim—"*Lalita,purākalik galpo, tathā mānas*"—and to the book's advertisement. Having quoted the text in full, the reviewer proceeds to a detailed analysis of its language:

> Had the above advertisement appeared as a question on a B.A. exam, everyone would have assumed it to be an invention of the examiner to deliberately provide a grammatically incorrect composition. But that is not so. It is written by Bankimchandra himself, the same who goes on to be the king of prose ... By the time Bankimbabu composed this advertisement, Bengali prose was already on full display in Bengal, and it had become a pedagogic instrument as well as a means of entertainment ... Reading this 1856 advertisement by Bankimbabu, one gets the feeling that Bankimbabu had completely ignored this treasure trove of prose.[48]

Akshaychandra's criticism of Bankim's early prose rests on the latter's propensity for removing Bengali from the sphere of everyday life. The deliberate flaws he identifies in the advertisement result from what he perceives to be either excessively pedantic or dry legalese—both of which, according to the reviewer, demonstrate a certain desire to show-off on Bankim's part, but not necessarily his artistic talent. Akshaychandra does not provide a reading of the poems themselves because they are, for him, of a much better quality than the prose. Bankim, he feels, fails to inspire life into his prose at this early stage because he is embroiled in, ironically, archaic practices of grammar that rob the text of its lucidity.

---

[48] Akshaychandra Sarkar, "*Bankimcandrer Pratham Gadya Racanā*" ("Bankimchandra's First Prose Composition"), *Bankim Prasanga*, 79–80, translation mine, 1901.

Becoming a Reader   107

This final objection appears to introduce a contradiction in the reviewer's perspective—does Akshaychandra criticize Bankim's prose for failing to be grammatically correct, or is there an overabundance of grammar thus rendering the text pedantic and stilted? The above quote is from a review Akshaychandra publishes in the magazine *Sāhitya* in 1901, and one finds an explication of the conundrum in his "Bankimcandra ō Bangadarśan" published three years later in *Bangabhāśār Lekhak*. In this chapter, he implicitly states that the faults present in Bankim's first prose composition recur in his early novels. *Durgeśnandinī* and *Kapalkundalā* suffer because the prose distances itself from living Bengali by focusing too much on following the conventions of Sanskrit grammar. The question of being grammatically incorrect thus takes on a new dimension— Bankim's prose in these novels is grammatically flawed from the perspective of the kind of Bengali accessible to the ordinary reader. Bankim's language, which Akshaychandra claims appears only when the novelist begins to write *Biśabriksha*, combines the high seriousness of Sanskrit grammar with the colloquial vernacular, without either being overtly in awe of the first or indulging in the vulgarity of the second. This middle language—Akshaychandra defines it as *"madhyabartinī bhāśā"* or language which occupies the middle position— becomes evident when Bankim relinquishes his Sanskrit-oriented Bengali. The prose, free from linguistic pretensions, appeals to the common reader and captures the poetry of the ordinary:

> Poetry that can touch the Bengali's heart must be in Bengali. The capacity ordinary descriptions and words have to express emotions is denied to one who is a devotee of Sanskrit ... In Biśabriksha, Bankimbabu began to use [colloquial] phrases such as "herding cows," and both kinds of language [the Bengali modelled after high Sanskrit, and that of everyday use] met. This was while Biśabriksha was a handwritten, unpublished manuscript.[49]

As a scholar of Sanskrit, Akshaychandra is acutely aware of the incongruence of a phrase such as "herding cows" in serious prose; the word *gōru* or cow is intrinsically Bengali, and herding barely captures the latent vulgarity of *thyangāite lāgilen*. Yet it is this incongruity that marks the prose as accessible because *gōru thyangānō* has no aspirations to be Sanskrit, it appeals to an activity familiar to the Bengali—herding cows—in a language that is unambiguous. All at once, the reader is removed from the grandly

---

[49] Akshaychandra Sarkar, "Bankimcandra ō Bangadarśan" ("Bankimchandra and Bangadarshan"), *Bankim Prasanga*, 87, translation mine, 1901.

descriptive opening paragraph of *Durgeśnandinī* in which the hero rides across a vast open plain, seeking shelter from an imminent thunderstorm, or the description of Kapalkundalā, heavily inflected with rules of Sanskrit poetry, into the mundane and recognizably Bengali world of landlords and peasants. This is certainly not to suggest that *Biśabriksha* lacks high prose, but the novel makes a conscious attempt at tempering Sanskritist Bengali with the colloquial. Thus the reviews by Akshaychandra index more than the minutiae of Bankim's prose style—they represent a reading practice that asserts Bengali as a respectable literary language while simultaneously demonstrating its evolution from Sanskrit.

This sense of teleological progression is of import to the Sanskritist because it serves two purposes—the first is to position Bengali as a modern language in touch with its roots, and the second is to wrest Sanskrit and its influences from the clutches of the grammarians and the pedants. The irony of this claim is not lost on me given Akshaychandra's own pedanticism, but it is worth stressing the distance between his version of over-exacting approach to language and the dogmatism of Sanskrit pundits. The latter marks a place of conservatism which cannot accord Bengali anything more than the status of a vernacular, and within whose worldview, a genre such as the novel is too experimental to be considered high literature. The respectability of Bengali—something that is gained when Bankim can combine the mundanity of the cowherd with the high sentiments espoused by the narrator describing the pastoral scene—provides the language and its readers with a buffer against the vulgarity of popular literature. A fear of the vulgar, which is implicit in Akshaychandra's reviews of Bankim's prose, becomes more apparent in the texts discussed below, and Akshaychandra is acutely aware that *bankimī* Bengali must walk a fine line if it is to lose whatever little protection offered by conservative Sanskrit pundits.

However, the Sanskritist reading practice, though concerned primarily with language, does not restrict itself to linguistic studies, as a number of reviews from *Āryadarśan* show. The journal with a predominantly Bramho focus publishes reviews and essays aimed at reviving the status of the Arya or the caste Hindu, and the bias is evident in the responses to Bankim's novels. The reviews, which often span several issues of the magazine, provide detailed character sketches, and the emphasis is often on the women in these novels and Bankim's talents at constructing them. The following anonymous review, signed *"ekjan cāśā"* or "a farmer"—the moniker being a variation on the theme of the reviewer's obvious

Becoming a Reader

attempt at self-deprecation—captures the journal's manifesto in the opening lines. The review of Bankim's first social novel *Biśabriksha* begins thus:

> Bankim babu's talent at drawing characters has made him both the foremost among novelists in Bengal, and a name worshipped in every household, in every heart. His prowess in drawing the interior world of the character in unparalleled. There have been very few such artists born to India after Balmiki, Byas, Bhababhuti, Kalidas, and Banabhatta … True, Bankim babu has not depicted the low propensities of revenge, hatred, and unrealizable desires, or the higher tendencies such as love for one's own kind, love for humanity, and mercy following Shakespeare, Schiller, and Fielding. Nor has he depicted the myriad transformations caused in the human heart by excitement, or the many deeds effected by humankind. But he has unknowingly created a wonderful moral revolution in Bengal by raising love to a higher station from the depths it was cast into by the disgusting sensuality of Bharatchandra.[50]

The allegiances held by this author are unambiguously presented—Bankim follows in the footsteps of classical Sanskrit authors from the supposed golden past of India, and, despite the depiction of higher human qualities in the works of European authors, the Bengali novelist does not use them as his models. The canon of which Bankim is a part consists of Sanskrit epics—Balmiki is credited with the composition of the *Rāmāyana*, and Byas authors the *Mahābhārata*— and classical poetry, and represents the best India has to offer. The nation thus constructed is Hindu—given *Āryadarśan*'s explicit religious bias—and there is little doubt that the moral revolution Bankim's novels have brought about is religious in nature.

A curious move can be observed in the last sentence of the above quote, in which the reviewer distances Bankim from existing Bengali literature in general, and Bharatchandra in particular. The objection against excessive sensuality is one which Bankim himself shares, and it suggests a puritanical reading whereby sensuality is equated with vulgarity and moral deprivation. Bharatchandra, an eighteenth-century Bengali poet, is best known for *Annadāmangal*, which is itself a part of the *mangal kābya* tradition in Bengal in which are narrated the lives of various deities indigenous to the region. The reviewer, along with most conservative Bengalis of the age, probably has in mind the second part of *Annadāmangal*, in which Bharatchandra narrates the love of Vidya and Sundar in what is considered to be graphic details. The distinction between Bharatchandra's

---

[50] Anonymous review, "Biśabriksha," *Āryadarśan*, Māgh 1284, 436.

110   *The Novel in Nineteenth-Century Bengal*

treatment of love and Bankim's approach to the same is necessary given the content of *Biśabriksha*. It is a tale of a married man's (Nagendra) illicit attraction toward a beautiful young widow (Kundanandini), and his wife's (Suryamukhi) self-sacrifice in bringing the two lovers together. The presence of the cad (Debendra) who tries to unsuccessfully lure Kundanandini, and successfully trap Heera, a maid in Nagendra and Suryamukhi's household, not only creates narrative tension, but brings the novel perilously close to depicting moral vices. The review, like the novel, must assure its reader that woven through this tale of love and betrayal is a lofty moral position. To accomplish this, the review draws upon Bankim's ability to create believable characters, and the rest of the text is dedicated to carefully unravelling each character in the novel to show that despite appearances, it is only Debendra who is an unreformed soul; the novel's protagonists, Suryamukhi, Kundanandini, and Nagendra are merely misguided till the narrative's end brings Kunda to her death, and reunites the married couple.

The nature of the moral revolution is further clarified if one considers the Sanskrit poets the reviewer likens Bankim to. These poets provide points of reference for the reading practice performed by the reviewer—they are all noted for composing love stories, but each of these stories represents a virtuous mode of being in the world. The eighth-century Sanskrit poet Bhababhuti, whose *Malatī-mādhava* serves as a model for Bankim's eponymous heroine in *Kapalkundalā*, presents the perfect amalgamation of the various *rasas*,[51] such that the predominant erotic or *sŕngāra rasa* is both complemented and highlighted. Similarly, Banabhatta's *Kādambarī* (seventh century CE) and Kalidasa's *Abhijyanaśankuntalam* (between first century BCE and fourth century CE) narrate tales of love that transcend all obstacles, but do so only because of the virtuous nature of the lovers. The reviewer urges his reader to keep in mind this illustrious lineage not only to receive a purified vision of love, but to perceive themselves as being an inheritor of the Sanskrit (Hindu) worldview. Like the Anglicist reader, the Sanskritist reader too is asked to inhabit the world they read about, but unlike their Eurocentric counterpart, they are not encouraged to identify with the characters. They are either so elevated or denigrated as to be beyond human reach; rather, the reader approaches them as one would gods

---

[51] The aesthetic theory developed around Sanskrit dramatic and literary arts, literally translated as "flavor." It is first recorded in Bharat Muni's *Nātyaśāstra* (*The Dramatic Arts*) which he began composing around the third century BCE and was then modified, adapted, and expanded by later theorists.

and monsters.[52] Thus, Suryamukhi's love for her husband is mythic, and the reader worships her (in much the same way, the reader worships the author of the novel) and buys into the purity of her love, while Debendra comes across as too far fallen to be worthy of redemption, and Heera, perhaps the only accessible character, serves as warning for women straying from the path of virtue.

The reasons for reading Bankim as one in a continuous line from classical Sanskrit to modern Bengali are as well-documented as those prompting an Anglicist reading, but perhaps a brief glance at some of the available texts on colonial education is necessary to provide a context. Both Akshaychandra and the anonymous reviewer of *Āryadarśan* share an interest in the Bengali Bankim employs in his novels, and this is the predominant characteristic of the Sanskritist reading practice. The language used by the novelist is seen as productively reworking the rigidity of Sanskrit rules of composition, while never straying too far from this originary language. Like the classical Sanskrit poets, the language itself is perceived as providing Bengali with a cultural heritage rivalling that of the west. The Sanskritist reading practice seeks to wrest Bengali from Anglophone influences, and to establish Bengali as a Sanskritic language. To one using the language in the twenty-first century, this seems an unnecessary battle—after all, Bengali uses the Indic script, and its root language is very clearly Sanskrit. However, the nineteenth-century Bengali reader does not have the luxury of certainty that I do, given the emphasis placed by the colonial government on anglicizing the language. Charles Trevelyan, a British civil servant posted in Kolkata in the mid-nineteenth century, is instrumental in propagating a policy of supporting European learning over Sanskrit, Arabic, and vernacular education. In his treatise *On the Education of the People of India*, Trevelyan founds his arguments on the "Resolution of Government, dated 7th March 1835," in which the colonial administration states its desire to promote "European literature and science amongst the natives of India."[53] This, by itself, is not entirely novel, although the proposed plan of not supporting indigenous students financially if they pursue any form of schooling other than European causes some resentment in both European and Indian circles.[54] The threat posed

---

[52] I discuss this in greater detail in Chapter 3.

[53] Charles Trevelyan, *On the Education of the People of India*, 13.

[54] Under the old system, students are provided a stipend to encourage them to attend schools funded at least partially by the government, whether they be Hindu *pāṭhśālās* or Islamic *madrasās*, and teachers in both forms are salaried employees of the colonial government. For more, see Introduction and Chapter 1 of this work.

by the new policies concerns the relationship between the vernaculars and English. Sanskrit and Arabic, Trevelyan acknowledges, are languages of some historical merit—mostly because they are studied as such by European scholars of the time—but, Sanskrit, being a dead language, has little practical utility, and neither of these two languages can be considered fit vehicles for imparting European learning. However, Trevelyan also points out the problem of first teaching indigenous students English before they can be exposed to higher forms of learning. Like most educators of his generation, Trevelyan believes in the Indian (and, peculiarly enough, the Russian) student's ability to learn languages, but this extends only to being able to parrot the most rudimentary forms of English. The actual learning, if it is to be imparted, can only be comprehended by the Indian student in his or her vernacular, and the government's goal, then, becomes the Anglicization of regional languages. The vernaculars themselves offer no resistance since they are seen to have "nothing ... fixed; every thing is yet to be done, and a new literature has to be formed, almost from the very foundation."[55] The blank spaces left in the vernaculars cannot be occupied by Sanskrit, because the language contains no useful learning, and the only logical alternative is therefore English. What Trevelyan proposes is a hollowing out of vernaculars such as Bengali, and filling it with English; the resulting language is Bengali only in name as the ideas it conveys, and many of the words it uses, are English in nature.

Against this backdrop, Akshaychandra's somewhat petty quibbles with particular words used by Bankim take on a new meaning. For the Sanskritist reader, the very existence of Bengali as a language is at stake, and in order to oppose the gradual Anglicization of Bengali, he must invest in Sanskrit grammar and rhetoric. The decision to use *upākhyan* or *kābya* in the place of novel is no longer a matter of linguistic preference, but rather the act of claiming literature being produced in Bengali as having a heritage of its own, and thus being fixed, contrary to Trevelyan's claims. When the anonymous reviewer refers to Bhababhuti, and by induction *Malatī-mādhava*, he is asking for a reader familiar with the references, but also for one willing to read *Malatī-mādhava* as Bankim's source text rather than *Ivanhoe*. This is perhaps closest to the reading Bankim himself embeds in his novels but he is by no means a wholehearted champion of the same. The Sanskritist reader still reads Bankim's novels against the grain because this reader wishes to distance the texts from European influences,

---

[55] Charles Trevelyan, *On the Education of the People of India*, 122.

while the texts themselves advocate a more nuanced position. For this reader, the novels' primary task is to allow them to cultivate a viable Bengali Hindu persona, by simultaneously modernizing the values of the Hindu scriptures, and creating a continuous link between pre-colonial and nineteenth-century Bengal. Positioning Bankim's linguistic and aesthetic choices within the world of classical Sanskrit literature becomes a way for the Sanskritist reader to claim that the Bengali, too, has a literary heritage capable of supporting a genre as modern as the novel.

IV. Conclusion

Rather than take the Bengali novel as inevitably moving toward a reading suggestive of Victorian mimicry, or as a genre representing a stable, singular version of national modernity, or even as a renewal of a golden Hindu past, we as scholars ought to be attentive to the practices of reading contemporary to these novels. My interest in documenting the Anglicist and the Sanskritist reading practice is to demonstrate how even a single novel could, and did, exist within multiple practices of reading, and to suggest that there were available other practices not addressed in this chapter. One of these, the Perso-Arabic, is the subject of Chapter 4, but even with the inclusion of the third we cannot possibly have covered the gamut of reading practices present in nineteenth-century Bengal. As scholars of the period, we have to come to terms with the fact that we cannot know precisely how these novels were read, and that our best option is to infer the contours of these practices by looking at documents and institutions invested in cultivating novel literacy. However, being faced with this challenge also forces us to look beyond received narratives about novels and their readers, and to question efforts which seek to channel the act of reading into an inevitable, teleological trajectory. This is not to say that the Sanskritists and the Anglicists did not seek to impose an order on the kinds of reading available to the nineteenth-century Bengali reader. Indeed, they frequently marked certain readings as off limits while placing other in a continuous chain which is often causal. But it is to argue for both these practices existing alongside others, each striving for dominance, and each seeking to define the Bengali novel's present and future. What is at stake, then, has less to do with whether or not the Bengali novel reader read like their Victorian counterpart, or how the novel was made to tell the story of the emergent Indian nation. Telling the story of the novel and

available practices of reading as this chapter does shift our focus to the larger worlds of which the above-mentioned elements were only minor aspects.

In the chapter that follows, I take up that practice of reading which definitively falls out of favor by the start of the twentieth century, so much so that we come to forget how significant it was during the early years of the Bengali novel's history. The Sanskritist reading practice allowed readers to be novel literate as soon as *Durgeśnandinī* is published, and it explains the genre's popularity which cannot be accounted for by arguments based on the influence of Victorian novels given how few readers would have had access to them. By turning away from essays and reviews about novels to the novels themselves, we see the push toward producing and consuming novels in light of classical Sanskrit literature and the *rasa* theory, but the theory used such that it draws on the Bengali reader's lived experience of Sanskrit as a cultural and religious rather than a literary language. In the novels of Bankim, we see in action that ideal version of Sanskrit which appeals to the reader's heart, and which provides the reader with clear signposts rendering the new genre intimately familiar. Bankim as a conflicted champion of the Sanskritist reading practice uses elements of Sanskrit *kāvya* literature thus training the reader to read the Sanskrit past as encoded in the text, and coexisting with the Westernized colonial present, albeit in a difficult relationship. It is telling that Bankim and his contemporaries position the novel as *upākhyan* or *ākhyāyikā*, and rarely refer to the genre with its English name. The unfamiliarity of the term "novel" might be appealing to the few readers equipped with the English language or at least English-literate adjacent, but for the vast majority of the readers, it is not a term that contains much meaning or attraction. The novel thus becomes a reworking of Sanskrit prose forms such as the *kathā* and the *ākhyāyikā*, and emerges as a genre less in conversation with European models than from classical Sanskrit and a quotidian familiarity with the same.

3

Dear Reader, Good Sir: The Reader and Bankim's Novels

When the British publishing house Macmillan launched its *Colonial Library* series on the 1st of March 1886, it was Maurice Macmillan's way of capitalizing on the colonial readers' growing fascination for Victorian novels. The Colonial Library series gave its readers the works of novelists such as William Black, Hugh Conway, and Mary Anne Barker. In colonial Bengal in particular, the series contributed to a distinct spike in the book trade, and one that had doubled between 1850 and 1890.[1] In the same period, the Imperial Library (now the National Library of India) in Kolkata was adding more fictional than non-fictional works to its holdings to whet the Bengali reader's appetite for novels. The reader's love for English language novels—and Bengali ones inspired by the same—meant that when Bankimchandra Chattopadhyay came to publish the first Bengali novel *Durgeśnandinī* in 1865, she perceived in that work the shadow of Walter Scott's *Ivanhoe*, and conferred upon Bankimchandra, the moniker of the "Scott of Bengal."

It appears from such a reading of novel production and consumption patterns in early nineteenth-century Bengal that the Victorian novel inevitably prefigures the Bengali novel, and the Victorian reader represents the model to be emulated by the Bengali reader. The latter and their responses to texts are trapped within originary reading practices which are invariably European and British, thus condemned to emulate the Victorian novel reader; the Bengali reader is assumed to read *like* a Victorian reader, learning the proper way to be in the world. This chapter perforates the narrative by examining an alternate

---

A version of this chapter appeared in *Comparative Literature*, vol. 73, March 1, 2021.

[1] Priya Joshi, *In Another Country*, 143, 2002.

reading practice—one founded in Sanskrit aesthetic theories—championed by Bankim and his early readers.[2]

The market-driven impetus of the *Colonial Library* series fits neatly into the policies of the Imperial government in Bengal, which sought to hollow out Bengali of its Sanskrit tendencies and fill it instead with one of the languages of European Enlightenment—English. While Lord Macaulay infamously suggested English replace all the Indic languages in his 1835 "Minute on Indian Education," on the ground, the British found it far more practical to retain vernaculars as the medium of instruction for the colonized masses and replace the content imparted rather than overhaul entire linguistic traditions, using English only to educate the elite upper classes of Indians. As I discuss elsewhere in this work, education reformists such as William Adam sought to bolster the vernaculars so as to use existing pedagogical structures to impart Western knowledge, thus saving the colonial government considerable effort and capital. The novel plays a key role in the pedagogical policy by providing an entertaining shorthand to Victorian tastes and morals, governing social passions through the medium of literary prose.

However, looking closely at Bankim's novels and essays reveals a very different story, one which is systematically rendered absent by colonial practices by the end of the nineteenth century. My interest lies less in the forces effecting this erasure than in recuperating an alternative narrative of reading practices in mid-nineteenth-century Bengal. In what follows, I argue for a practice of reading rooted not in Victorian England and Enlightenment principles but in Sanskrit literary and aesthetic traditions. I examine the period between 1865 and 1894—beginning with the publication of *Durgeśnandinī* and ending with Bankim's

---

[2] At this juncture, I would like to note that there is a more complex history of the Victorian novel's "rise," to borrow from the staples of novel theory, Ian Watt and Michael McKeon, than discussed here. Michael McKeon—in *The Origins of the English Novel* and *The Theory of the Novel* (the latter being a collection of essays edited by McKeon, and important for the range and scope of theories presented therein)—uses what he terms his "dialectical method" to examine the Victorian novel as a product of epistemological and social continuities and discontinuities, rather than focusing on the "birth" of the novel as a moment of sharp disjuncture. As his work shows, one witnesses in England during the period from 1600 to 1740 two parallel moves—the epistemological move from romances to skepticism, via naïve empiricism, and the "socio-ethical" move from locating individual worth in birth to merit. According to McKeon, these two strands are revealed in the novel, which both draw on existing narrative modes—such as the early modern romance—and enact the crisis of individual worth, while creating for itself an identifiable, coherent identity. He argues that a multiplicity of specific narrative practices come together during this 140-year period of socio-cultural upheaval to bring the novel into "cultural consciousness." His work is significant in that it demonstrates how the Victorian novel speaks not merely to the system of modernity, but is equally indebted to past epistemological, social, and cultural practices.

death—and suggest a relationship between Bankim and his readers unique to a Sanskritized Bengal. Bankim provides his readers with signposts in his novels drawn from Sanskrit *rasa* and *kāvya* aesthetics, and the popularity of the novels indicates both a recognition and an appreciation of the same by his readers. This practice of reading allows both the novelist and the readers to imagine a viable modernity in which Sanskrit traditions coexist with and even dominate Enlightenment principles.

I. Sanskrit as Lived Experience

"Is there even a farmer in Bengal who does not understand the meaning of the words *dhānya* (crop), *pushkarinī* (pond/lake), *gṛha* (house) or *mastak* (head) etc.," asks Bankim in the 1877/8 *Jaiṣtha* edition of the Bengali literary periodical *Bangadarśan*? The farmer in question is a stand-in for the average Bengali who, according to Bankim, comprehends Sanskrit words (the words glossed in the quote are in Sanskrit) even when there are Bengali equivalents for the same. Bankim acknowledges that this is not true for all Bengali words, and there are instances when the Bengali form of a Sanskrit word is too enmeshed in the former language to bear replacing. It is this intrinsic relationship between Bengali and Sanskrit that Bankim champions both in this particular essay and in his larger body works. For Bankim, Sanskrit as the originary language contains all that one can desire in its "word stores filled with jewels," and as such, forms the skeleton of the Bengali language. The linguistic—and by consequence, cultural—stability that Sanskrit can lend Bengali cannot be derived from any other language, and again, it is the language comprehended by the masses, unlike English or Arabic. One should, he continues, use all available linguistic resources be they "English, Persian, Arabic, Sanskrit, rural, wild" to write beautifully and simply, and not use Sanskrit for the sake of sounding grand or in the name of tradition. However, the natural foundation for Bengali remains Sanskrit, and the Bengali writer must return to this.[3]

The nuances of Bankim's arguments regarding the affinities between Bengali and Sanskrit—in terms of linguistics and literary aesthetics—are lost by the time we come to the generation of writers immediately following him. For authors such as Rabindranath Tagore, Bankim's language is experimental,

---

[3] Bankim, "Bāṅglā bhāṣā," 317–21, unless otherwise noted all translations of Bankim are mine.

marking the period of transition between premodern and modern Bengali rather than indicating a continuous, organic relationship with Sanskrit. Rabindranath reads him as abjuring the beautiful, yet affected, Sanskrit past of Bengal in favor of a robust engagement with the modern—read, Western— and establishing the language as emerging from its nonage.[4] Following this argument, the nineteenth century, and Bankim's works along with it, forms the precursor to modern Bengali literature in an inevitable teleological progression—the Sanskrit past is gradually worked out of Bengali literature's system to make room for the modern anglicized present and future. Later Bankim scholars, such as Sudipta Kaviraj and Amitrasudan Bhattacharya, adopt a similar position, implying Bankim as effecting a radical break between the Sanskrit past and the anglicized present. Kaviraj, for example, reads this in-between position as revealing itself in a "sharp sense of historical rupture" in Bankim's "reflections on the discourse on literary taste" (Kaviraj, 170). The colonial present, though cruel in its destruction of Bengali sovereignty, is undeniable and, if one follows Kaviraj's argument, instrumental in Bankim's artistic decisions.

It is interesting to note that this sense of sharp rupture is all but absent when it comes to a discussion of *battalā* or cheap popular presses in nineteenth-century Bengal. Bankim and his readers inhabited a world which effortlessly mixed the high and the low—Sanskrit aesthetics representing the high, and the *battalā* texts the socially and the morally low. I would like to refer to the following theoretical texts in particular—Sukumar Sen's *Battalār chapa o chabi* (*The Prints and Images of Battalā*), Sripantha's *Battalā*, and Gautam Bhadra's *Nyara battalāy jay k'bar?* (*How Often Does Nyara Go to the Battalā?*), alongside Sukumar Sen's four volumes entitled *Bānglā sāhityer itihās* (*The History of Bengali Literature*)— to underscore the sense of continuum evident in nineteenth-century Bengali literary history. These works engage with the robust tradition of prose writing in Bengali that predates the popularity of the Victorian novel in Bengal, and provide textual evidence to support the claim that the origins of the Bengali novel lay not exclusively in Britain, but in a layered body of texts produced and consumed by the elite and the everyday reader. As Sen, Sripantha, and Bhadra argue, nineteenth-century readers familiar with proto-novelistic texts such as Pyarichand Mitra's *Ālāler gharer dulāl* (1858), Kaliprasanna Singha's *Hutam pyancār nakśā* (1861–2),

---

[4] Rabindranath Tagore argues that Bankim rouses Bengali from a Sanskrit-induced somnolence, and frees it from the shackles of the past.

and the anonymous *Hemlatā-Ratikanta* (1847) or *Kaminīkumār* (1856) would have had models other than British novels to draw on.[5]

However, since the above discussion focuses primarily on *battalā* presses, Bankim and the Bengali novel only get tangential mentions, and along with colonial pedagogical policies and later Postcolonial scholarship, this body of texts fails to account for the pace and extent of the popularity Bankim's novels achieve during the author's lifetime. As Jogeshchandra Bagal, the editor of Bankim's collected works, notes, *Durgeśnandinī* undergoes thirteen reprints in Bankim's lifetime. How does a genre so new become so popular in such a short span of time? There are few readers with access to either the English language or British novels,[6] and none of the proto-novelistic texts in Bengali, such as *Ālāler gharer dulāl*, command the popularity of *Durgeśnandinī*.[7] Even Bankim's first novel, *Rajmohan's Wife*, written in English and published just a year before *Durgeśnandinī* fails to gain a substantial body of readers. My contention is that the popularity of Bankim's novels can be explained through the following argument—Bankim is not counting on a base of readers familiar with English and the conventions of reading Victorian novels, but is rather drawing on elements of aesthetic literacy possessed by existing readers of Bengali in order to present the new genre of the Bengali novel as more familiar than alien. He rightly assumes his readers' familiarity with Sanskrit literary aesthetics not as Sanskrit pundits but rather as part of their everyday lived experience, and decants the new wine of the Bengali novel into the existing bottle of Sanskrit literary traditions. In doing so, he is true to his desire both to establish a continuum between Sanskrit and Bengali and to rectify the mistake made in *Rajmohan's Wife*—of modeling the Bengali novel along the lines of the social and domestic novel of Victorian England.[8]

---

[5] See also Chapter 1 of this work.

[6] While Joshi documents the sharp rise in the profits made from selling English language novels between 1850 and 1899, combining this information with Adam's *Report on Vernacular Education* reveals a fairly small body of readers, limited mostly to the presidencies.

[7] I must also mention Chandranath Basu's essay "Nabel bā kathāgranther uddyeśya" (Novel or the aim of prose texts) to acknowledge the debate surrounding novel reading during the latter part of the nineteenth century. A number of late-nineteenth-century thinkers, such as Basu, Akshaychandra Sarkar, and Purnachandra Chattopadhyay, to name only a few, are invested in allocating Bankim's novels to the Sanskritist or the Anglicist camps. I take up their reviews of *Durgeśnandinī* in Chapter 2.

[8] Bankim is not alone in experimenting with genres; Michael Madhusudan Dutt, for example, charts a similar path when he creates modern Bengali poetry as an amalgamation of classical Sanskrit and Miltonic styles. Bankim himself begins his literary career by writing verse in a volume entitled *Lalitā tathā mānas* (1856), which I discuss briefly in Chapter 2. Throughout the nineteenth century we note the presence of changing modes of writing (see Introduction for more), and this creates in readers the appetite for newer genres. Thus this is the moment when one sees the emergence of genres as varied as self-help books, letter writing manuals, blank verse poetry, alongside the Bengali novel.

120   *The Novel in Nineteenth-Century Bengal*

As a novelist trained in Sanskrit aesthetics and Enlightenment principles alike, the tension between the so-called East and West is palpable in Bankim, but the predominance of the former is undeniable. Most Bankim scholars agree that there is marked transition in his thinking from the publication of "*Sāmya*" in 1876 to that of *Kṛṣṇacaritra* in 1886, when his investment in Hindu revivalism becomes overt, and he clearly moves beyond his Enlightenment attachments (notably Auguste Comte and John Stuart Mill). "*Sāmya*," published in the journal *Bangadarshan*, is the work of a younger Bankim who draws on the principles of the French Revolution, among other things, to argue for social equality between men and women. However, by the time we come to the Bankim of *Kṛṣṇacaritra*, the hagiography of Krishna, the earlier version of the author has been repudiated, and he has moved overtly in the direction of Hindu philosophy mediated by Sanskrit aesthetics. I would claim that in this more mature Bankim we find a man who has not only refused to reprint "*Sāmya*" (as Sureshchandra Samajpati notes in *Bankim Prasanga*), but has found a precarious resolution for the tension between Sanskritist and Anglicist tendencies—he is able to recast principles of Sanskrit aesthetics to connect his present to a Sanskrit past that is not *atita* (a past that is inert and distinct) but *agama* (a past that produces the present and is contiguous with it). Hence we find his last novel, *Anandamath* (1882), guided by the *śanta* (tranquil) *rasa*—*śānti* (tranquility), *sneha* (non-sexual love), and *daya* (compassion) are the sustainable sentiments that Bankim relies on.[9]

In keeping with his multifaceted training, Bankim draws inspiration from all available sources but the material is arranged such that the reader recognizes in the text aesthetic signposts from Sanskrit literature, guiding the act of reading and rendering the text as part of a known universe. Bankim signals a unique moment in Bengali colonial history when the traditional and the modern are both viable aesthetic options, and indeed when the practices of Sanskrit *kāvya* literature are the dominant structural and aesthetic elements of the Bengali novel. I locate my claim in the reader as invoked by the texts to suggest that

---

[9] Bankim's relationship with Sanskrit aesthetics reveals itself in two more distinct, yet related, ways. In "*Uttarcarita*," he comments on his uneasiness with the term *rasa*, given Bengali literature's fascination with obscenity or the *aslil*, and of the Bengali reader's propensity toward favoring the *ādirasa*, a euphemism for lust or sensuality. His aim is to identify and condemn those traditions of Bengali literature that have corrupted classical Sanskrit aesthetics—and have become low and vulgar as a result—and push the readers toward a better (read, more modern) understanding of these aesthetic principles. The second is his desire to express that which is referred to by the *rasas*, but given the mire of connotations surrounding the word *rasa*, to simply use another term. He does not wish to do away with the *rasas* or Sanskrit aesthetics but to avoid the sexual overtones acquired by the term *rasa* itself.

Dear Reader, Good Sir   121

Bankim's novels train her to read the Sanskrit past as encoded in the text, and coexisting with the modern present, albeit in a difficult relationship. The presence of Sanskrit aesthetics indicates not so much a desire to provide the modern Bengali reader with a newly minted literature that can compete with English, but rather the belief that the reader and the author share a cultural past which they inhabit at the same time as the present. This is not a past that "perfumes" the present, to use Kaviraj's words, as the present hurtles toward modernity, but rather one that is lived on a quotidian level through communal recitations of the *Rāmāyana* and the *Mahābhārata*, through an offhand knowledge of Kālidas' poem *Abhigyanaśakuntalā*, or the poetic oeuvre of Vidyapati and Jayadeva.[10] By approaching Bankim's relationship with his reader as more than one of training the future subject of the Indian nation,[11] one is able to explore both his texts and his readers' responses to them in light of alternate reading practices, ones which exist independent of colonial pedagogical policies or received reading from Britain.

Bankim's training in Sanskrit aesthetics, and influence of the same in his novels, has been documented by scholars but the discussion has been mostly restricted to discovering whether the novels repurpose original British source material.[12] Studies of the *bankimī* novel's reader are more difficult to find, and when the reader *is* mentioned she is assumed to be female or adolescent (since the novels are mostly romances written in the vernacular).[13] Memoirs of nineteenth-century readers—almost exclusively male[14]—are revisited to

---

[10] As a scholar of reading practices, however, I understand all too well the ephemerality of reading, and the fragmented nature of the nineteenth-century Bengali reader. This chapter is cognizant of the lines that would have separated Bankim from his readers. Of the former, we have a vast body of textual material—composed both by him and his friends and followers—chronicling the tendencies evident in how he read, while of the latter we have significantly fewer direct textual records. Will all of his readers have read him with Sanskrit aesthetics in mind? Probably not—Sanskrit would have been a more lived rather than an intellectual experience for many of his readers, and the very debate over the provenance of *Durgeśnandinī*'s story stands testimony to the sometimes prospective nature of Bankim's readers. However, it is possible to reconstruct the reader and their reading practices using the texts as coded clues—we have factual evidence of the immense popularity of his novels, numerous reviews of and responses to the novels from contemporary readers, and a sustained, if not growing, use of Sanskrit aesthetic principles in the novels themselves. This third claim, in conjunction with the first, provides us with substantial resources to imagine the reader, and to use the reader as a theoretically viable site for this work.

[11] The dominant line in Bankim scholarship, cf. Rochona Majumdar, Jashodhara Bagchi, and Amiya P. Sen.

[12] Amitrasudan Bhattacharya provides an extensive discussion of Bankim's source material, 82–8 (1998).

[13] For a discussion of Bankim's novels being received as romances see Amiya P. Sen's *Bankim Chandra Chattopadhyay: An Intellectual Biography* (2008).

[14] Rassundari Debi is a notable exception, and I discuss her as a reader in the Conclusion to this work.

discuss the legitimacy of Bankim's Bengali language with reference to Sanskrit grammar, or the proximity of the content of his stories to British sources.[15] Yet the publication history of Bankim's novels does not support the argument for the gender and age of his reader,[16] and the references to Sanskrit are more deeply entrenched than merely at the level of linguistic experimentation. In this chapter, I argue for a fuller examination of Bankim's relationship with his reader in light of Sanskrit aesthetics, namely *rasa* theory. Contrary to the school of thinking that claims a radical break between the Sanskrit past and the Westernized present in Bankim's novels, I suggest that the novelist attains mythic levels of popularity by encoding the novel not as a foreign genre, but as one the nineteenth-century Bengali reader would have been already familiar with. Bankim relies on his reader's knowledge of the Sanskrit *kathā* and the *ākhyāyika*, and the various *rasas* (roughly translated as flavors or moods, but also affective tones) evoked by literary works.[17] His reader is not one who imitates their Victorian counterpart, but is rather a *rasik*—one who is aware of, and participates in, evoking the *rasa*. In order to satisfy the *rasik*, Bankim employs several methods prescribed by *rasa* theorists, and I examine two of these techniques—evoking the *śṛngāra* (erotic) *rasa*, and introducing verse in longer works of prose. I restrict my discussion to three novels by Bankim—his first, *Durgeśnandinī* (*The Chieftain's Daughter*, 1865), *Biśabṛksha* (*The Poison Tree*, 1873), and one of his last novels, *Anandamath* (*The House of Bliss*, 1882)—to demonstrate Bankim's commitment to *rasa* aesthetics, and his readers' participation in the same. As a note, I use *rasa* theory as applicable to literature as a whole, and not just the dramatic arts.

---

[15] Cf. Amiya P. Sen and Amitrasudan Bhattacharya.

[16] Literacy, even in the vernacular, while on the rise for women, was far from being the norm in nineteenth-century Bengal, and one wonders whether most women or adolescents contemporary to Bankim would have been buying/subscribing to the magazines in which the novels were published, or the novels when they were published as independent books.

[17] The first essay in the collection titled *Bankim Prasanga* (*On the Subject of Bankim*, 1922), by Rabindranath Tagore, narrates Tagore's first meeting with Bankim at a literary meet near Kolkata. As with most of the essays, Tagore's "Bankimchandra" is anecdotal in nature, and recounts the event as memorable not because the author met his literary hero, but owing to Bankim's pained response at a speaker using the *bibhatsa* or the odious *rasa*. Bankim apparently covers his face and moves away from the crowd, thus imprinting on the young Tagore the sensitive nature of the poetic soul. Such casual but specific reference to *rasas* is a common feature of a number of the essays, including those by Chandranath Basu, Haraprasad Sastri, Akshaychandra Sarkar, and Sureshchandra Samajpati, again to name only a few. My claim is that while these are the elites of Bengali intelligentsia, *Bankim Prasanga* is not designed to be a scholarly volume; it collects stories and reminiscences by those who knew Bankim best, and as such is intended for the general public. As late as 1922, references to the *rasas* in particular, and to Sanskrit aesthetics in general, would have appealed to the average Bengali, so it is not too far off the mark to assume the presence of the same in lived experience of the Bengali reader in the second half of the nineteenth century.

Dear Reader, Good Sir   123

In this, I follow practices established by classical and contemporary Sanskrit scholars who note the presence of the *rasas* in literary texts, dance forms, and musical compositions. Given my focus on literature and reading, I refer to the audience as *pāthak* (reader) rather than *darśak* (spectator).

Instead of a complete rejection of the modern in favor of a mythic indigenous past, this chapter suggests that the traditions of *rasik* principles, generic conventions of Sanskrit literature, and a linguistic fluidity between Bengali and Sanskrit are a part of the lived experience of both Bankim and his nineteenth-century reader. His novels retain enough of the familiar to provide the reader with points of reference, both in terms of aesthetics and structure, and are thus new enough to be attractive and fashionable while still bearing the marks of the comfortably known.

II. The *Rasik Pāthak* and the Model Reader

Durgeśnandinī occupies a mythic position in the canon of modern Bengali literature for a number of reasons—it is the first self-consciously crafted novel in the language and in a remarkably short span of time grants its author, Bankim, the honor of being a superstar in the intellectual life of nineteenth-century Bengal. Tilottama, the novel's heroine, however, is largely overshadowed by Bankim's later female protagonists; she has none of Kapalkundala's enigmatic charm, nor Kundanandini's ill-fated passion, nor is she as fully formed a character as Prafulla. Yet Tilottama has one unique feature—she is the first character to appear as a reader in the genre, and through her practice of reading, Bankim guides the readers of *Durgeśnandinī* in particular, and of the Bengali novel in general. As she reads, the invoked reader—addressed simply as *pāthak* (the masculine for "reader" in Bengali)—occupies a voyeuristic position and learns that this strange new genre can, after all, be read in a comfortably familiar way. Through her, the reader is invited to note in *Durgeśnandinī* the evocation of the *śṛngāra rasa* that orders the novel's narrative and stylistic contents in accordance with classical Sanskrit aesthetics, and situates the text not as recklessly moving toward an unorthodox modernity, but rather as organically reworking elements of Sanskrit tradition. Bankim's technique of enframing Tilottama before presenting her as a reader of a deliberately chosen set of Sanskrit texts isolates her as the ideal reader who inhabits the *pāthak's* psyche both as a guide and as a dimly recollected past. This invoked reader is urged to fall in love with Tilottama both because of her

124   *The Novel in Nineteenth-Century Bengal*

own allure and her ability to remind the reader of someone he has intimately loved in the past, and because of the familiarity of the reading she performs. This love for Tilottama depends upon the reader deciphering the code embedded in her practice of reading—the *rasik pāthak* will understand that she is formed after Kadambari, Vasavadatta, and Radha and, like these women, can only be truly appreciated if she evokes the sentiment of *śṛngāra* in the *pāthak*. The reader, then, has to read like Tilottama so as to be able to fully comprehend her charm, and by induction the beauty of *Durgeśnandinī*.

At first glance, Tilottama is the quintessential romantic heroine, intended to be the object of the male gaze of the author, the hero, and the invoked reader. We first see her inside a Hindu temple on a predictably stormy night, framed by the light of a lamp and her veil, when she encounters the novel's protagonist, Jagatsingha. It is love at first sight for both, but she must return to her father's castle with her chaperone, Bimala, and he must go away to defend Bengal against the Pathans, acting on behalf of the Mughal emperor Akbar. Following a brief foray into the history of the region in the late sixteenth century—the novel's temporal setting, referred to as the *ākhyāyikābarnita kāl*[18]—the narrator returns the reader to Tilottama and the prospect of learning more about the romance. Bankim paints her as lovesick and distracted, and invites the reader to recall his love from his adolescence to fully experience Tilottama's beauty. The passage, evocative in its use of *alamkār* (ornamental figures of speech), describes the archetype of innocent, youthful, feminine beauty, and leaves both the reader in no doubt of the author's intentions—to underscore that Tilottama is, indeed, beautiful (*sundar*). This beauty is both seen and experienced by the reader,[19] and these are as central to the passage as the descriptions of the protagonist herself.

The passage commences with the phrase "Tilottama is beautiful" but it immediately transitions to the vocative case as the *pāthak* is asked if he has ever, in his youth (*kiśōr bayese*), seen with/in his "eyes of love" (*premcokkhute*) such beauty as Tilottama's.[20] The *pāthak*'s access to her is conditional upon an affirmative response to the above question—"Only if you have seen [such

---

[18] The phrase translates to "the time described in the *ākhyāyikā*" but given the complex relationship between history and imagined narratives in the *ākhyāyikā* and the *kathā*, I explore this phrase more fully later in the chapter in relation to *Durgeśnandinī*.

[19] I advisedly conflate the invoked reader with the reader of the novel or the actual reader, as the former is meant to represent the latter. Using the figure of the invoked reader allows Bankim to keep the reader in close proximity to the text, and call on him at significant moments in the narrative. The goal is, what the *pāthak* learns under Bankim's direct tutelage, the actual reader learns by proxy.

[20] *Durgeśnandinī*, 11, translation mine.

Dear Reader, Good Sir   125

a figure]" the narrative claims, "can you feel in your mind the true nature of Tilottama's form."[21] This act of seeing is said to occur in a memory that is almost dream-like, as Bankim effects a conjunction of reading, remembering, and seeing. As the reader reads, he is urged to both remember and dream the ideal that is Tilottama; the adjectives used to describe her call to mind something very familiar, yet there is a certain unknowability that places her in the realm of the reader's dream.[22] By itself, the passage is far from extraordinary—by delimiting Tilottama to the reader's dream and memory, the author ensures that, while enticing, she is preserved by her innate virtue for the sole consumption of the hero.

However, what Tilottama does immediately following this description undermines the apparently straightforward nature of the passage. It grows dark outside, and the return of the lamp (reminiscent of our introduction to her in the temple) compels her to turn to her room, and to her books. This is a strange, even scandalous, action for a female character in the middle of the nineteenth century, and Bankim is acutely aware of that.[23] He hastens to add, "Tilottama knew how to read; Abhiram Swami [her father's political and spiritual advisor] had taught her to read Sanskrit."[24] Tilottama being a literate woman is a fairly novel concept for Bankim's audience in an age when the education of women is far from an accepted norm, and later in the novel, Bimala too must also explain her ability to write letters. Thus part of the sentence's effect is to establish the plausibility of Tilottama's action. Of interest to my argument is the language of instruction—she knows Sanskrit. This too is not extraordinary in itself; Tilottama is the daughter of a wealthy landowner whose political affiliation with the Mughal court is distinct from his explicitly articulated Hindu identity, and Sanskrit is an integral part of that process of Hindu self-formation.

My contention is that the choice of Sanskrit allows Bankim to model through Tilottama, a particular practice of reading which would be far more familiar to the *pāthak* than either the novel genre imported from the West, or the particular example of *Ivanhoe*. Among other things, this practice assumes the reader's

---

[21] Ibid.
[22] Tilottama is "serene, constant, soft-natured" who travels the paths of the reader's memory like a dream, *Durgeśnandinī*, 11.
[23] Popular satires, such as "*Miss Binobibi B.A.*" and "*Novel Nāyikā*," capture what was a commonly held belief—a woman ought not to be allowed to read works of fiction, novels, and romances in particular, by herself in the seclusion of her room. In such a circumstance, the woman would be without supervision and free to indulge in the moral depravity encouraged by these texts.
[24] *Durgeśnandinī*, 11.

126 *The Novel in Nineteenth-Century Bengal*

knowledge of Sanskrit prose romances and stylistic elements of the same. As Tilottama reads, the reading list becomes more than mere intertextual reference:

> Tilottama left off worrying and sat near the lamp with a book ... The book was *Kadambari*. After reading for a while, she expressed annoyance and rejected *Kadambari*. She got another book; Subandhu's *Vasavadatta*. She read, thought, read again, thought distractedly; she didn't like *Vasavadatta* either. Setting it aside, she started reading *Gītgōvinda*; she liked *Gītgōvinda* for a while. She smiled coyly while reading, then threw the book away.
>
> (Durgeśnandinī, 11–12)

Bankim introduces three texts through his model reader—Bānabhatta's *Kadambari* (first half of the seventh century CE), Subandhu's *Vasavadatta* (also seventh century but before Bāna), and Jayadeva's *Gītgōvinda* (twelfth century CE). Both *Kadambari*[25] and *Vasavadatta* are prose romances in classical Sanskrit, while *Gītgōvinda* is in verse, and all three appear to have been inserted to inform the reader about Tilottama's romantic sentiments. The works by Bāna and Subandhu refer specifically to instances of well-known lovers, initially suffering *biraha* (separation owing to fate and circumstance) but ultimately achieving *milan* (united thanks to their virtue, faith, and divine intervention). *Gītgōvinda* narrates the love of Radha and Kṛshna in the *Vaishnava* tradition, celebrating the divine couple and rewarding Radha's devotion to the sometime unfaithful, yet eventually penitent, Kṛshna. The thematic structure of these three texts prioritizes *milan* following *biraha*; each couple must undergo separation and prove their fidelity through prolonged—often seemingly interminable—periods of waiting before experiencing *milan*. This echoes the narrative of *Durgeśnandinī* in which Tilottama and Jagatsingha are separated when the Pathans attack and capture her father's castle. Their reunion occurs only after a prolonged separation during which Jagatsingha must be convinced of her fidelity, and both must suffer physical and emotional privations.

 The texts stand in for more than a narrative foretelling owing to the dominant *rasa*—*śṛngāra*—evoked in each, and by implication in *Durgeśnandinī*. According to the *Nātyaśastra* (composed orally and transmitted to writing between 100 BCE and 100 CE) by Bhārata,[26] there are eight dominant or fundamental feelings

---

[25] It is also interesting to note here that Bankim is not alone in his fascination with *Kadambari*. Tarashankar Tarkaratna translates the text into Bengali, also naming his work *Kadambari* in 1861, merely four years prior to the publication of *Durgeshnandini*.

[26] I follow the convention of attributing the *Nātyaśāstra* to Bharata, even though it is generally agreed that the text is a composite.

(*sthāyībhāva*) which exist in a latent form in all human beings. He names them as follows—Delight (*rati*), Laughter (*hāsa*), Sorrow (*śōka*), Anger (*krōdha*), Heroism (*utsāha*), Fear (*bhaya*), Disgust (*jugupsa*), and Wonder (*vismaya*). The eight *rasas* correspond to the eight *sthāyībhāvas*. In the *Nātyaśastra*, the *rasas* are the Erotic (*śṛngāra*), the Comic (*hāsya*), the Pathetic (*karunā*), the Furious (*raudra*), the Heroic (*vira*), the Terrible (*bhayanaka*), the Odious (*bibhatsa*), and the Marvellous (*adbhuta*).[27] Later a ninth *rasa*, the Tranquil (*śānta*), is added to this list, probably by the theorist Abhinavgupta around the tenth century, and is gradually accepted as being the highest *rasa* an author must strive toward, although during the period of Bana and Subandhu, the pinnacle of the *rasas* is *śṛngāra*. The *Nātyaśāstra* outlines a set of practical rules by which the composer may successfully express a *sthayibhāva* through the text, which is then aesthetically transformed into a *rasa* experienced by the audience. When the *rasik* audience encounters a *sthāyibhāva* in art, she feels particular pleasure, and it is this feeling that Bhārata names *rasa*. Aesthetic experience involves the audience being first aware of the *sthāyibhāva*, and then tasting the *rasa*, which is born of the union of the text and its performance.[28] For a work of art, there should a dominant *rasa*, which dictates all the other elements, and provides an affective framework for the audience.

Of significance to my argument is the *śṛngāra rasa*, and it is worth quoting the *Nātyaśāstra*'s description at length:

Of these [the *rasas*], the Erotic (*śṛngāra*) Sentiment proceeds from the Dominant State of love (*rati*) and it has as its basis (lit. soul) a bright attire; for whatever in this world is white, pure, bright and beautiful is appreciated in terms of the Dominant State of love (*śṛngāra*). For example, one who is elegantly dressed is called a lovely person (*śṛngārin*) … Hence the Erotic Sentiment has been so named on account of its usually being associated with a bright and elegant attire. It owes its origin to men and women and relates to the fullness of youth.[29]

The text places as much emphasis on "a bright attire" (*ujwalveshhātmak*) as it does on love and the "fullness of youth," and leaves open a considerable room for interpretation. This juxtaposition of the erotic with vibrant attire can be explained in part by the range of meanings encompassed by the word *śṛngāra*. As

---

[27] I draw on Gnoli's translation here.
[28] For a more detailed discussion of the transition from the state of awareness to that of savoring the *rasa*, see Kathleen Marie Higgins' "An Alchemy of Emotions."
[29] Bharata, chap. 6, verse 45.

128   *The Novel in Nineteenth-Century Bengal*

the entry in the *Monier-Williams Sanskrit-English Dictionary* of 1872 indicates, *śṛngāra* simultaneously refers to love, amorous passions, sexual union, as well as elegant attire, and in particular, a dress suitable for amorous purposes or the act of dressing up for such an event.

I wish to dwell on the implicit meaning here; *śṛngāra* connotes beauty (*soundarya*) and the beautiful (*sundar*). In a twentieth-century commentary on the *Nātyaśastra*, the classical Bharatnātyam dancer, V. P. Dhananjayan, elaborates upon Bhārata's cryptic passage by equating *śṛngāra* with *soundarya*; amorous love based on physical attraction can only serve as the initial moment of the *rasa*, but for the work to achieve the culmination of the *śṛngāra rasa*, there must be an exploration of that which is truly beautiful, both in the mind and the body. According to this commentary, the love thus born between two individuals is able to overcome any obstacles, and because it is another form of truth, it is suitably elevated to be the subject matter of great art.

It is this definition of the *śṛngāra rasa* that colors both Bankim's description of Tilottama and the *pāthak*'s perception of her. If one keeps in mind Dhananjayan's commentary, then Bankim's repetition of the word "beautiful" in relation to Tilottama becomes more than mere word play:

> Tilottama was beautiful [*sundari*] ... Tilottama's body, though beautifully proportioned [*sugathan*], was not fully developed; whether it was because of her young age, or the natural built of her body, this beautiful body [*sundar dehe*] was more slender than plump. Yet every part of this young girl's body was perfectly rounded [*sugol*] and delicately soft [*sulalita*]. Gem bracelets on her perfectly rounded wrists [*sugol praoshthe*]; a diamond studded ornament on her perfectly rounded arms [*sugol bahute*]; a ring on her perfectly rounded finger [*sugol angulate*]; a *mekhala* on her perfectly rounded thighs [*sugol urute*]; a golden necklace on her beautifully formed shoulder [*sugathan angsopare*]; a gem necklace on her beautifully formed neck [*sugathan kanthe*]; everything beautifully formed [*sarbatrer gathan sundar*].[30]

This passage is clearly meant to demonstrate Bankim's ability to mold Bengali into an ornate and rhetorically charged language. The use of *anupras* (alliteration) bears this out—every descriptive unit begins with either *sugathan* (beautifully formed) or *sugōl* (perfectly rounded), and the repetition of the syllable "*su*" employs *shabdalamkār* (ornamentation based on the sound of the word). The alliteration, however, perfectly captures the interpretation of the *śṛngāra rasa*

---

[30] *Durgeśnandinī*, 11.

Dhananjayan alludes to. "Tilottama is *sundar* (beautiful)" cues the reader into both a description of her physical self and the dominant *rasa* of the work. The *sugathan* of her body echoes the first syllable of *sundar* and its meaning, as do *sugōl* and *sulalita* (delicately soft). The choice of the alliterative syllable is similarly telling—"*su*," much like the Greek "eu" refers to that which is auspicious, good, and, by implication, inherently beautiful. Bankim evokes the *rasa* by enhancing each portion of *sundar* Tilottama with an ornament, thus coupling the *alamkār* (ornament) of the language with a physical adornment. Each member of her body is decorated with an appropriate ornament, and together they infuse the prose with the appropriate *rasa*. The catalogue of jewels further obeys the dictates of the *Nātyaśāstra* by presenting the heroine in glittering attire. While Tilottama's jewels help the reader gauge her social status, at the level of aesthetic theory, the ornaments are as necessary as Tilottama being in the "fullness of youth" in enhancing her beauty and evoking the *śṛngāra rasa*.

This play on *alamkār* is present in *Kadambari* as Bāna surrounds the heroine with handmaidens, each of whom is both bejeweled as well as a jewel herself[31]; Kadambari's beauty is reflected in the jeweled pavement, walls, roof, and figures carved into the roof of her pavilion.[32] For Bāna, Kadambari abandons childhood in favor of youth the moment she falls in love and becomes a woman the poet can describe as the erotic ideal,[33] but Bankim very consciously refuses to cross that line. Tilottama, though ornamented, is the archetype of innocent adolescence, and hence her body, though beautifully formed is not fully formed. Thus while Bāna's text plunges into a vivid description of Kadambari's heavy breasts which are jewel-like, Bankim prudishly restricts himself to Tilottama's arms, fingers, shoulders, and neck. The *śṛngāra rasa* is to be evoked, but within the bounds of Bengali decorum.

Tilottama, however, is not an isolated instance of the *śṛngāra rasa* in *Durgeśnandinī*. After the reader is invited to gaze upon her beauty, he disappears for two chapters, reappearing when Bimala, Tilottama's chaperone, is performing

---

[31] *Kadambari* narrates the tale of two pairs of star-crossed lovers, Mahāswetā and Pundarik, and Kadambari and Candrapida. Using the structure of stories nestled within stories, Bana describes how both couples are separated by fate, with the heroes either dead or suddenly called away. As a result both heroines feel compelled to die following the departure of their beloved, but are urged by the gods to believe in rebirth, and are finally rewarded for their patience by being reunited with their lovers. The moment in the narrative I discuss above occurs when Chandrapida first encounters Kadambari, and both are captivated and physically weakened by their love for the other.

[32] *Kadambari*, 59–62 (Kane translation), 217–19 (Layne translation).

[33] *Kadambari*, 60 (Kane translation), 218–19 (Layne translation).

her toilette, or the act of *śṛngāra*. The author asks the *pāthak* to contemplate the more mature, self-consciously erotic beauty of Bimala.[34] She is also ornamented, but the prose used to describe her is far less poetically charged; Bimala is the erotic incarnate, the more sensual element of the *rasa*, and Bankim is clearly anxious to contain her sexuality. By the end of the narrative, Bimala is widowed and shorn of all her physical charms, but not before she employs those very charms to seduce Katlu Khan (the lascivious and cruel Pathan villain) to his death. In Bimala one notices the novelist's hesitance with fully exploring the bounds of the *rasa*; it is too erotic, too sensual to be emulated completely. Tilottama's presence mitigates what to Bankim are the cruder aspects of this *rasa*, as she can be relied on to filter *śṛngāra* through the *sundar* (beautiful), and allow the novelist to reinterpret a classical theory for the modern reader. Thus Tilottama does pick up *Kadambari* first, but abandons it with annoyance soon after; Bankim's use of the verb *parityāg* describes Tilottama's rejection of the text connoting an explicit rejection of the text.

The work she takes up next, *Vasavadatta*, is more appealing. Subandhu's *Vasavadatta* recounts the romance between Kandarpaketu and Vasavadatta, both of whom have a vision of the other in their dreams which serves as a catalyst to their meeting. Like *Kadambari*, *Vasavadatta* too subjects the lovers to a separation, when the heroine accidentally wanders into a hermitage, and is turned into stone by an ascetic whose penances are interrupted by her excessive beauty. Kandarpaketu, having lost Vasavadatta, is on the brink of committing suicide when a divine voice assures him of reunion; his search leads him to her statue which returns to life on his touch. The narrative is much shorter than *Kadambari* and the structure less intricate, but here too the dominant *rasa* is *śṛngāra*, as becomes evident from the author's introduction of Vasavadatta— "(Kandarpaketu) saw Vasavadatta brilliant with a pair of legs <reddened feet> as grammar has <rubricated *padas*>; with <goodly joints> as the *Bhārata* has <a hundred books>."[35] This translation by Louis H. Gray is notable for its attention to Subandhu's style, and in particular the latter's reliance on *slesha* or paronomasia. According to Gray, Subandhu declares his mastery of this particular form of *alamkār* in the text's introduction, claiming that he is able to arrange "a series of paronomasias in every syllable."[36] In this particular section,

---

[34] *Durgeśnandinī*, 14.
[35] Subandhu, 113–14.
[36] Gray, Introduction, 17.

the extended *slesha* compares Vasavadatta to various classical Sanskrit texts and
rhetorical devices, thus textualizing the body of the woman, and extending the
śṛngāra rasa to the literary arts. Vasavadatta's beauty is comparable to the true
beauty of the *pada* (lit. feet, here referring to the quarter divisions of Panini's
treatise on grammar). Subandhu puns on the multiple sense of the word *sundar*;
Sundarkāṇḍa refers to the fifth book (*kāṇḍa*) of the *Ramayana*, but *sundar* as
beauty also stands in for *śṛngāra*. The mention of Bharata reminds the reader
that the author is punning on descriptions from the *Nātyaśāstra*. Unlike Bana
who introduces Kadambari with the help of visual ornamentation, Subandhu
relies on the *alamkār* (ornaments) of literature and the arts. He follows the
conventions of the blazon by comparing each portion of the heroine's body with
a beautiful object, thus enhancing the attractiveness of the body, but replaces the
traditional lexicon of precious gems and heavenly bodies with rhetorical devices
and the *śāstras* (religious or secular treatises).

Little wonder then Tilottama prefers *Vasavadatta* to the more sexually
explicit *Kadambari*. The essence of the *rasa* is filtered through the literary arts,
and as the reader, Tilottama chooses to identify more with the textualized beauty
of Vasavadatta than the explicit sexuality of Kadambari. More importantly,
Bankim's reader hears echoes of Subandhu's description and perceives Tilottama
as the beautiful Vasavadatta. The intertextual reference elevates *Durgeśnandinī*
to the level of *Vasavadatta*, from where it can then be compared to the body of
classical Sanskrit texts, in the same way that Bankim's heroine can be compared
to Subandhu's. The reader who recognizes this connection between the two
texts finds in Bankim a modern practitioner of a classical *rasa* and notices the
Bengali novelist rinsing the sentiment of its overt sensuality. Tilottama, and by
extension the reader, prefers that iteration of the *śṛngāra rasa* which focuses on
the *sundar* as not merely transcending the bodily but conflating the corporeal
with the textual. In *Kadambari*, the *alamkār* used in the prose evokes the *rasa*,
but the object of the sentiment is always the beautiful woman; in this passage
from *Vasavadatta*, the *alamkār* of *slesh*, by virtue of equating the body of the
woman with the text, makes the prose as much an object of the *rasa* as the body.

Bankim's style makes the language itself an object of the *śṛngāra rasa*. Like
Tilottama, like Bimala, Bankim's prose possesses the beauty worthy of evoking
in the reader the *rasa*, and it is most evident in the description of the novel's third
female character, Ayesha. As the daughter of the Pathan Katlu Khān, Ayesha is
necessarily in the wrong camp, but that does not prevent Bankim from lavishing
some of the most beautiful language in the novel on her. She also forms the third

side of the love triangle when she falls in love with Jagatsingha after he has been taken prisoner by her father, and her unrequited love for the hero, along with her beauty, wins the reader's sympathy. Bankim again addresses the reader after seemingly forgetting her in the heat of narrative's action. He then displays his mastery of *slesha*, as he plays upon the idea of painting a picture of Ayesha for the reader. If he were an artist, Bankim says, he would take up a brush and paint her complexion, outline her forehead, her ears, her mass of beautifully parted black hair, draw her eyes and her lips. However, as one reads the passage, one begins to note the insertion of the verb "I would write" (*likhitām*) for the verb "I would paint" (*ānkitām*). The construction plays with the reader's expectation; the writer is writing a picture, but using verbs associated with painting an image.[37] By the end of the passage, the only verb used is "I would write" but the construction is still that of "I would paint." The word play Bankim effects relies on the reader noticing the syntactical incongruity upon a careful perusal of the passage, but humoring the author nonetheless as he conflates the two verbs and paints a word picture. The elaborate pun culminates in the author's somewhat perplexing confession; having described her incomparable beauty, he says, "[I]f I could write it [the extent of her beauty] all, even then I would not touch the paintbrush."[38] Such is the force of Ayesha's beauty, that any effort to capture it in words or lines is in vain, and yet this false modesty merely serves to intensify the exquisiteness of the prose that, through this syntactical confusion, evokes the *śṛngāra rasa*. If Ayesha's beauty is worth the reader's attention, the allure of Bankim's prose is a formidable competitor; the latter might ostensibly serve as the vehicle for evoking the sentiment for the former, but in its beauty, it is as much an object of the *rasa* as Ayesha herself.

The audience for all three moments when the *śṛngāra rasa* is evoked through a description of feminine beauty is Bankim's reliable *pāthak*. At these moments, the narrative takes on the aspects of a dramatic performance, as the author invites the *pāthak* to direct their attention to the performer on stage, and marvel both at her beauty and at the perfection of the composer's craft. As with the portrayal of Ayesha, with the reader too Bankim plays on the verbs; he calls on all of the reader's senses, thus constructing reading as an act that transcends the restrictions of the medium, and becomes one performed by the body and all its senses. The reader sees the words on the page, but she also imagines,

[37] *Durgeśnandinī*, 41.
[38] Ibid.

hears, and tastes them, and this entire encounter is the *pāthak* experiencing the *śṛṅgāra rasa*. The *rasik* reader transcends the worldly and specific moment in the text toward a depersonalized, universal articulation of emotions and senses. Bimala's description captures the centrality of *rasa* for the audience-like reader; she is not young, much like the *pāthak*, but age has not tarnished her beauty because her mind (*man*) brims with *rasa*. Bankim uses rhyming ideophones (*dhyanātmakśabda*) to further cement the equivalence between beauty (*rūp*) and *rasa*. Hence, Bimala's body overflows (*dhalodhalo*) with beauty because her mind overflows (*talotalo*) with *rasa*. Age, for Bankim, only serves to make the *rasa* perfectly digestible, and the reader who is past her prime can attest to this.[39]

In many ways, Victorian critics also allude to reading as a fundamentally bodily experience; G. H. Lewes, for example, suggests reading is a physical act governed by the temporal rhythms of both the body of the reader and the sequence of words on the page. Indeed, the Sensation novel as a genre specializes in addressing the nerves rather than the readers' rational faculties. However, the argument presented is in favor of viewing the reader's body as a machine—so as to echo industrialized Victorian England—not the visceral, organic experience espoused by the Bengali novelist. The physiological theory of Lewes and the characteristics of the Sensation novel further indicate attempts to create theoretical tools exclusively for the novel, and not borrowed from older literary genres such as the epic and the lyric.[40]

For Bankim, however, the immersive experience of consuming the text is a conscious situating of the novel in the non-novelistic tradition of classical Sanskrit. In using culinary terms such as *"paripāk"* (digestion), and coupling them with ideophones evocative of vessels filled with liquid (*dhalodhalo*, *talotalo*), the novelist draws on a parallel evoked by the *Nātyaśāstra* between reception of art and consumption of food. *Rasa* in Sanskrit means juice or flavor, and in using this term to indicate aesthetic principles the *Nātyaśāstra* suggests that the *rasik* audience's body performs an act similar to the ingestion of flavorful food—it takes aesthetic pleasure from the emotional and physical satisfaction of eating good food.[41] The text consciously asks the reader to

[39] Ibid., 14.
[40] Dames, 9–12; also see Vanessa Ryan's *Thinking without Thinking in the Victorian Novel* (2012). Ryan's work is reminiscent of Dames'—in both we are reacquainted with George Henry Lewes and William James, and their impact on novelists such as Henry James and George Eliot who envision reading to be an act intimately tied to the reader's body.
[41] The relationship between art and food is discussed by both Royona Mitra and Kathleen Marie Higgins, with particular reference to the *rasa* theory and Indian classical dance forms.

134   *The Novel in Nineteenth-Century Bengal*

model herself along the lines of the *rasik sahṛdaya* (empathetic) audience who necessarily tastes the myriad flavors (*rasas*) of a work of art while consuming the text. It is this satisfaction that Bankim's reader derives while voyeuristically gazing on Bimala, Tilottama, or Ayesha through the act of reading. For the *pāthak*, like the audience of classical Sanskrit drama, the act of consuming the aesthetic object produces the sensory delight in the same way as that produced by the partaking of a "flavorful meal." Thus the deliberate confusion of verbs attunes the invoked reader of the novel to the extent to which the theory of the *rasas* informs the text she is reading, and assures the reader that *Durgeśnandinī* as a work of art follows conventions familiar to her; the organization of the elements into a genre may be new, but the elements of which the reader knows well.

III. The *sahṛdaya pāthak*

The *Nātyaśāstra* delineates the rules a work of art must follow in order to convey affective states to the audience. However, no matter how competently the author may depict a *sthayibhāva* so as to allow the audience to experience it as a *rasa*, the *rasa* cannot be achieved without the participation of the audience. For the *rasa* to be experienced, the work requires an ideal spectator, one who is defined as being not only of "high birth," "good character," and "proficient in drama," but also capable of experiencing "gladness on seeing a person glad, and sorrow on seeing him sorry … [feel] miserable on seeing him miserable."[42] In other words, the audience capable of experiencing *rasa* must be *sahṛdaya* (lit. possessing of heart) or have the ability to be in sympathetic resonance with the emotions depicted in the work. The *sahṛdaya* audience may sympathize with the characters (*hṛdayasamvada*), and even identify with the situation (*tanmayibhāva*), but the very experience of *rasa* is maintaining an aesthetic distance from that which is depicted, and aesthetically relishing this resonance instead.[43] By asking his reader to be a *rasik pāthak*, then, Bankim is necessarily writing for a *sahṛdaya pāthak*—if they are to fully experience the *rasa* they must sympathize with the novel's protagonists and their predicaments, but always maintain an aesthetic distance from the same.

---

[42] Higgins, 50 (2007).
[43] For more see Masson and Patwardhan (1970), Higgins.

The significance of such a reader becomes obvious in light of the charges leveled against novels in both Victorian England and nineteenth-century Bengal. The arguments accusing novels and novelists of corrupting readers by exposing them to narratives of lax moral standards are too well known to require restating in detail here. Even a cursory glance at works by theorists such as Priya Joshi and Anindita Das—to name only two—reveals that both the nineteenth-century Bengali novel and its Victorian counterpart are thought to be harmful for the average reader.[44] Jane Austen's Catherine Morland faces criticism for believing in lurid Gothic imaginations, while the heroine of the popular Bengali satire *Nabel nāyikā* (*The Novel Heroine*) becomes a social outcast after reading romances such as Bankim's. These accusations are founded upon the novel's ability to immerse the reader and compel them to identify with the characters they read about, so much so that they are unable to tell reality from fiction.

However, the reader of Bankim's novels is not called on find themselves in the texts—rather, as the *rasik pāthak*, they can aesthetically enjoy the sympathetic connection with the characters and the situations depicted while keeping a morally unambiguous distance from that which they read. In invoking the reader, Bankim returns to the conventions of dramatic staging—the characters perform before the audience-like reader, unmindful of their presence, and the reader is aware of seeing them at a distance from themselves. The *pāthak* is connected to the action on the page/stage as though they occupy the same spacio-temporal location, but their aesthetic experience of the characters ensures that they never identify fully with the characters or their situations.

Vijaya Subramani traces the roots of the *rasa* theory in the Vedantic tradition of Hindu philosophy which seeks to find a "balance between indiscriminate indulgence and self-starving asceticism" by urging the individual to enjoy without the desire for ownership.[45] She suggests that the audience who is truly *sahṛdaya* enjoys the aesthetic experience by being in harmony with the *rasas* or the emotions in common with universal humankind, instead of seeking ownership of that particular emotion through the aesthetic object. Thus in a text like Kālidāsa's *Śakuntalā*, the *sahṛdaya* audience does not desire ownership of the erotic sentiment they experience through the performance of the play, or

---

[44] For a more detailed discussion on Victorian readership, and the rich reading lives of Victorians, see Louis James' *The Victorian Novel* (2006), Vanessa Ryan's *Thinking without Thinking in the Victorian Novel*, Rebecca Mitchell's *Victorian Lessons in Empathy and Difference* (2011), and Grace Moore's *The Victorian Novel in Context* (2012).

[45] Subramani, 244.

seek to be in the same situation as the lovers so as to feel in reality the erotic. Rather, their experience of the aestheticized emotion relies upon their ability to perceive it as not belonging to anyone in particular; it is not the audience's personal emotion, or that of the character, performer, or even the composer. It is the universal feeling of the erotic produced within the emotional space of the text which the audience shares with all others experiencing the aesthetic object. Watching King Dushmanta professing love to Śakuntalā allows the audience to experience what being madly in love feels like, without inducing the desire to own that feeling for themselves; the experience is entirely aesthetic without moral or ethical consequences since the *sahṛdaya* audience is not tempted to follow in the characters' footsteps.[46] This sense of detached enjoyment thus prevents the audience from fully identifying with the representation they encounter, and the understanding that what is being experienced is fleeting further distances them from uncritically emulating the aesthetic object. The aesthetic object itself, while depicting nature—and by extension emotions and life—does not imitate nature. The *sahṛdaya* audience becomes aware of the *sthayibhāva* or the fundamental feelings in the text, but experiences them not as textual imitations of everyday emotions, but rather as a means of transcending the mundane toward a higher, universal expression of emotions.

Given the range of fairly risqué subjects in Bankim's novels, the aesthetic distance the reader places between themselves and the text is of significance. The presence of the *sahṛdaya pāthak* capable of deriving aesthetic pleasure from the situations represented on the page allows the author to introduce characters who prioritize desire over morality, become willing accomplices to seduction, and go against codes of social behavior, without the fear of providing the reader with bad role models.[47] The recurrence of the *śṛngāra rasa* in particular, in texts aimed at the conservative Bengali reader during an age when it was taboo for the wife to even meet her husband during the day, suggests that the reader is expected to maintain a certain distance from the situations and emotions depicted, a detachment which owes its origin to the *sahṛdaya* audience of classical Sanskrit aesthetics.

---

[46] For a detailed analysis of the transcendence and aesthetic experience see Arindam Chakrabarti's "Play, Pleasure, Pain: Ownerless Emotions in Rasa-Aesthetics."

[47] I should emphasize that Bankim does not rely exclusively on his reader's willingness to be *sahṛdaya* to ensure that she does not suffer from the moral repercussions of his narratives. There is a didactic strain prominent in his novels that defies *rasa* aesthetics, and it becomes evident in the construction of Tilottama as the reader to be emulated, or of Kamal and Shrishchandra as the model of companionate marriage in *Bishabṛksha*.

In *Bishabṛksha*, for example, Bankim chooses as his protagonist Kundanandini, a woman who, compelled by fate and her own desires, falls in love with her benefactor, Nagendra. Their illicit relationship almost destroys Nagendra's first marriage, when his wife Suryamukhi chooses to sacrifice herself for the sake of her husband's happiness. The moral world appears to be inverted when the reader finds Suryamukhi destitute and on the verge of death while Kundanandini, already widowed, becomes Nagendra's second wife. While polygamy is still a fairly common practice among the landed gentry in nineteenth-century Bengal, Kundanandini's story assumes a peculiarly scandalous edge because the reader is made privy to her uncontrolled desire for Nagendra while he is still *parpuruś* (lit. someone else's husband, but also a man outside the inner chambers of the house). Even when Suryamukhi initially throws her out of the house—before inexplicably bringing her back in—the reader learns of her plan to return for a single glimpse of Nagendra, the wave of love (*pranaysrōt*) overcoming that of shame (*lajjasrōt*).[48] Yet despite this non-normative admission of desire, Kundanandini remains the novel's heroine and the subject of both pity and admiration. When Kundanandini hears of Suryamukhi's apparent death, the reader—whom Bankim here addresses as *thakurāni* (a term used to address female elders, also suggestive of a social acquaintance)—is chastised for being gleeful at the death of a *satin* (co-wife), but the heroine mourns.[49] The narrative attains closure only when Kundanandini consumes poison, thus leaving the legitimate couple to continue unhindered, but it still treats her with considerable poignancy while reinscribing the warmth of her passions; she dies as a virtuous wife, having gained both the love of Nagendra and the forgiveness of Suryamukhi.

The novel leaves little doubt as to which character sustains the reader's attention; Suryamukhi, the only other contender, physically disappears for a significant stretch of the narrative, while Kundanandini, even at the height of her shame, remains a constant presence. She is the aesthetic object who evokes the *śṛngāra rasa* even when she first elicits an extramarital confession of love from Nagendra. We see her in a garden, and the beauty of her surroundings echoes her own as the *pāthak* witnesses the blossoms caressing her body. Bankim introduces the *rasa* with the word *sundar* (beauty), but unlike *Durgeśnandinī*, here Kundanandini ascribes the quality to everyone but herself—she thinks everyone is *sundar* while she has no attractive qualities at all. The effect on the reader,

---

[48] *Bishabṛksha*, 244–5.
[49] Ibid., 270–1.

138   *The Novel in Nineteenth-Century Bengal*

however, is the opposite. The more she laments that Suryamukhi, Haramani, Bishu, Mukta, and all the members of the household, down to the conniving and morally destitute maid, Hira, are prettier than she is, the more the reader perceives her as the model of innocent yet doomed beauty.[50] Yet this beauty is also dangerous, as Kundanandini's contemplation of death demonstrates. She has this initial chance to kill herself, thereby removing the threat posed by her allure, but as the narrator wonders at the close of the chapter, "why [doesn't] Kunda kill herself by drowning?"[51]

Despite her perilous beauty, Kundanandini can thrive in the novel as the reader is shielded from emulating her self-destructive passion by her aesthetic distance from the text. The reader derives pleasure and thrill from seeing Kundanandini challenge fate and social customs, without becoming embroiled in the world of the novel. Her death at the moment she transgresses would preserve the moral universe but detract from the *rasa*, and so the narrative chooses instead to minimally contain the damage by suggesting she kill herself while emphasizing her fragile beauty that is evocative of both desire and death. The reader feels what it is to give in to a forbidden love, but the experience of the *rasa* prevents them from identifying with Kundanandini or desiring to be in the same situation as the novel's heroine. As the *sahṛdaya pāthak* they recognize the *rasa*'s emphasis is not mimetic (*anukaran*) but detached appreciation, and their aesthetic distance from the text allows Bankim to accentuate the taboo and the erotic.[52] Like Kālidāsa's audience, Bankim's reader sympathizes with Kundanandini, but they do not see themselves in the character; the *sahṛdaya pāthak*'s morality suffers no damage from their experience of reading the novel.

IV. *Kathā*, *Ākhyāyikā*, and a Sanskritized Bengali

One significant difference between Bankim and Kalidasa is their choice of artistic medium. The latter composes in the highest of genres—verse—while the former employs a relatively new and secondary genre in Sanskrit literary history—prose. If the texts read by Tilottama—in particular *Kādambarī* and *Vasavadattā*—provide Bankim's reader with an aesthetic reference point, they

---

[50] *Biśabriksha*, 230–2.

[51] Ibid.

[52] Chakrabarti's chapter is a good reference here, in particular the discussion on page 196.

also situate his novels within the tradition of classical Sanskrit prose narratives. He describes *Durgeśnandinī* as an *ākhyāyikā*, which is one of two available modes of Sanskrit prose narratives, the other being the *kathā*.[53] This choice of descriptor is significant as Bankim does not merely identify the text as a *kāhinī* or a story; he selects a specific genre, one which his reader would be more familiar with than the foreign form of the novel. The word "novel" itself becomes assimilated into the Bengali language soon after the publication of *Durgeśnandinī* and enters colloquial use to the extent that popular, cheap satires regularly refer to the ill-effects of reading "*nātak-nabel*" ("plays, novels").[54] Yet Bankim persists in his use of the term *ākhyāyikā* in texts as late as *Ānandamath* (1882) and *Debi Chaudhurāni* (1884), assuming his readers' familiarity with the form even when the novel as a genre and a term is well-established in Bengal.

However, before examining how *Kādambarī* and *Vāsavadattā* are employed to create a literary lineage for the Bengali novel, it is worth looking briefly at the history of prose in the Sanskrit literary tradition, given the primacy of verse compositions and the wealth of commentary surrounding poetic texts. The record of Sanskrit prose is a contentious one, not least because it is rarely accorded the literary merit associated with the more illustrious poetic tradition. Sanskrit scholars situate prose as an inferior art form, composed in the shadow of poetry, following the accepted hierarchy in Sanskrit art; poetry is the repository of beauty or *alamkār* and characterized by *rasa*.[55] The history of prose is dependent upon that of poetry because the artistic features of prose are almost exclusively derived from poetic compositions, and it is a history narrated through difference rather than identity. Sanskrit prose is initially described as the absence or limited use of verse, and consequently lacking the rhetorical sophistication of poetry, while its content is seen as a smaller subset of the subjects fit for poetic composition. Even in such classic texts as *Kādambarī* and *Vāsavadattā*, prose is frequently interspersed with stanzas of verse which either indicate a break in the narrative or—and this is more often—express the more creative articulation of the *rasas*.

The status of prose improves when the seventh-century Kashmiri rhetorician, Bhamaha, addresses *kāvya* or poetry and its variations based on structure, subject matter, and the manner of composition, in the most significant treatise on classical Sanskrit rhetoric, *Kāvyalamkāra* (*The Ornaments of Poetry*).

---

[53] *Durgeśnandinī*, 5.
[54] *Nabhel Nāyikā Bā Śikkhita Bou* and *Miss Bino Bibi, B.A.* are only two such examples.
[55] Cf. Hrishikesh Bose, *Kadambari ō gadya-sāhitye śilpa-bicār* (1968).

Bhamaha suggests that the word *kāvya*—traditionally taken to mean poetry or verse compositions—is a combination of word and meaning, rather than a literary form, and as such, can be composed as verse or prose.[56] He establishes aesthetic rules particular to prose, and demarcates historical and imaginative prose writing—*itihās* as the former, and *kathā* and *ākhyāyika* as the latter. While the distinctions between *kathā* and *ākhyāyika* become a matter of considerable debate among prominent theorists of ancient India such as Dandin, Lollata, and Rudrata, the two are generally accepted to be the class of fictional prose narratives to which both *Kādambarī* and *Vasavadattā* belong. The rules of composition encompass both form and content, and the essential ones require that the *kathā* and the *ākhyāyika* be literary compositions, written primarily in prose using "words pleasing to the ear (*sravya*) and agreeable to the matter intended (*prakrtanukula*)." Verse should be used "in *vaktra* and *apavaktra* metre" to provide "a timely indication of the future happenings in the story." The *Kavyalamkāra* also recommends the theme for such compositions to be the "abduction of a girl (*kanya-harana*), a fight (*samgrama*), a separation (*vipralambha*), and the (final) triumph (*udaya*), apparently of the hero," and the narrative to be divided "into several pauses called *ucchvasas*" so as to allow the narrator time to breathe.[57] Most commentaries on *Kādambarī* and *Vasavadattā* as archetypes of prose narrative agree that the tenor of these works is dictated by their central theme—*kanyālābha* (winning of the maiden) or *kanyāharana*, which gives "free scope to the delineation of the amorous sentiment" (*śṛngāra rasa*).[58] This furthers the idea that the prose texts are fundamentally inventions of the composer, and can be read as examples of romantic fiction in the Sanskrit canon. The *udaya* marks the victory of love as much as it does of the hero with the removal of the cause of separation and the union of the lovers. There is added emphasis on the *śṛngāra rasa* when theorists such as Rudrata and Vishwanatha insist on *sarasa vastu* (subject matter imbued with *rasa*, but also implying a contrast between the flavor of fiction and the dryness of historical accounts) as substance fit for the form.

The difficulties of applying the tenets of classical Sanskrit poetics to a set of texts written in nineteenth-century Bengal are obvious, not least of all given

---

[56] Bhamaha, 6.

[57] For more, see Sisir Kumar Das's "The Ākhyāyikā and the Kathā in Classical Sanskrit" (1924).

[58] Rudrata's version of the *Kāvyalamkāra* replaces *kanyaharana* (abduction of a maiden) with the less valorous *kanyālabha* (winning of the girl), but the emphasis on the hero acquiring his beloved remains.

that the Sanskrit theorists assume both prose and verse compositions to be initially oral. This transition from orality is perhaps most evident in the absence of *ucchvāsas* or pauses for breath in the novels. Bankim follows later conventions in conflating some of the distinctions, choosing to focus more on the *rasa* of the *kathā* while still retaining the historical allusions of the *ākhyāyikā*, thus modifying the genres to suit his treatment of historical romantic fiction. Given the difference in stress between Bengali and Sanskrit as languages, the meters are also different, and neither the *vaktra* nor the *apavaktra* meters occur in Bankim's texts. However, despite these differences, most of Bankim's novels do follow Bhamaha's dictates in using verse to foreshadow future events in the narrative, use language both lofty and pleasant, and have lovers' union following an enforced separation as their overarching theme.

The technique of preparing readers for future events through sections of verse is most notable in *Bishabṛksha*, in which Bankim contends with a subject matter peculiarly thorny for a conservative Bengali audience. I wish to focus in particular on two such instances when the novelist presents one of the characters in disguise whose songs cue the reader—and all other characters except the naïve Kundanandini—to what is about to happen. Debendra, the narrative's black-hearted villain, intent on seducing and ruining innocent beautiful women, particularly Kundanandini, gains access to the inner chambers or *antarmahal* of the house she lives in by disguising himself as a *baiśnabī* (a female mendicant, usually followers of the god Vishnu, and often noted for their singing talent). He introduces himself as Haridāsi and offers to sing and entertain the women of the household. Harisdāsi pointedly asks Kundanandini what she would like to hear, thus ensuring the audience (and the reader) knows who the song really is for. He sings a *kirtan* (semi-religious songs about Radha and Krishna's love), and the following lines foretell the crisis about to occur:

> Unless you look at me again,
> I'll go off to the shore of the Yamuna,
> I'll break my flute, give up my life,
> Let your vanity go now[59]

Debendra turns Kundanandini into Radha, while he assumes the voice of Krishna, and implores her to look at him again—she has already refused to meet him—and threatens to kill himself if she continues to ignore him.

---

[59] *Biśabriksha*, 217.

The sentiment is an oft-repeated one in *kirtans*, and in itself not particularly notable. In the context of the narrative, however, it presages the future; even when physically threatened, Kundanandini stands her ground and rejects Debendra's advances. He ultimately dies of liver cirrhosis, driven to excess by his failure to conquer her. The song applies not merely to Debendra and his fate; it encodes the future of Kundanandini's story with Nagendra as well. The roles are reversed, and Kundanandini is now the one professing love to the sometime reluctant Nagendra, but like Debendra, she too must die of unrequited love.

The method of encoding future events in verse is not exclusive to the tradition of Sanskrit prose, but in this context, it allows one to understand the repeated intrusion of verse in Bankim's otherwise emphasis on prose.[60] In almost all his novels, he includes verse stanzas and they predominantly serve the same function as in *Bishabṛksha*. If one takes into account the requirement that the verse additions reflect the tenor of the section which they either begin or are a part of,[61] their utility in helping establish the dominant *rasa* of the narrative becomes evident. In the above example, the song explicitly articulates the erotic sentiment, and serves to reinforce the emotion that has already been invoked for the reader through the heightened descriptions of female beauty and love. In *Durgeśnandinī*, Bankim utilizes the descriptions of the female characters to highlight the *śṛngāra rasa*; in *Bishabṛksha*, a more mature novelist reintroduces the *rasa* through the subtle use of predictive verse.

Perhaps the most famous example of verse in Bankim's novels is from his last work, *Ānandamath*. "*Bande Mātaram*" ("I bow to thee, Motherland") has acquired a life independent of the novel because of its association with Indian nationalism. In part, "*Bande Mātaram*" owes its popularity to the role played by the novel in imagining the nation as the motherland demanding service from its seventy million children.[62] The song lies at the heart of the narrative as a prayer

---

[60] What is also unique about Bankim's use of verse in this instance is the mélange he effects between the highly Sanskritized Bengali and the everyday common—occasionally vulgar—Bengali of folk songs. Akshaychandra Sarkar praises this version of *bankimī* Bengali when he calls is *madhyabartinī bhāṣā* or the language of the middle path. For readers such as Akshaychandra, this form of the language retains the beauty of Sanskrit while still appealing to the heart of the average Bengali reader, and shows the craft of a mature novelist fully in control of the language. As these examples from *Biśabriksha* demonstrate, the narrative incorporates the low into the high in ways that are generative in terms of both form and narrative content. For more on Akshyachandra's discussion, see Chapter 2. For a related discussion on the incorporation of the low into the high in Mosharraf Hossain's *Biśād Sindhu*, see Chapter 4 of this work.

[61] Sisir Kumar Das discusses this construction in detail in his work, and in particular on page 512.

[62] The song can be found on page 663 of the novel.

to the motherland who is *dharma* (faith, purpose) and *marma* (meaning), foreshadowing the guerrilla war waged by the Hindu *Santan* (lit. children, referring to men who fashion themselves as the *Sanyasis* or the ascetics, serving the motherland) against both the British and the Muslim rulers of Bengal. Set against the 1771 Bengal famine, the narrative follows Mahendra and Kalyani as they try and survive in a land destroyed by hunger and consequent rebellions. They are given shelter by the *Sanyasis* who show them the vision of the motherland as she was (glorious, fertile, like the goddess Jagaddhatri), as she is (denuded, dark, like Kali), and as she will be (renewed, golden, like Durga). The narrative culminates in a battle between the *Sanyasis* and the British, as the former attack a fort and, despite all odds, win their first victory against the *rājā* (king, ruler).

The importance of *Ānandamath* to the project of Indian nationalism, and as an example of Bankim's brand of revolutionary politics is well documented;[63] of interest here is the language of "*Bande Mātaram*." Similar to the verses used in *Bishabṛksha*, "*Bande Mātaram*" too establishes the dominant *rasa*, which here is the *vira rasa* (heroic) culminating in the *śānta rasa* (tranquil). By appearing at a key moment in the narrative—soon after Mahendra has been rescued by Bhabananda, one of the *Sanyasi* leaders, close to the start of the novel—the verses inform the reader of the actions to follow and the ultimate victory of the *Sanyasis* in establishing a glorious motherland. Bankim's linguistic choice is a distillation of the Sanskritized Bengali he employs in his prose, and is emblematic of the *bankimī* style in its infusion of the two languages. The verse, like the prose, uses language intended to be pleasing to the ear and fit for the subject, thus meeting the criteria established by Bhamaha. This language, however, appears to be particularly impenetrable for a modern Bengali reader as it practically disappears from literature after Bankim's death, and also because it requires at least a passing familiarity with Sanskrit. In the first line of the verse—"*bande mātaram*" ("I bow to thee, Mother")—the script is Bengali, as is roughly the syntactical structure, but the words Bankim uses are Sanskrit. To emphasize this distinction, most editions of the novel either use the diacritic mark *hashanta* after the final "m" in "*mātaram*," which represents a consonant sound without an inherent vowel, or replace the "m" with "ng," thus creating a nasal sound. Both forms are common in Sanskrit but rare in Bengali. The words that follow—

---

[63] Jashodhara Bagchi's "Positivism and Nationalism" (1985) and Meenakshi Mukherjee's "Anandamath: A Political Myth" (1982), to name only two.

"*sujalāng sufalāng malayajaśītalāng śaśyaśyāmalāng*" ("richly watered, fertile, cooled by the gentle south winds, green with the harvest")—are Sanskrit in form, both in terms of the "ng" endings as well as the compound words, yet comprehensible in Bengali. A pattern begins to emerge in this song which is present in all of Bankim's Bengali works. The language uses the Sanskrit style of compounding words (*samās*), often resulting in entire phrases being constructed as single word units. This technique of using *samās* is a commonplace in Sanskrit compositions, and various regional styles are identified by their propensity for *samās* and *sandhi* (euphonic combinations). Bankim is almost unique in using *samās* as most of his contemporaries either rely on a form of Bengali mimicking the English grammar,[64] or write in the popular form of the language, which often incorporates the vulgar.[65]

As mentioned in the introduction, the story that the scholar of modern Bengali literature has inherited positions the language of "*Bande Mātaram*," and by implication that of the novels, as innovative yet anomalous since it forms merely one stage in the teleological progress of Bengali literature.[66] Yet the *bankimī* style of Bengali containing the complexities of *alamkār* and *rasas* has a long history in early modern Bengali literature, and in many ways, Bankim is perhaps its final practitioner. For an audience familiar with, if not competent readers of, authors such as Bharatchandra Ray, Rama Prasad, and Ishwar Gupta,[67] Bankim's style of writing in Sanskritized Bengali would have produced the linguistic pleasure Bhamaha advises even though they occupy a world in which Sanskrit has become increasingly inaccessible.

The final text Tilottama reads in *Durgeśnandinī*, Jayadeva's *Gītagōvinda*, is a perfect example of this comingling of Sanskrit and Bengali as the following lines demonstrate:

> *Lalitā-lavanga-latā-parisilana-kōmala-malaya-samire*
> *Madhukara-nikara-karambita-kōkilā-kujita-kunja-kutire*
> The gentle clove leaf pursues the soft southern wind
> The humming of bees is echoing and the cuckoo sings in the hut and in
>   the garden[68]

---

[64] *Ālāler gharer dulāl.*

[65] *Hutam pyāncār nakśā.*

[66] Cf. Sudipta Kaviraj's "Two Histories of Literary Culture in Bengal" (2003).

[67] For a detailed analysis of the relationship between Bengali, Sanskrit, and Prakrit, see Dinesh Chandra Sen's *History of Bengali Language and Literature* (1911).

[68] Jayadeva, xli, translation mine.

The language Jayadeva uses is Sanskrit, but the lines can be read in Bengali as each word is *tatsama* or identical in meaning in both languages. A reader of Bengali would read the last four words "*kōkila-kujita-kunja-kutire*" ("the cuckoo sings in the hut and in the garden") as Bengali, thus making the language of the poem ambiguous. Compare this to a few more lines of "*Bande Mataram*":

Saptakō Tīkan Thakalakalaninādakarāle
Dwisaptakō Tībhūjairdhṛtakhara-karabāle
Seven million voices in unison
Twice seven million hands bearing arms[69]

In syntactical form, the lines appear to be in Sanskrit; yet, the language is clearly Bengali. Each component of the compound is a Bengali word that is either *tatsama* or *tadbhāva* (derived from Sanskrit). The alliterative sound in the segment is "k," and Bankim is able to play with it because of the alliterative effect created in the previous segment ("*sujalāng sufalāng malayajaśītalāng*"). In that, the rhyme is based on Bengali using a single "sh" sound for both *s* and *ś*, even though the words are Sanskrit, and would not rhyme if pronounced in that language. The linguistic play here draws on the literary culture that exists among the Bengali-speaking readers who inhabit the junction of both these languages and are able to appreciate Bankim's texts for their continuance of this tradition.

V. Concluding Thoughts

The study of the British novel has benefited from a multifaceted literary history, but significant work remains to be done on the histories of novels from Britain's erstwhile colonies. This chapter is one such attempt at engaging with the larger project of revising the literary history of former colonial spaces by placing the Bengali novel in conversation with non-Western practices of reading. This novel is premised on a rejection of the English language novel by the same readers who enthusiastically embrace the former. Bankim's first novel, *Rajmohan's Wife*, published in 1864, one year before *Durgeśnandinī* is largely forgotten by all but Bankim scholars, and even when his readers compare his first Bengali work to *Ivanhoe*, there is no evidence to suggest they even draw on *Rajmohan's Wife* to support their claim that Bankim is indeed trying to imitate the British form.

---

[69] *Anandamath*, 663.

The Sanskritist reading practice aligning the genre with classical Sanskrit literary traditions clearly resonates with readers who still inhabit these traditions as part of their present. That this does ultimately give way to the Anglicist practice bears testimony to the pervasive and violent nature of colonial rule and the degree to which its ideologies infiltrate and inform native practices.

While the Bengali novel emerges after the introduction of its Victorian counterpart, the former is a product of engagement with tensions foreign to the British novel. Examining the connections shared by readers, reading practices, and the novel provides an opportunity to re-evaluate the genre of the postcolonial novel, and to approach it neither as an allegorical form passively reflecting anticolonial ideologies, nor as just another cultural artifact among others. As the texts by Bankim suggest, the novel can instead be understood to actively create a reading public and instruct it on how to read the text, and in the process, be created as a form distinct from the British novel.

4

Another World of Reading: Hossain and Islamic Bengali Prose

I. From the Global to the Local: Mosharraf Hossain's *Biśād Sindhu*

My grandmother, who was originally from undivided Bengal, moved to Kolkata around the partition of India in 1947, and brought with her stories from her native city of Comilla.[1] One of these stories was about reading Mir Mosharraf Hossain's novel *Biśād Sindhu* (*Ocean of Sorrows*) and watching its narrative performed on the banks of the Dharmasagar (a lake in the city) during Muharram.[2] For her, as a young Hindu girl, the act of watching the ritualized mourning of the fall of Husayn Ibn Ali and his brother Hasan evoked the same emotional response as that of reading of their martyrdom in the pages of *Biśād Sindhu*; the pathos of the story brought tears to her eyes, whether it was by watching the mourners in public or reading the novel in private. As she recounted this story to my mother during the second half of the twentieth century, the world of the novel, of the religious performance, and her own affect would merge to create an indistinguishable whole. For her, the transition between reading and watching this narrative was seamless, and the novel continued to be one of her favorites despite being an avid reader of world literature. This is a story I have inherited as family lore which, for the longest time, was a marker of my grandmother's connection with Bangladesh and of her personal sense of losing her homeland. It represented one individual's relationship to a text which I assumed was born of her attachment to Comilla rather than a quality of the novel itself.

Years later, when I sat down to write this book, *Biśād Sindhu* reappeared as one of the first Bengali novels written by a Muslim author, Mosharraf Hossain.

---

[1] Following the partition of India, city is now in Bangladesh.

[2] For Shia Muslims, Muharram marks the death of Husein Ibn Ali, the Prophet Mohammad's grandson, at the Battle of Karbala, and is a period of mourning and remembrance.

Originally published in three parts in 1885, 1887, and 1891, this novel generated considerable interest among late nineteenth-century readers, leading to critical discussions and advertisements in contemporary periodicals such as *Hitakarī*, *Sādharanī*, *The Education Gazette*, and *Bangadarśan*. Soon after, it was adopted as a textbook in various schools across Bengal, and continues to be on school and college curricula in both West Bengal and Bangladesh. In short, the novel became integrated into Bengali print culture immediately following its publication, like most other late-nineteenth-century Bengali novels. However, I also discovered that unlike most of these other novels, being read in print formed only one part of *Biśād Sindhu*'s life as both its pre- and post-publication history exceeded the print medium by referring to modes of consumption similar to those my grandmother recounted. Despite his own claims to the contrary, Mosharraf Hossain did not take as his inspiration quasi-historical texts such as the Persian classic *Maqtal Rawzat al-Shuhada* (1504) by Husain Waiz Kashifi or its articulation in Bengal titled generically[3] *Maqtul Husayn* by Muhammad Khan (eighteenth or early nineteenth century), but instead chose Bengali folktales on the story of Hassan and Husayn as his source.[4] These folktales were sometimes to be found preserved in *punthis* or manuscripts,[5] and frequently performed as *jārigān*—a folk music performance—during either Muharram or other religious ceremonies. Once the text of *Biśād Sindhu* is published, the novel's language is adopted by *jārigān* performers, and Mosharraf Hossain's written text became a mainstay of their repertoire. Thus the same performances that served as the novel's inspiration began to use the novel's language to tell the story of Husayn and Hasan. These are the same *jārigān* performances my grandmother recalls having attended in the late 1920s and 1930s in Comilla, suggesting that this relationship between print, performance, and manuscripts lasts well beyond the novel's initial entry into Bengali literary history. The merger of various modes of perception, then, is far from one person's memory of a lost homeland—it is an intrinsic part of

---

[3] *Maqtal* as a genre refers to narratives of the Battle of Karbala and Husayn's martyrdom.

[4] As several scholarly sources including Fakrul Alam's introduction to the English translation of *Biśād Sindhu*, and Anisujjaman's discussion of the novel's publication history suggests, I comment on this at length later in the chapter.

[5] It is also worth noting here that for Islamic texts, *punthi* refers to not only the form of the book but to its language as well. This language, known variously as *misra bhāśā*, *dōbhāśā*, or *Musalmānī bāṅglā*, is a mix of Persianate languages and Bengali. Frequently associated with the lower classes, *misra bhasha* was looked down upon by upper-class Muslims and Hindus alike, but it formed a significant part of nineteenth-century Bengali life because of its abundant use in oral performances such as *jāri* and later in cheap *battalā* texts.

the world in which the text is published and read, performed and watched. This was the way the novel was read, as part text and part performance, narrating a significant moment in Bengali Islamic history with its pathos appealing to Hindus and Muslims alike.

Exciting as this discovery was on a personal front—it allowed me to see my grandmother as belonging to a particular time and place with their own tangible traditions—it also led me to the set of literary historical questions informing this chapter. What was it about this first self-identified Islamic Bengali novel that allowed it to straddle multiple perceptive worlds? What might one say about the practice of reading a novel such as *Biśād Sindhu*, and what did it mean to be literate in the Perso-Arabic reading practice of which the novel was a part? What were the traits peculiar to this reading practice which differentiated it from the Sanskritist or the Anglicist practice? As one begins to answer these questions, the paucity of the archive becomes evident; there are very few novels being written by Bengali Muslim authors in Bengali during the nineteenth century. The predominance of Bengali Hindu authors, whether Sanskritists or Anglicists, has obscured the legacy of Bengali Muslims writing long prose narratives during the period, such that we are left with only a handful of names and works. In this group are authors such as Nawab Faizunnesa whose part autobiographical poetic composition *Rupjālāl* (1876) is one of the first by a Muslim woman in Bengal, journalist Reazuddin Ahmed who is responsible for editing periodicals such as *Islam Pracārak* and *Sudhakar*, and novelist Rokeya Sakhawat Hossain who publishes her first novel *Sultana's Dream* in 1908. We also find proto-novelistic texts such as Shamsuddin Mohammad Siddiqi's *Uchit Sraban* (1860), and satires or sketches by a range of authors including Golam Hussain, Sheikh Ajimuddin, and Ayen Ali Sikdar.

However, Mosharraf Hossain appears as the only Bengali Muslim writing novels in Bengali in the nineteenth century, and it is with his novel *Biśād Sindhu* that this chapter concerns itself. *Biśād Sindhu* and later novels by Mosharraf Hossain are part of a different reading practice—what I am calling the Perso-Arabic practice—that sets them apart from novels written within either the Sanskritist or the Anglicist practices. Hindu readers are perfectly adequate readers of these novels, and as the discussions[6] in the periodicals of the day show,

---

[6] *Somprakash*, for example, praises the novelist for eschewing Persianate languages in review of the novel dated March 29, 1886, and the sentiment is echoed by the *Magh* 1888 issue of *Bharati o balak*, and the *Ashwin* 1886 issue of *Bangadarśan*.

they read the texts just as they would Bengali works that are overtly or covertly Hindu, or European.[7] That Mosharraf Hossain's novels can accommodate the reader who has little to no knowledge of Islam or its stories is evidenced by their popularity among even conservative Hindus such as Bankimchandra Chattopadhyay or Akshaychandra Sarkar who take from these texts examples of heightened human emotions, critiques of social ills, or descriptions of rural Bengal written in chaste (read, Sanskritized) Bengali.

For the Bengali Muslim, however, the novel inaugurates a practice of reading that is simultaneously global and local, and fundamentally performative in nature. The text encourages reading as a form of pious practice by drawing on the principle of *adab*—broadly defined as a code of conduct, but that meaning is far from exhaustive—thus urging the reader to view themselves as part of the larger Islamic *umma* or community invested in proper *adab*. The novel being set in Medina and Damascus, telling the story of Hasan and Husayn as one of the central narratives of Islam aids in this process of identification, but as I argue in this chapter, it is *adab* that serves as the conceptual foundation allowing the Bengali Muslim to feel connected with Muslims outside their immediate local context. At the same time, *Biṣād Sindhu* is related to another kind of performance—the *jārigān* tradition—that is unique to Bengal. As a folk performance, *jārigān* narrates the events at Karbala as ritual theater, inviting the community to take part in a shared expression of grief venerating the *pak panjatan*, or the five sacred figures of Islam, the Prophet, Ali, Hasan, Husayn, and Fatema. The novel both draws on one of the first *jāri* texts, Heyat Mahmud's *Jārijungnama*, and itself becomes an integral part of the *jāri* repertoire. The reader of *Biṣād Sindhu* participates in this integration of print and performance through the act of reading the novel as they are part of the community that consumes both the text and *jārigān* performances. This form of reading *Biṣād Sindhu* is performative not only because it resides in the same perceptive world as that of *jārigān*, but because the narrative encourages the same pathos-laden response as it presents the reader with the story of Hasan, Husayn, and their family.

The reason behind *Biṣād Sindhu's* success in integrating reading as performance lies in the story it chooses to tell. The sectarian split between Shias and Sunnis can be traced to the battle of Karbala which marks a key moment in the debate over inheriting the prophetic line. In 680 AD, the Prophet's grandson,

---

[7] Anglicized Bengali is seen as representing Europe rather than Christianity, while Hindu is often perceived to be the neutral (secular?) form of Bengali.

Husayn, is killed at Karbala, and for Shia Muslims mourning the event becomes ritualized as Muharram. As the event gets embedded in oral and written literature, it also provides a way for Islam to transmit itself as it travels across the world, forming a core of belief for those moving outward from their homelands as well as for those newly converted. In South Asia, and in other parts of the Islamicate world with a predominantly Shia population, these narratives of the Prophet and his family as told by the Sufi pirs[8] come to be the authoritative religious source given that, for many local communities, the sacred texts of the Qur'an and the *Hadith*[9] do not exist in vernacular translations till late into the nineteenth century.[10] Alongside this narrativized version of Islam, Muharram rituals of chest beating and loud laments of *"Hai Hasan Hai Husayn"* create an affective whole capable of attracting a population becoming familiar with the religion. These rituals gradually become the basis of the folk poetic traditions of the *marsiya* and the *nauha* in South Asia, both of which mourn the martyrdom of Husayn. These two forms are formally adopted by Muslims in Bengal as space and time within the *hussainiya*[11] are accorded to mourners to sing *marsiyas* and *nauhas* during Muharram.[12] *Jāri*, though born of this same tradition, is not one of the designated rituals within the *hussainiya* as it continues to exist just outside structured religion, in a syncretic space occupied by rural, Bengali-speaking, Hindus and Muslims.

Biṣād Sindhu narrates the story of Karbala as it is known to this rural community thanks to the prevalence of *jārigān*. In the preface or the *"mukhabandha"* to the first edition of *Biṣād Sindhu*, Mosharraf Hossain tells his readers that the novel draws on the story of Muharram when Hosen (Husayn)[13] and his family are killed by Ejid's (Yazid) soldiers at Karbala. The narrative is divided into three parts titled *"Muharram parba"* ("Muharram Episode"), *"Uddhar parba"* ("The

---

[8] Saints.

[9] A narrative record of the sayings and customs of the Prophet and his companions.

[10] One of the earliest mentions of the Qur'an in Bengali, for example, appears as late as 1891 in the magazine *Indian Nation*, and even there, the reviewer notes that the text is not considered to have religious authority by the Muslims since it was translated by a non-Muslim scholar of Arabic.

[11] A communal hall built to house mourners during Muharram, and for other religious observances. Originally in eighth-century Iran, mourners performed in open public spaces, and gradually shelters were built to protect them against the elements, leading to the formalization of *hussainiyas*, also known as *Imambaras*.

[12] See for example Ahmad Hasan Dani's *Dhaka: A Record of Its Changing Fortunes* for more on the Muharram rituals in Dhaka.

[13] A note on Bengali transliteration of Perso-Arabic names. When referring to characters in the novel, I use the Bengalicized forms of Arabic names to be faithful to Mosharraf Hossain's text. Outside the novel, I use the Arabic names.

Rescue Episode"), and *"Ejid badh parba"* ("The Episode on killing Ejid"), and as the introduction or the *upakramanika* informs us, the novel exemplifies the inevitability of the divine plan. The Prophet Mohammad foretells the death of his grandsons Hasan and Hosen at the hands of Ejid, and as each part unfolds, Mosharraf Hossain shows how this prophecy comes to be. Ejid's desire for Hasan's wife Jaynab (Zainab) leads to Hasan and Hosen's death in the *"Muharram parba"* as the reader is shown the follies not just of lust but also the treachery of women. The following part, *"Uddhar parba,"* narrates how the rest of Hasan and Hosen's family is saved, and how the great warrior Mohammad Hanifa swears to avenge Hosen's death. This promise leads Mohammad Hanifa to engage in a slaughtering spree where he kills both the innocent and the guilty living in Damascus, the city ruled by Ejid. Finally in *"Ejid badh parba,"* the novelist describes the fate of an imprisoned and repentant Ejid who, along with Mohammad Hanifa, must burn in eternal hellfire for their crimes. The novel ends on the note that sinners must always pay for their sins, and the virtuous will be rewarded even though theirs is a path of suffering.

Despite the clearly Islamic overtones, discussions of *Biśād Sindhu* in nineteenth-century literary circles are telling of the ways in which the novel is co-opted into Sanskritist reading practices which focus almost exclusively on Mosharraf Hossain's ability to use *bishuddha* or pure Bengali. Such is the force of this narrative that many reviewers suggest "Mosharraf Hossain" must be a *nom de plume* of a Hindu writer because no Muslim author can use Bengali so beautifully.[14] Even when critics accept the novelist's religious identity, they praise him for couching Arabic terms in ways that are pleasing to the Bengali reader, thus cementing Hindu Bengali as the neutral or normative position. Yet outside this co-option lies a very different reading practice, one which is attentive to Persianate languages and Islamic aesthetic structures, and my interest in *Biśād Sindhu* lies in the novel's ability to grant us access to this Perso-Arabic reading practice. In this chapter, I argue for reading *Biśād Sindhu* through a practice of reading rooted in the concept of *adab* and one of its folk manifestations in Bengal, the *jārigān*. I suggest that Mosharraf Hossain's novel incorporates aesthetic markers which direct the knowing reader on how to read the text so as to acquire the knowledge necessary for an ethically correct life. While *adab* allows *Biśād Sindhu* to be part of a larger Islamicate world which includes

---

[14] Included in this list are the *Education Gazette* and the *Calcutta Review*, both nineteenth-century periodicals.

novels in Persian and Urdu, its relationship with *jārigān* returns the narrative to the familiar context of Bengal and to the ways in which the sacred becomes a function of a community. Examining these two aspects of the Perso-Arabic reading practice provides us with the unique opportunity of understanding how Bengali Muslims engaged with, and entered, literary modernity in late-nineteenth-century Bengal.

II. *Adab* as the Implicit Code, or How to Read *Biśād Sindhu*

When the first part of *Biśād Sindhu*, "*Maharam Parba*" ("Muharram Episode"), is published in 1885, the following review of the novel appears in the Bengali periodical *Education Gazette*:

> The novelist has collected the gist of the original event from Persian and Arabic texts and has beautifully written the book in clear Bengali. There is not even the whiff of Islamic language [*Musalmani bhasha*] in his book. He has described the events in pure pleasant Bengali [...] The novel is filled with *karuna rasa*, even the burning effect of *vir rasa* is apparent in it.[15]

The reviewer praises Mosharraf Hossain for not only avoiding the use of "*Musalmani bhasha*," but goes so far as to see in the novel the aesthetic principles of *rasa*.[16] The various adjectives used to describe Bengali—pure, pleasant, clear— draw the reader's attention to not *Hindu bhasha* but to *bhasha*, in this case Bengali, or language in general. According to the review, the novelist is successful in creating a novel that the reader wants to read from start to finish because he has told a story many "average" ("*sadharon*") Bengalis are unaware of in a language that is simple, using a literary structure that this average reader knows well. One notes similar reviews of Mosharraf Hossain's first novel, *Ratnabati* (1869), in periodicals such as *Rahasya Sandarbha*[17] and *Calcutta Review*.[18] A few years later, the author published his play *Jamidar Darpan* (*A Mirror Held to the Landlords*, 1873) to yet again the same remarks, this time from the literary periodical *Bangadarshan*. The magazine found no trace of "*Musalmani bangla*"

---

[15] *Education Gazette*, June 12, 1885, translation mine.
[16] See Chapter 3 for a detailed discussion of the *rasa* theory.
[17] "*Natun granther samalochana*" ("Review of new books"), 5 *parba*, 54 *khanda*, 1869, in *Sambad-samayik Patre Unish Shataker Bangali Musalman Samaj*, pp. 490–1.
[18] Vol. 50, 1870, in *Sambad-samayik Patre Unish Shataker Bangali Musalman Samaj*, pp. 489–90.

("Islamic Bengali") in the play, suggesting that its linguistic merit was its use of unalloyed Bengali even though it was written by a Muslim author.[19] While both reviews are anonymous, their authors' religious affiliation is not hard to gauge. Bhudeb Mukhopadhyay, the editor of *Education Gazette*, and Bankim, the editor of *Bangadarshan*, are both upper-caste Hindu men, and book reviews were nearly always the task of a magazine's editor. Bhudeb and Bankim read Mosharraf Hossain's texts as desiring entry into Sanskritized Bengali in order to become part of mainstream Bengali literature. From the perspective of Bhudeb, that the novel in particular is able to evoke *karuna* (compassionate) and *vir* (heroic) *rasas* adds to the ease with which it might be seen as simply "Bengali" without the need for the descriptor "Muslim." This emphasis on the text using pure Bengali, matched only by the reviewers' surprise at a Bengali Muslim's ability to write in such a register, represents the Hindu Bengali's parochialism toward the language and its literary productions.[20]

However, when we consider Mosharraf Hossain's own remarks regarding the supposed purity of Bengali, he seems far from advocating for the erasure of *"Musalmani bhasha"* from his works. In the July 2, 1892, issue of the journal *Hitakarī*, Mosharraf Hossain responds to a letter to the editor asking him to explain why, in a publication otherwise using *"bisuddha"* or pure Bengali, there are articles using *"Musalmani katha"* (Muslim words, referring to Urdu and Arabic words).[21] He defends the periodical's language policy on two fronts: first, he says, there are Muslim authors who contribute to *Hitakarī* regularly, and second, he resents the day's fashion of intermingling of Bengali and English, saying that he would rather fuse Bengali (*matribhasha* or mother tongue) with Urdu (*bhratribhasha* or brother tongue).[22] *Hitakarī* is not overtly Islamic in its mission, unlike more conservative publications such as *Islam Pracārak* and *Sudhākar*, but as the editor of a journal conscious of its Muslim reader base, Mosharraf Hossain refutes the suggestion that Sanskritized Bengali is either

[19] *Bangadarśan, Bhadra* 1873 in *Sambād-sāmayik Patre Uniś Śataker Bāngāli Musalmān Samāj*, p. 493.
[20] Mosharraf Hossain is far from being the sole recipient of such comments remarking on the Bengali Muslim's ability to successfully mimic their Hindu counterparts. For example, when a group of students from Mohsin College in Hooghly launch their periodical, *Ajijan Nehar* in 1874, the publication receives considerable praise from the government sponsored and Hindu edited *Education Gazette* for being the first Muslim-led journal to use *"saral bangala bhasha"* or simple Bengali.
[21] *"Sampādakiya mantabya"* ("Editor's notes"), *Hitakarī*, July 2, 1891, p. 287.
[22] *"Sampādakiya mantabya,"* p. 288.

the definitive form of the language or the only one used by Bengali Muslims. Instead, he juxtaposes Bengali and Urdu as *bhrātribhāśā* thus effecting a familial connection between these two languages, and incorporating the Muslim reader into the fold of the Bengali. He creates a metaphor whereby Bengali as the *mātribhāśā* is mother to all her children, regardless of whether they speak Bengali or Urdu, are Hindu or Muslim. Mosharraf Hossain repeats the verb *mesānō* or to mix when referring to the relationship between *mātribhāśā* and *bhrātribhāśā*, but he is careful to not suggest that this mixing produces something new. After all, *misra bhāśā* or mixed language has deeply negative connotations for Hindus and Muslims—for both, it is the language spoken by the uneducated and illiterate peasantry and boatmen, and as a result, it bears the marks of vulgarity, obscenity, and a form of religious syncreticism suspicious to both religions. Instead, *Hitakarī's* editor suggests an addition which retains the individual identity of both Bengali and Urdu, thereby allowing both Hindus and Muslims to participate in reading and writing on equal terms. This natural affiliation between Bengali and Urdu underscores the Muslim reader's familiarity with both languages, providing us with a way to understand how a novel such as *Biśād Sindhu* is shaped by the aesthetic structures inherent in Urdu rather than those that are Sanskritic by nature.

Jettisoning, then, the Hindu Bengalis' claims to linguistic purity, we are free to look more closely at the aesthetic paradigms available to Mosharraf Hossain via his relationship with Islam and Persianate languages such as Urdu. Looking at the world of Urdu literature is particularly instructive at this juncture as *Biśād Sindhu* enters the public imagination within a few years of the publication of a set of three Urdu novels which significantly reshape the Indian literary scene. These three texts *Mirat-al-arus* (*The Mirror of the Bride*, 1869), *Banat-an-nāsh* (*Daughters of the Bier*, 1872), and *Taubā-an-nāsuh* (*The Repentence of Nasuh*, 1874), all by Nazir Ahmad, are some of the first novels to be written in Urdu. He responds to a call for "useful works in the vernacular" issued by William Muir, the lieutenant-governor of the North-West provinces in 1868.[23] Muir offers a cash reward to any writer capable of producing work in either "Oordoo [Urdu] or Hindee [Hindi]"[24] that was not sectarian or overtly religious, and could be used for the intellectual amelioration of native readers. There is an added emphasis on texts aimed at women, and in response, Nazir Ahmad writes three

---

[23] The notice as quoted in C. M. Naim's "Prize Winning Adab," 292–3.
[24] C. M. Naim's "Prize Winning Adab," 292–3.

156   *The Novel in Nineteenth-Century Bengal*

novels which essentially conduct books for women. *Mirat-al-arus*, in particular, becomes hugely popular across the Indian subcontinent, finding its way into Urdu syllabi (where it remains till this day), and being translated into a number of languages, one of which is Bengali.[25] We find advertisements for Urdu and Bengali versions of the novel in not only *Hitakari* but also other contemporary Bengali periodicals such as *Sōmprakāś* and *Ādarinī*, and in Persian newspapers such as *Aina-e-Sikander*, suggesting that it had considerable reach among readers in Bengal. Even readers in rural Bengal who may not have adequate knowledge of Urdu thus had access to Nazir Ahmad's novel. With *Mirat-al-arus*, Muslim readers in India find one of the earliest iterations of a novel which allows them a point of entry into a modern literary genre through Indian vernacular languages, while still being guided by the principles of Islamic *adab* literature.[26] It provides its readers domestic and spiritual guidance through a narrative that foregrounds the aesthetic structures of *adab*, thereby placing itself in a continuum with literature in classical Persianate languages.

Mosharraf Hossain's early works appear to bear little resemblance to Persianate realm of Nazir Ahmad's novels. *Ratnabati*, Mosharraf Hossain's first novel, is described by reviewers as "a romantic tale designed to shew that knowledge is of greater importance than wealth."[27] In it, he narrates the story of a prince, Sukumar, who is a rich, spoilt young man, and who gets imprisoned because of his own folly. When he discovers that his wealth cannot save him, he has to rely on his friend, the minister's son Sumantra, who, though not very wealthy, is intelligent enough to free him, thus demonstrating the moral of the story. The narrative—both in form and content—is Sanskritized enough to lead yet another reviewer from *Rahasya Sandarbha* to claim Mosharraf Hossain the equal of any *pundit* (teacher) of the Sanskrit College.[28] Indeed, what the novelist writes is a Bengali Hindu fairy tale, often referred to as *thākurmā'r galpa* or grandmother's tales, putting his characters through their paces in a world that would be intimately familiar to a Bengali Hindu. Four years

---

[25] Frances Pritchett, in the afterword to her English translation of *Mirat* (1985), as well as Ralph Russell in his *The Pursuit of Urdu Literature* (1992) note the popularity of Nazir Ahmad's novel and the speed with which it was translated into multiple Indian languages, including Bengali, Gujarati, Kashmiri, and Punjabi.

[26] Following scholarly custom, I use this term to refer to literature on *adab* as well as texts based on the principles of *adab*.

[27] *Calcutta Review*, vol. 50 1870 in *Sambād-sāmayik Patre Uniś Śataker Bāṅgāli Musalmān Samāj*, pp. 489–90.

[28] *Rahasya Sandarbha*, 5 *parba*, 54 *khanda*, 1869 in *Sambad-sāmayik patre unish śataker bāṅgāli musalmān samaj*, pp. 490–1.

Another World of Reading

later, Mosharraf Hossain's play *Basantakumārī* (1873) delineates a similarly Sanskritized landscape with characters who have distinctly Hindu names such as the protagonist Basantakumari, the princess of Bhojpur, and her beloved, Narendranath, the prince of Indrapur. The play opens with a *prastabana* or a prologue, an intrinsic component of Sanskrit *nataka* (play) which makes its way into Bengali theater, thus infusing the form with Sanskrit aesthetic modes. The only moment of dissonance arises when Mosharraf Hossain has the Nati or the female actor in the prologue exclaim the impropriety of performing a play written by a Muslim before Bengali (implicit: Hindu) audiences. The Nata, the male actor, chastises her for being so communally divisive, and the play begins.[29] If one reads these two early texts by Mosharraf Hossain—*Ratnabati* and *Basantakumārī*—one would be forgiven for thinking that the author wishes to produce works that are mainstream because they are aimed at Bengali Hindu readers with the awareness that Bengali Muslims are perceived as alien or foreign. The reviewer from *Calcutta Review* who assumed "that the author has concealed his real name under the nom de plume of a Musalman,"[30] in this context, appears to be voicing something obvious—Mosharraf Hussain wishes to write like his Hindu compatriots.

Biśād Sindhu, however, disrupts any such easy narrative of assimilation, and not just because the novel is about the Battle of Karbala. With *Biśād Sindhu*, one notes a turn away from the overtly Sanskritic style in Mosharraf Hossain's oeuvre, a turn which persists in the texts he goes on to write after the novel, including the semi-autobiographical *Gāji Miyār Bostāni* (1899) in which he depicts late-nineteenth-century rural Muslim life through a critique of an oppressive Muslim landlord. The *"Bostani"* in *Gāji Miyār Bostāni*, for example, alludes to Mir Taki Khayal's eighteenth-century *dāstān* or tale titled *Bostan e khayal*, thereby suggesting an explicit allegiance with Persian and Urdu literary traditions. Similarly, *Biśād Sindhu* contains the markers of a *dāstān* but complicates these allusions by drawing from Bengali *punthis*. However, what is more important than identifying particular generic traits in these texts is to place them as examples of literary *adab*. In the wake of Nazir Ahmad's popularity, a Bengali novelist such as Mosharraf Hossain can rely on a market that is receptive to long prose works providing both entertainment and moral

[29] *Basantakumārī*, 11–12.
[30] *Calcutta Review*, vol. 50, 1870 in *Sambad-sāmayik patre unish śataker bāngāli musalmān samaj*, pp. 489–90.

guidance to the Muslim reader. In *Mirat-al-arus*, Muslim readers find a text in an Indian vernacular investigating the limits of moral propriety, and it is in this tradition that I wish to read *Biśād Sindhu*. Mosharraf Hossain's novel is not a straightforward etiquette narrative like *Mirat* or *Banas* but like them, it, too, aims at guiding the Muslim reader toward knowledge which can produce correct behavior. It is only when we read *Biśād Sindhu* thus that it becomes apparent that those elements of the novel deemed inexplicable by Bengali Hindu readers—such as the insertion of Persian, Urdu, or Arabic words, or the supernatural and coincidental portions of the narrative—are far from being anomalies. These are the markers embedded within the text that indicate it be read as part of a Perso-Arabic reading practice rather than as a Muslim author's attempt at entering the Sanskritist reading practice. Rather than find in the novel examples of *karunā* or *vir rasa*—using an aesthetic frame imposed on it by those within the Sanskritist practice—it is more productive, then, to take seriously the text's adherence to the principles of *adab*.

The concept of *adab* has a rich history in classical and modern Islamic thought. The term in Persian has a range of meaning broadly converging along the lines of civility and its expression in one's actions, and there are ethical, social, and intellectual components to it. *Adab* articulates the moral expectations for all Muslims and the external behavior whose practice leads to the embodiment of these expectations. Thus one encounters the *adab* of princes[31] and of the common person,[32] while Ansari's *Mukhtasar fi adab assufiyya* (1393) describes codes of behavior particular to the *sufis*. In the context of South Asia, we find notable examples in Yusuf Gada's fourteenth-century ethical treatise *Tuhfa i nasaih* in which the author posits *adab* as "embrac[ing] both moral authority and etiquette in the individual's ordinary daily behaviour."[33] The extensive body of scholarship on the concept of *adab* compares it to the Greek notion of *paideia* as both remark on the individual's modes of comportment in accordance with ethics.[34] The register of *adab*, however, exceeds that of social conduct to include the literary; *adab* "is both polite learning and its uses."[35] The literariness of *adab* comes to be consolidated from the nineteenth and twentieth centuries onward

---

[31] *Qabusnāmā* (*Mirrors for Princes*, 1082).

[32] al-Ghazzali's *Ihya ulum ad-din* and Miskawaih's *Tahdib al-akhlaq*, both from the premodern period.

[33] Simon Digby, "The *Tuhfa I nasaih* of Yusuf Gada," 104.

[34] Peter Brown, "Late Antiquity and Islam" (1984), Ira M. Lapidus, *Knowledge, Virtue and Action: The Classical Muslim Conception of Adab and the Nature of Religious Fulfilment in Islam* (1984).

[35] Bray, "Adab," *Medieval Islamic Civilization: An Encyclopaedia*, 13 (2006).

Another World of Reading 159

when *adab* comes to mean not only literature, but becomes institutionalized "as a modern discipline" in places such as Egypt[36] and India.[37]

Yet as Barbara Metcalf Daly reminds us, *adab* is not a unitary concept with a coherent definition that is independent of context. She suggests that "[a]*dab* not only comprises various strands within itself but is also potentially challenged by other Islamic styles."[38] As Islamic history demonstrates, a preoccupation with explicit codes of moral conduct and the founding of the individual on the same is not always evident. Various Islamic societies emphasize an adherence to *adab* to greater or lesser extent at different moments in time. The contradictions within the concept, along with the multiplicity of meaning, suggest that *adab* may or may not have been at the forefront when it came to individuals living their lives in most periods of history. In fact, since *adab* is frequently associated with a variety of professions, ethnicities, non-Islamic social groups, or other ways of being Islamic, it appears that individuals could, and did, perform the forms of behavior sanctioned by the concept without being self-conscious about this performance, nor was there an emphasis on coherence.

When looking at these moments in history when *adab* is implicit rather than explicit, comfortable in its lack of unity, when individuals are indifferent toward the technicalities of *adab*, what strikes one is the congruence of political and religious stability. It becomes apparent that the meaning of *adab* and its practice close ranks and shed their multifarious—often experimental—nature during moments of crisis and change. Thus the social upheavals within Muslim communities following the Abbasid revolution led to the need for articulating an Islamic ideal, and its result was the *Qabusnāmā* (*Mirrors for Princes*, 1082) advising princes on appropriate codes of conduct. This is also the period referred to by historians as the Golden Age of Islam, during which the religion encounters Greek philosophy. A consequence of this interaction is the founding of the Mu'tazilah, a speculative school of Islamic thought, which along with Greek philosophy poses a challenge to Sufism and its belief in an a-rational relationship with divinity.[39] This crisis leads Sufis such as Abu Nasr as-Sarraj to compile the tenets of Sufism in his *Kitab al-lumā* (988), in which the principles of *adab* are propounded to teach the believer the means of acquiring the

---

[36] Michael Allan, *In the Shadow of World Literature*, 76 (2016).
[37] For example in the Calcutta Madrassa College.
[38] Daly, "Introduction," *Moral Conduct and Authority*, 15 (1984).
[39] Tanvir Anjum, "Sufism in History," 235 (2006).

intuitive knowledge needed for reaching God. Here *adab* as practiced behavior for an emotional understanding of God is made explicit so as to serve as a buffer against the predominance of reason.

Little surprise, then, that *adab* would be expressed more and more unambiguously over the course of the nineteenth century as the British completed their dislodging of the Mughal Empire, plunging into crisis Muslim communities across India. The first of Nazir Ahmad's prize-winning novels, *Mirat al-arus*, appears scarcely a decade after the first war of Indian independence during which the Mughal Empire's final claim is quashed, and it comes at a time when the Muslim reader requires the articulation of something that is distinctly Islamic. *Adab* satisfies this need by giving this reader not just a means to being a good Muslim but the support of an epistemic structure. It is a means of knowing and being in the world that is uniquely Islamic and bears the weight of literary, cultural, political, and religious history, as made evident in classical Persian and Arabic texts. That first *Mirat al-arus* and then *Biśād Sindhu* vernacularize the aesthetic paradigm of Islamic classics becomes significant when read in light of this history of articulating *adab* more forcefully during periods of crises. Ronit Ricci's work on the Islamicization of South India is particularly instructive on this front. Ricci formulates the notion of "literary networks" that connect "Muslims across boundaries of space and culture" that comprise a range of texts "crucial to the establishment of both local and global Islamic identities."[40] Her argument that literary works—however one conceives of the term "literature"—helped foster a sense of belonging to a translocal community, allowing Muslims in South India to feel part of both their local contexts but also the wider Islamic *ummā*, can be applied to nineteenth-century Bengal as well. Bengal had always been an outpost of the Mughal Empire, but Bengali Muslims, as part of the ruling elite, had enjoyed considerable social and financial privileges till the Battle of Plassey in 1757. With the loss of power at the hands of the East India Company, Bengali Muslims now found themselves doubly marginalized, as the minority community vis-à-vis Hindu domination, and as the dislodged ruling class vis-à-vis the British. As I discuss elsewhere in this work, Bengali Muslims felt the need to overcome the sense of alienation imposed upon them by the rising Hindu intelligentsia, and one way to achieve this was to look outside Bengal to the community of which they considered themselves to be an integral part—the

---

[40] Ricci, *Islam Translated*, 1–2 (2011).

Islamic *umma*. *Adab* as the repository of aesthetic and religious traditions, of communal memory articulated as codes of behavior, and of Persianate literature provided a connection to that *umma*, and with it, a sense of belonging.

III. *Adab* as a Window to the World

One of the signal qualities of *adab* literature is that the text be both informative and entertaining. The roots of this combination can be traced back to some of the earliest examples of the concept in Abd al-Hamid bin Yahya al-Kateb's eighth-century epistles or *rasa'el*. As a secretary to the last Umayyad caliph, Marvan bin Mohammad (744–50), Abd al-Hamid is in a position to offer advice both to the heir apparent, Prince Abdallah, and to future secretaries in the Caliphate. The "Epistle of advice to the heir apparent" is an early instance of the "mirror for princes" genre[41] (of which *Qabusnāmā* is perhaps the best-known example), while the "Epistle to the secretaries" is an advice manual for secretaries. In the latter, Abd al-Hamid instructs secretaries to "[l]earn to write well, as that will be an ornament to [their] letters" but to temper eloquence with thought as their task is to "set up everything in its proper, customary form." The goal for the secretaries is to not only incorporate information—accounts, dates, land, and tax deeds—in their texts, but to do so in a manner that transmits poetry.[42] The *adab* of the secretary thus emphasizes a particular use of language such that the text is composed in beautiful language, regardless of the mundanity of the subject matter conveyed by it.

This stress on linguistic charm is not reserved for the *adab* of secretarial writings alone; it becomes evident in both literary and non-literary genres, including histories, biographies, fantastical tales, and religious narratives. For example, when Ibn Battuta returns to Fez in 1354, the Sultan of Morocco invites him to write an account of his travels and pairs him with Mohammad ibn Juzayy al-Kalbi who transcribes Ibn Battuta's narrative. The text, *Rihla* (*Travels*, 1355),[43] relies partly on Ibn Battuta's memories and partly on Ibn Juazzy's use

---

[41] The function of the form is to provide academic, administrative, and moral guidance to princes and rulers.

[42] Abd al-Hamid bin Yahya, "Epistle to the secretaries," translated from Arabic by Franz Rosenthal (747).

[43] Its full title is *Tuffāt al-Nuzzār fi Ghara'ib al-Amsar wa Aja'ib al-Afsar* which can be roughly translated as "A Gift to Those Who Contemplate the Wonders of Cities and the Marvels of Travelling." Ross E. Dunn's work on Ibn Battuta is of note here.

of other historical descriptions of those places visited by Ibn Battuta, and is a complex mixture of travelogue, memoire, and history. Of interest to me here is Ibn Juazzy's addition of poetic language to ensure that the experience of reading *al-Rihla* is a pleasant one. Ibn Juazzy inserts verses into the narrative in order to elevate the language of text, thus beautifying it. A similar melange of form and content is the basis of Abd al-Qadir ibn Umar al-Baghdadi's *Khizānat al-adab wa-lubb lubāb lisān al-Arab* ("Library of Literature and the Door of the Heart of the Arab Language"), a seventeenth-century encyclopedia of Arabic literary heritage. This list of texts underlining the importance of using language beautifully to convey ideas and information could be endlessly proliferated, signaling that *adab* "requires a knowledge of history, poetry, ideas, proverbs, parallels, precedents, and *the correct and pleasing use of language.*"[44]

What this engagement with ornate language demonstrates is a continued interest in Islamic texts in *how* the reader reads a text. If *what* a text contains is significant, then of no less importance is *how* this content is made available to the reader through the language used by the text. In both premodern and modern Islamic texts, one notices a careful curating of language so as to make the latter more beautiful and, often, poetic. The craftsmanship contained in language serves a deeper purpose than creating a pleasant work—it positions the reader as an *adīb* or a practitioner of *adab*. As an *adīb*, the reader appreciates the civility conveyed by the text's language, and through this appreciation cultivates the proper mode of being in the world. The moral virtue of *adab* manifests itself in the linguistic choices made by the author, and in reading these choices, the reader, too, can learn or continue the process of being virtuous. During moments of religious or political crises, the *udābā* (pl. of *adīb*) take on the task of safeguarding cultural and behavioral norms such that on the appearance of calmer times they can rebuild a cultural and morally just society based on *adab*. The reader as an *adīb* is capable of such a social reconstruction because having practiced *adab* through the act of reading, they are closer to the human ideal than others who are *be-adab* or without *adab*.[45] Thus beautiful language is not merely a theme of *adab* literature but one of its intrinsic qualities which allow the reader access to the correct moral path.

The role played by *adab* in shaping Islamic culture in South Asia is undeniable as evidenced by numerous texts explicating this practice of piety. From the

---

[44] Bray, "Adab," *Medieval Islamic Civilization: An Encyclopedia*, 13, emphases mine.
[45] By no means are readers the only *adīb*; any Muslim who practices *adab* in any form, be it in art, statecraft, devotion, or in other avenues of life, is an *adīb*.

writings of *sufi* saints to those by *muftis* (experts on Islamic law) to literary texts we see the repeated emphasis on *adab's* linguistic element. One way to understand the recurrence of ornate language is to understand the evolution of *adab* in the context of South Asia where the concept comes to be associated with Islamic values. By the time we get to the nineteenth century, the term's semantic polyvalence atrophies as it becomes attached with the idea that practicing *adab* upholds values which are essential for social respectability. The move toward respectability owes part of its origin to the elaborate *adab* of the Mughal court as the codification of courtly etiquette comes to identify linguistic politeness and dexterity as the hallmark of the *adīb*, and as a necessary prerequisite for professional advancement.[46]

To add to this, one must also take into account the term's journey from Arabic and Persian into Urdu. In Urdu, *adab* morphs to mean "respect" or "regard," thus narrowing the concept from its Arabic meaning of "code of behaviour."[47] For Bengali Muslims, *adab* (now with the rounded Bengali vowel) gets attached to the word *qaidā*, roughly translated as sanctioned or authoritative norms, thereby buttressing respect with authority. Not only does the importance of proper language use remain unchanged through the process of semantic evolution, it becomes increasingly indispensable to articulations of *adab* in literary texts. Thus, for example, Nazir Ahmad opens *Mirat* with the need for a well-written book of moral instruction for women "which should improve their ideas and correct their habits [...] and yet which should be in a form sufficiently attractive to prevent their being discouraged or dismayed by its perusal."[48] A few decades later, *Mirat* finds itself on the list of "harmful books" in Maulana Ashraf Ali Thanawi's didactic treatise *Bahishti zewar* (*Heavenly Ornaments*, 1905) because Thanawi deems novels to be morally detrimental for all Muslims, and for women in particular. However, despite this fundamental difference in approach to literature between Nazir Ahmad and Thanawi,[49] both authors emphasize the intimate relation between form and content as necessary for the reader to be

---

[46] For more, see J. F. Richards' discussion of the hierarchies within the Mughal imperial system of administrative and military officers in "Norms of Comportment among Imperial Mughal Officers" (1984) and Mana Kia's "*Adab* as Ethics" (2014).

[47] I borrow this semantic distinction from M. Khalid Masud's "*Adab al-Mufti*: The Muslim Understanding of Values, Characteristics, and Role of a *Mufti*" (1984).

[48] Nazir Ahmad, *Mirat*, 2, translated from Urdu by G. E. Ward (1869).

[49] These differences extend to the need for women to be educated. Nazir Ahmad is a proponent for educating Muslim women, while Thanawi opposes the idea, citing the importance of only providing religious education to women.

164   *The Novel in Nineteenth-Century Bengal*

able to identify and thus learn from. Thanawai, for example, rejects most novels, but retains Nazir Ahmad's third novel, *Taubā-an-nāsuh*, because of its eloquent articulation of morals suitable for women.[50]

At this juncture, I would like to reintroduce the remarks made by nineteenth-century reviewers of *Biśād Sindhu* on the novel's use of *biśuddha* or chaste Bengali. They are right in noting the Sanskritic overtones in Mosharraf Hossain's Bengali which are present from the very opening of the novel. The novelist titles the introduction with its Sanskrit name, *upakramanikā*, has his characters use the Sanskrit vocative case—*Prabho*—when referring to the Prophet Mohammad, and all of this happens on the first page alone.[51] The gap between the text's language and its narrative, however, becomes apparent when the reader is introduced in Chapter 2. Having learned of Ejid's all-consuming desire for Jaynab, his father Mabia consents to sending a messenger to Abdul Jabbar, Jaynab's husband, to lure him to Damascus. The narrator says,

> Reader! Even though the *kāsed* is a messenger, don't mistake him for a runner (*dāk harkarā*) or a letter carrier (*patrabāhak*) from Bengal. A royal messenger, but civilised and wise—that is whom great Muslim writers have referred to as "*kāsed*" ... But between a *dūt* and a *kāsed* there is but little difference, "*kāsed*" is not as well respected as *dūt*.[52]

The narrative identifies the reader as Bengali and as someone familiar with modes of communication prevalent in colonial Bengal, such as the runner or the *dāk harkarā* who were tasked with conveying or "running" messages as part of the British postal system. Similarly, the reader knows the Sanskrit/Bengali word for emissaries (*dūt*), a term harking back to Hindu Bengali folk and fairy tales. The unfamiliar term, and the one chosen by Mosharraf Hossain, is *kāsed* and as the narrator suggests, the word suits this context because famous Muslim authors used it. The subtle aligning of the narrator with Persianate terminology via texts by Muslim authors is one of the first indications we get that while the novel's language may appear to be Sanskritized Bengali, its aesthetic affiliations lie within the world of Islamic literature. At the same time, the narrative chooses to use the Bengali form of the word *kāsed* rather than the Urdu *qasid*. This technique of Bengalicization is evident in character names as well where the novelist follows folk conventions in morphing the names to fit the sounds of

---

[50] *Behishti zewar*, book 10.
[51] *Biśād Sindhu*, 1.
[52] *Biśād Sindhu*, 15, translation mine.

Another World of Reading 165

Bengali vowels and consonants.[53] With the first mention of the reader, then, Mosharraf Hossain makes evident the juxtaposition of Bengali as *mātribhāṣā* (mother tongue, in this instance Sanskritized Bengali) and Urdu as *bhrātribhāṣā* (brother tongue).

Yet as a novelist in Hindu-dominant Bengal, he is aware that a significant portion of his readers are Hindus, and to be commercially successful, the novel must be legible to this population. Thus when we next meet the reader in *Biṣād Sindhu*, we meet Hindu readers in particular. Having reached the court of Damascus, Abdul Jabbar is invited to divorce Jaynab and marry the princess Saleha, an invitation which he readily accepts. The narrator interjects by adding that "[h]ere I have something to say to the Hindu readers. If our wedding rituals are not explained in brief, it will require some effort to comprehend this present business of marriage."[54] Over the course of the next two pages, the text provides a detailed description of Islamic wedding rituals before returning to the narrative. The narrator provides a similar description of Islamic widowhood and the process of re-marriage,[55] and of funeral rituals when Mabia dies.[56] These moments of disruption are anthropological, allowing the Hindu reader to observe the community while firmly placing this reader as the outsider. Armed with these explanations, the Hindu reader can understand the plot's progression, and the novelist can be confident of capturing the Hindu market. However, what is important to note here is the division between "us" and "them" as insiders and outsiders. It is the "us"—the "our" of the above quote—who does not require explanations of fundamental social rituals, and who can read the text effortlessly as an insider to its literary and cultural heritage.

This reader is a Bengali Muslim who can appreciate Mosharraf Hossain's interplay with Bengali and Urdu, and who comes to the text knowing the story of Muharram. They are attuned to the profound religious significance of the narrative while being attentive to the element of entertainment inherent in a novel. The merger of information and pleasure is available to the Bengali Muslim reader alerting them to the novel's self-positioning as *adab* literature. The ornate nature of *Biṣād Sindhu*'s language, interspersed as it is with Bengalicized Urdu and Arabic words, is a manifestation of a signal theme of *adab* rather than a Muslim author merely mimicking his Hindu counterparts. The presence of

---

[53] I discuss more of this folk influence in the section on *jārigān* later in this chapter.
[54] *Biṣād Sindhu*, p. 25, translation mine.
[55] *Biṣād Sindhu*, pp. 34–5.
[56] Ibid., pp. 55–6.

166   *The Novel in Nineteenth-Century Bengal*

Sanskritized Bengali indicates the novelist relying on the most courteous or refined form of Bengali available to him so as to compose in a language suitable for conveying the respectability required of *adab*. Take, for example, one of the epithets used to describe Jaynab as Abdul Jabbar formally divorces her:

> Pen and paper were ready. Abdul Jabbar first wrote the name of God (*parameśwarer nām*), then writing the name of the Prophet Mohammad (*prabhu Mohammader nām*) he divorced (*tālāk dilen*) the husband-devoted (*patiparāyanā*) innocent (*niraparadhinī*) faithful (*satisadhwī*) co-religious (*sahadharminī*) Jaynab.[57]

At first glance, there is nothing out of place in Jaynab's description—the terms used are typical referents for married Bengali Hindu women. Except Jaynab is Muslim, her Islamic identity is highlighted by narrator explaining what a *talāknāmā* is just before the quoted section. A parenthetical note informs the Hindu reader that a *talāknāmā* is a "*strīparityag patra*"[58] literally translated as a letter of rejecting one's wife. The phrase "*strīparityag patra*" rings awkwardly in the ears of a Hindu reader as, conceptually, such a document is impossible within the faith. The descriptor *satisadhwī* strikes an equally discordant note because the idea of a wife as faithful as the goddess Sati comes from one of the 108 names of the goddess Durga. The phrase, used in colloquial Bengali, comes from *Shrī Dūrgāśtōttarsathanāmā Stōtram* (*Ode to Durga's One Hundred and Eight Names*), and in referring to Jaynab as a *satisadhwī* Mosharraf Hossain is consciously positioning her as one would a Hindu wife. The sense of discord, however, disappears when one reads the passage as an example not of Hindu adjectives being applied to a Muslim woman, but of the most poetic language available to a Bengali novelist to describe a married woman who has been rejected by her husband through no fault of her own. Mosharraf Hossain is using the highest form of Bengali available to him not because of its explicitly Sanskrit (read, Hindu) overtones, but because by doing so he can fulfill the dictates of an aesthetic structure which is distinctly Islamic.

As the *adīb*, the reader's role is to parse this ornate and interrelated language as articulating the image of the ideal Muslim. The beautiful framework created by the novelist serves as a vehicle for conveying religious exemplars, and it is through the act of reading that the *adīb* can comprehend this ideal. For the refined reader, descriptive scenes, such as the one involving Jaynab's moral purity, act

---

[57] *Biśād Sindhu*, p. 27, translation mine.
[58] *Biśād Sindhu*, p. 27.

as signals indicating that in perceiving Jaynab's goodness through the beautiful language, the reader is enacting moral transformation for themselves. Those who read the language as purely superfluous would thus deprive themselves of reaching the depths of the text, mistaking for mere surface ornamentation the path to piety. In conceptualizing the relationship of reading and *adab*, I draw on Mana Kia's discussion of the ethical and social implications of *adab* in Shaykh Mushrif al-Din Shirazi's *Gulistān* (*Rose Garden*, 1258). Kia notes that in the process of creating literature that would inform via entertainment, writers of *adab* literature such as Shirazi, better known as Sadi, had perfected a mode of composition in which "asthetics *is* ethics" [*sic*].[59] A reader accustomed to Persianate literature—whether in the Persianate languages or in translation into the vernaculars—would anticipate moments of proper ethical behavior to be couched in high literary language such that the text's aesthetics is never overwhelmed by the teachings contained within it. The *adīb* draws an ineluctable relationship between the language of the text and the ethical message conveyed by it, and in performing the reading thus, the *adīb* participates in the process of virtuous self-transformation.

Thus in *Biśād Sindhu*, whenever one encounters instances of didacticism, one notes a concomitant elevation of narrative language. Listing all such moments would lead to a chapter nearly as long as the 500-page novel, so I will briefly mention three of significant narrative import here—Hasan forgiving one of his wives Jayda on his deathbed despite the latter poisoning him (pp. 126–30), Hosen getting ready for battle following the death of his son, Ali Akbar (pp. 256–63), and the description of the hellish prison in Damascus within which Ejid and fellow sinners are incarcerated (pp. 503–6). Each scene is of heightened emotions with characters in tears bemoaning the fate of those near to them while accepting divine omnipotence and human beings' limited understanding of the same. In the first example, the bitter pill the reader must swallow is that even one as pure as Hasan can be betrayed by one closest to him, in the second, accept that a father may not be able to save his son's life, and in the third, get a glimpse into the punishment awaiting sinners in this life. The cue for the reader that one now approaches a portion of the narrative from which one should draw an ethical lesson is Mosharraf Hossain's use of a string of adjectival phrases to describe both atmosphere and emotion. The adjectives are frequently alliterative, and often repeated with different words to create a series of related images. For

[59] Mana Kia, "Adab as Ethics," 289.

example, the noun structuring the prison scene is *lōuha* or iron and within a single paragraph, it appears in conjunction with *śringkhal* (chains), *perek* (nails), and *śalakā* (bars). The same paragraph then transitions to *driśti* (sight) as the primary noun and verb as we are told of the prisoners' sightless eyes.[60] Finally, the narrative voice tells the *pāthak* or the reader that these scenes are too cruel to behold, returning us to the verb *dekhā* (to see) with which the narrator had opened the passage, inviting the *pāthak* to see the prison in Damascus.[61] The passage guides the reader's vision to scenes of torment, encases this vision through a variety of iron chains before releasing the reader to continue with the narrative flow. It is a masterful display of adjectival phrases trapping the reader to pay attention to the fate of sinners while simultaneously providing the careful reader with clues to see their way out of the prison.

It is worth noting the extent to which these scenes rely on the reader's active participation and willingness to read imaginatively. As Hasan lies on his deathbed, he calls his brother Hosen to speak with him for one last time. Hasan narrates his final dream in which he mentions seeing his grandfather, the Prophet Mohammad, and through this dream takes the reader back to the novel's introduction and the vision had by the Prophet of Hasan and Hosen's death. That vision now appears as Hasan's dream, thus enabling Hasan to foretell not only his own death but that of his brother as well. As Hosen rages against fate and repeatedly asks his brother for the name of the person who poisoned him, Hasan invites him to abjure his anger and accept the divine plan. At the scene's closing, the reader learns of Hasan hearing again his grandfather's call to join him in heaven and dies. Through this lengthy section, the reader is presented with several pieces of information—the cause of both Hasan and Hosen's death, even though the second event is yet to come, and Hasan revealing that he knew Jayda was poisoning him all along. However, the narrative makes no distinction between vision and fact. In the world of the novel, the reader has to imagine a blending of the religio-fantastic with more tangible facts so as to accept an alternate form of reality in which both coexist, and indeed shape each other. Such a merging occurs several times in the novel, most notably when Hosen's dismembered head magically vanishes from Ejid's court.[62]

The intermingling of the real with the fantastical brings me to two interrelated genres of *adab* literature, the *qissā* and the *dāstān*, which are necessary to complete

---

[60] "[S]ightless in every direction, sight set only on the wide-open sky," 596, translation mine.
[61] *Biśād Sindhu*, 506.
[62] Ibid., 262–3.

Another World of Reading   169

any discussion of *Biṣād Sindhu*. Despite the novel being about the martyrdoms of Hasan and Hosen, it isn't typical of *Maqatil* (sing. *Maqtal*) literature which focus on the Battle of Karbala and on Hosen's death. Instead, Mosharraf Hossain chooses as his primary theme Ejid's fatal desire for Jaynab which allows him to draw on the features of the *qissa* and the *dastan*. In Urdu, both *qissā* (Arabic) and *dāstān* (Persian) mean "story" and refer to elaborate and long prose romances, and by the middle of the nineteenth century become popularized in translation in both Urdu and other Indian vernaculars such as Bengali, spreading from North India to the rest of the subcontinent. The reach of *dāstān*s and *qissā*s is attested to by the plethora of texts which circulate both for pleasure and instruction across Bengal, from *Dāstān-e-amir Hamzah* or the *Adventures of Amir Hamzah*, to *Qissā-e Gul-e bakavali*, and to *Qissā-e Hatim Tai*.[63] Such is the extent of their presence in Bengal that *qissā* becomes Bengalicized to *kecchā* and incorporated into folktale and prose narratives.

An essential element of the *qissā* and the *dāstān* is the blending of the fantastic and the real and incorporating both as part of the natural world. As in the realm of the *dāstān* so also in *Biṣād Sindhu*, the reader comes to expect reality to be elastic enough to include visions, angels, demons, and acts of magic, and the text's language to be capable of transmitting this flexible reality. Thus there is no discord when the magnitude of Ejid's sins dawns on him at the very moment when Hosen's severed head disappears from the former's court. The verb used to structure the scene is *dekhā* (to see), as the reader transitions from Hosen's family and followers calling on god to stop the spectacle of Ejid displaying Hosen's head and committing a sacrilege to its miraculous disappearance. As soon as the head disappears, the only person expressing surprise is the villain Ejid, who is dumbfounded at the power of divine intervention and terrified at the thought of impending doom. Hosen's loved ones—and by induction the reader for whose moral edification the scene is narrated thus—exclaim prior to the fantastic

---

[63] *Dāstān-e-amir Hamzah* finds repeated mentions in the Persianate periodicals coming out of Kolkata throughout the nineteenth century such as *Mirat ul Akhbar* and *Akhbar-i-Serampore*, while *Gulistān* was used as a Persian primer by the Fort William College. For more on the various translations and iterations of these two texts, see Frances Pritchett's work on *qissā* and *dāstān*, Jennifer Durbow and Maryam Wasif Khan's books on the Islamic cosmopolis in nineteenth- and twentieth-century India, and Mana Kia's work on *Gulistān*. The Urdu translation of *Dāstān-e-amir Hamzah* by Naval Kishore Press published in six volumes between 1893 and 1908 coincided with the publication of *Biṣād Sindhu*, and for educated Bengali Muslims, both texts would have formed a part of their literary world. For example, Rokeya Sakhawat Hossein, better known as Begum Rokeya, makes mention of both in Syed Emdad Ali's periodical *Nabanūr*, and we find references to *Dastan* in periodicals such as the Mohammedan Observer which also carried advertisements for *Biṣād Sindhu*, further suggesting that Bengalis were reading both.

moment that they cannot watch this desecration any longer, disassociating from the verb *dekhā*. The text attributes amazement to Ejid alone because only for him is this divine act surprising and terrifying; documenting the response of the rest of the characters is unnecessary because they have called on god to perform precisely such a miracle and thus have no cause for astonishment. In his characteristic way, Mosharraf Hossain indicates an edifying moment through the use of elaborate adjectives. The adjectives describing this scene, *tyej* (power) and *jyōti* (luminosity), are visual, in keeping with the verb *dekhā* and Ejid finds himself blinded by this light. Standing at a safe distance, the reader is able to appreciate the beauty of the language, even in a passage describing a severed head, while learning of the fear felt by a sinner in the presence of divinity. The aesthetic couches the ethical message even as the fantastic becomes one with the real. As noted by scholars such as Julia Bray and Frances Pritchett, classical Persian literature uses language so as to blur the boundaries between the real and the fantastic, making both part of the Muslim individual's lived reality. Mosharraf Hossain draws on his readers quotidian familiarity with the *dāstān* and the *qissā* as he situates *Biśād Sindhu* in a world where moral virtue is presented in words that are aesthetically pleasing.

However, not all readers of the novel find the novel's language satisfying on either an aesthetic or an ethical level. Some Bengali Muslim readers accuse Mosharraf Hossain of using language that is insufficiently attentive to the sanctity of Islam. The novelist opens chapter four of the second part, *"Uddhār parba,"* with a lengthy invective against those of his faith (*swajāti*) who have taken offense at his use of "Bengali words" (*"bāṅgālā bhāśāye byabahārja śabda"*) as prefixes to the names of the Prophet Mohammad, Hasan, and Husayn.[64] The implication is that as a Sanskritized language, using Bengali in the place of Arabic defiles these invocations. Around the time of writing *"Uddhār parba"* Mosharraf Hossain also faces criticism from Bengali Muslims for denouncing the killing of cows for meat in his essay *"Gō jīban"* ("Life of Cows," 1889), but the particular emphasis on language makes criticism of the novel unique. While he is forced to recant *"Gō jīban"* from his own magazine *Hitakarī* owing to pressure from more conservative Muslims such as Reazuddin Ahmad,[65] the novelist is far more adamant in his response to the linguistic censure. In fact,

---

[64] *Biśād Sindhu*, 302–3.

[65] Who writes at length against both Mosharraf Hossain and the essay in the periodical *Islam Pracārak*. I briefly discuss this in Chapter 1.

he positions the linguistic criticism just before a long description of all the heavenly hosts, including the Prophet Mohammad, Hasan, and all the saints coming down to Karbala to mourn Hosen. In keeping with previous scenes, the narrative identifies each saint with an elaborate description of their great deeds, but retains the Sanskritized appellations for these revered figures. Thus, the Prophet Mohammad is described as "*Mahārisī Prabhu Hajrat*,"[66] with the first word meaning a "great saint" in Sanskrit, the second being a Sanskrit, and the third an Arabic honorific. Similarly, Sakhina, Hosen's daughter, is described as "*mahādebī*" and "*satī*," both terms being Sanskrit in origin.[67] The juxtaposition of the criticism with this scene reveals the novelist to be openly mocking his critics, and continuing to use Sanskritized Bengali to convey Islamic beliefs.

That he considers this form of Bengali to not be the sole property of Hindus becomes evident in his responses to letters criticizing him for tainting Bengali with Persianate words.[68] His conviction that Bengali and the Persianate languages should be wedded so as to include the majority of Bengali Muslims into a larger community *as* Bengalis ensures that despite the hostility, the language used in *Biśād Sindhu* and his later works remains closer to Sanskritized Bengali. As he suggests in those responses, and indeed in all his literary works following *Biśād Sindhu*, Bengali is the perfect vehicle for communicating the principles of *adab* because it is the most aesthetically pleasing form of the language available to the Bengali Muslim author and reader, and a means to incorporate in Bengali the aesthetic principles shared by the larger Islamic world.

IV. Incorporating the Familiar: *Jārigān* and *Biśād Sindhu*

If *adab* allows the reader access to the larger Islamicate world, then *jārigān* provides a means of return to the familiarity of Bengal. As a genre, *jārigān* owes its origins to *azadari* or the ritual mourning of the fall of Husayn during the Battle of Karbala in 680 CE. *Azadari* is the performance (Persian, *dari*) of mourning (Arabic, *aza*), referring to the assemblage of Persian and Arabic cultures, and to the ceremonies of lamentation enacted by pious Muslims—primarily, though not exclusively, Shias—during Muharram. The practice starts

---

[66] *Biśād Sindhu*, 305.
[67] Ibid., 308.
[68] See Chapter 1 for a detailed discussion of this question.

in Iran in the eleventh century before traveling across South Asia to Bengal around the seventeenth century, and here, in the hands of the Sufi pirs,[69] the ritual of mourning becomes associated with folk poetic traditions.[70] While the early history of *jāri* is not well documented, one can deduce its formal features from two texts. One of the earliest examples of the amalgamation of the sacred with the folk can be found in Sheikh Faizullah's poem "*Jaynaber Cautisā*" composed sometime during the seventeenth century.[71] The text of the poem narrates the events of Karbala from the perspective of Zainab (or Jaynab) who laments the fall of Husayn as a personal loss. While not fully realized as a *jāri* text, "*Jaynaber Cautisā*" nonetheless explains how central the individual character's voice is in the folk perception of Islam in Bengal, and this focus on the individual goes on to be one of the primary characteristics of *jāri*. Toward the first part of the eighteenth century, the Sufi pir Heyat Mahmud recorded the events of Karbala in his manuscript titled *Jungnāmā* (1723) to which were later added the performative elements of *jāri*, and the name eventually morphed to *Jārijungnāmā*.[72] While Heyat Mahmud may not have intended his *Jungnāmā* to eventually become part of the *jāri* tradition, it is indisputable that he used the narrative to attract local inhabitants to Islam. The Battle of Karbala was frequently chosen by early Muslim proselytizers based on the narrative quality of the event which allowed them to present the tenets of Islam through a story full of elements of adventure and pathos.

Following scholarly consensus, I would also argue that the story-like rendition of religious history provided early Muslims with the ability to draw on aspects of existing folk beliefs to explain Islam in terms that would be readily comprehensible—and perhaps, attractive—to the masses being preached to.[73] The resulting syncreticism becomes a cause for concern for nineteenth-century Muslim reformers who are shocked by how closely intertwined Islam gets with

---

[69] Spiritual guides instructing their disciples in the path of Sufism or a form of Islamic mysticism. An extended description of Sufism is beyond the scope of this chapter, but it is worth noting its significance in Bengal, particularly as it allows for a syncretic version of Islam which moves away from religious orthodoxy toward a more communal and heterodox approach to Islam.

[70] For a detailed discussion of the history of *jārigān* in Bengal, see Epsita Halder's "Reading the 'Cheapness' of Cheap Prints: Karbala Narrative in the Early Print Culture" (2015).

[71] *Historical Dictionary of the Bengalis*, 185 (2013).

[72] For more on the history of *Jārijungnāmā*, and on the *jāri* tradition, see Epsita Halder's "Reading the 'Cheapness' of Cheap Print" and Mary Frances Dunham's *Jārigan: Muslim Epic Songs of Bangladesh* (1997).

[73] Epsita Halder and Ronit Ricci both discuss the syncretic nature of Islam in India, albeit with very different focal points.

Another World of Reading   173

Hindu and folk religions.[74] However, it is this syncreticism that leads to the immense popularity of the Karbala story in its various guises as it appeals to both Hindus and Muslims. *Jāri* performers continue the tradition of vernacularizing the story of Hasan and Husayn by drawing on *"Jaynāber cautisā," "Jārijungnāmā,"* and a variety of *pāncālīs*[75] with equal *élan*. The *pāncālī*, in fact, becomes the form of *jārigān* as performers use the rhythmic patterns of reciting *pāncālīs* to incorporate aspects of *chanda* (poetical metre) and *tāl* (musical measure).

As with other forms of Bengali folk performances such as *kabigān*, *kirtan*, and *pālā gān*, *jārigān* also mythologizes Islam, and in this act, becomes a communal performance. Thus *jārigān* performances were, and continue to be, seen as belonging to the community, with both performers and audiences coming from within a local group of people. This creates a sense of shared experience, requiring the audience to contribute to the performance, sometimes by clapping to the rhythm, sometimes by singing along, and in performing the ritualized mourning of Hasan and Husayn. What one also discovers when looking closely at *jārigān* is a lack of generic distinction. The audience and performers are less concerned about the relationship between *jārigān* and other forms of elegiac poetry such as the *marsiya* or the *nauha*—both of which are expressions of ritual grief during Muharram—and more with the performance itself. Thus frequently one finds the emphasis on personal grief, characteristic of the *marsiya*, to be embedded in the long descriptive narratives that otherwise characterize *jārigān*.

Each of these three elements—the communal nature of *jārigān*, its investment in lengthy descriptions of the Battle of Karbala, and the simultaneous ability to individualize religious history through a personal relationship between the audience and the characters in the story—is key to understanding Mosharraf Hossain's choice of source material for *Biśād Sindhu*. In the *mukhabandha* or the preface to the first edition of the novel, Mosharraf Hossain elaborates on his rationale for writing *Biśād Sindhu* and suggests what his source texts might be. It is worth quoting at length:

> Muharram is the name of the first month of the *Candramās* [lunar] year. On 8th Muharram of the Hijri year 61, the king of Madina, Hosen, along with the rest of his family arrived at Karbala following a sequence of events, and died on the

---

[74] The *Muhammedan Observer*, for example, notes with horror the prevalence of stories such as "Kali and Jummapeer were rivals, and that one day Jummapeer defeated the goddess and transplanted her in the Kalighat" ("The Muhammedan Community Needs a Girl School," April 26, 1894) in *Sambad-sāmayik patre uniś śataker bāngālī musalmān samāj*, pp. 263–4.

[75] A form of oral narrative, often used to tell the story of Hindu gods and goddess, but equally frequently used to narrate Islamic hagiography.

battlefield at the hands of soldiers sent by Ejid. This tragedy has become famous by the name of Muharram. What the origin of that event was, and why the terrible battle took place, the profound facts of these are perhaps known to many. "Biśād Sindhu" has been composed by taking the gist of the original event from Persian and Arabic texts. To perfectly imitate classical *kābya-grantha* [lit. poetic texts] maintaining the honour of the compositional skills of classical poets, and of the *shastras* [religious doctrines] is very difficult. For a person like me, the desire to properly preserve the majesty of these subjects is like "the dwarf reaching for the moon" [referring to a Bengali idiom]. But my primary objective is to make the original story of Muharram easily comprehensible (*sahaje hridayangam*) to the dear readers [both male and female] who love the Bengali language.[76]

Mosharraf Hossain identifies his readers as those "who love the Bengali language" further attesting to his desire to position Bengali Muslims as Bengalis, a point I discuss in the previous section. Of interest here, however, is the novelist's description of his sources. These, he says, are Persian and Arabic classics, and yet when one looks closely at the narrative itself, it appears that the real sources are Faizullah's "*Jaynāber cautisā*" and Heyat Mahmud's *Jārijungnāmā*. "*Jaynāber cautisā*" presents the events at Karbala in the form of Jaynab's lament for her husband and brother-in-law, and explains why a novel—ostensibly about Karbala—opens with Jaynab, spends the first 275 pages narrating the consequences of her marriage with Hasan, and places Ejid's love for Jaynab as the novel's driving force. On the other hand, *Jārijungnāmā* provides the narrative its structure as a *jungnāmā* or the tale (*nāmā*) of a battle (*jung*) whose primary generic feature is to present the story of Muslim heroes defeating armies of unbelievers. *Jārijungnāmā*, then, gives *Biśād Sindhu* the template for imaginatively reconstructing history.[77]

That, despite Mosharraf Hossain's claims, the novel's sources might lie closer at home comes through the novelist admitting to the difficulties of imitating classical Persianate poets. His decision to include a Bengali idiom is an interesting one here, even if one takes into account the display of modesty as an usual feature of nineteenth-century texts. It reasserts two significant things—one, the

---

[76] "*Mukhabandha*," *Biśād Sindhu*, n.p. translation mine.

[77] Here I follow the scholarly work of Anisujjaman, Sukumar Sen, and Munir Chaudhuri, among others, who agree that *Biśād Sindhu* is more likely a work based on *punthis* or indigenous manuscripts rather than on Persianate classics. Anisujjaman also cites Mosharraf Hossain's autobiography in which the latter confesses to knowing very little Persian and Arabic, as evidence for his novel not being derived from classical texts. Given that most of these classics were not translated into Bengali until later in the twentieth century, I am inclined to accept Anisujjaman's explanation.

novelist's stated identity as a Bengali comfortable with elevating very common Bengali sayings, and two, it connects with the later sentence invoking Bengali-loving readers, placing both the author and the reader in the same context. The first provides a clue that the sources, like the author, cannot dare do justice to either the classics or their high religiosity; to aim to do either would be akin to the dwarf reaching for the moon. All that the author wishes to do is to make the story easily comprehensible, but comprehensible in a manner that appeals to the reader's heart as suggested by the word *hridayangam* (*hriday* = heart). The implication is that the reader easily feels the story as much as they understand it. The emotional appeal aligns the novel with other such works narrating the Karbala events, not aspiring to be high literature but rather texts the average Bengali would read and enjoy. *Jārijungnāmā* and *"Jaynāber cautisā"* would be two such texts which had permeated Bengali Muslim imaginary and colored its perception of Muharram from the seventeenth century onwards. Mosharraf Hossain's familiarity with *punthi sāhitya* or folk literature[78]—a category to which both Faizullah and Heyat Mahmud's texts belong—further attests to the likelihood that the novel was based on the same texts used by *jārigān* performers.[79]

This discussion of *Biṣād Sindhu*'s sources allows me to make another observation regarding the novel's reader. This reader is positioned as Bengali loving so as to enable Mosharraf Hossain to include all classes of literate Bengali Muslims, many of whom, like the novelist himself, would have only passing knowledge of Arabic through reading the *Qur'an*, and equally tangential knowledge of Persian or Urdu. Those educated enough to have a reading knowledge of Persianate languages—belonging either to the upper classes or to more conservative families seeking to distance themselves from Bengali because of its association with Hinduism—are also appealed to by the elevated nature

---

[78] The translation of *punthi sāhitya* as folk literature is at best reductive. This is a rich and complex body of literature dating back to early modern Bengal and the name owes its origin to the practice of transcribing orally transmitted texts onto palm leaf manuscripts or *punthis*. The particular form of *Musalmānī punthi sāhitya* or Islamic *punthi* literature grew up around the regions of Kolkata, Hooghly, and Howrah where poets composed romances based on Islamic tales in a Bengali mixed with Persianate languages called *misrabhāṣā* or Mixed Language. The language came to be increasingly identified with lower-class Muslims, and thus found little truck with highbrow litterateurs, whether Hindu or Muslim. This, however, had little impact on the widespread popularity of *punthi sāhitya* which, by the end of the nineteenth century, had turned into one of the primary ways in which Bengali Muslims acquired knowledge of Islam if they did not read any of the Persianate languages. Abdul Khaer Shaikh's *"Musalmānī" punthi sāhitya* and Anisujjaman's *Muslim-mānās ō bānglā sāhitya* are excellent resources on this subject.

[79] Mosharraf Hossain mentions the same at various points in his autobiography.

176   *The Novel in Nineteenth-Century Bengal*

of the novel's Bengali, but by including the former group, Mosharraf Hossain is able to exponentially increase his reader base. These mostly middle-class Bengali readers would have access to novels by Hindus such as Bankimchandra Chattopadhyay, but in *Biśād Sindhu* they would have seen their own religious identity positively depicted for the first time in novel form.

In committing to print the Karbala narrative, *Biśād Sindhu* may have opened the floodgates for a host of prose and lyric renditions of the story in formal Bengali or *sādhu bhāśā*,[80] but by no means did it occupy such a pioneering position when it came to cheap *battalā* editions. Various versions of the Muharram story had been in circulation in print from the early years of the nineteenth century onwards, and as with popular Hindu mythological texts, these, too, were often reproduced in print in their manuscript form. Thus *Jārijungnāmā* existed in named and unnamed editions, often identified for the buyer with the publisher or the printer's name rather than that of the author. Another remarkably popular adaptation was Garibullah or Yakub's *Jungnāmā*, which continues to be in print, the text still being based on the original *punthi* form. These texts went a long way toward making the story of Karbala *hridayangam* to Bengali Muslim readers, and while Mosharraf Hossain aimed for a reader more refined than the one consuming Karbala *punthi*s in *Mishrabhāśā* (see footnote 71), he certainly sought to capitalize on the narrative's popularity in the print market.

What is interesting to note in this proliferation of print texts telling the story of Hasan and Husayn is the singular attention paid to two texts by the *jārigān* tradition—*Jārijungnāmā* and *Biśād Sindhu*. Of all these works in circulation, these two texts alone merge the world of print and performance as practitioners of *jāri* add *Biśād Sindhu* to their repertoire in the same way that they take on Heyat Mahmud's *Jungnāmā* and personalize it by making it into *Jārijungnāmā*. This bridging of modes of perception leads one to revisit the novel in light of a performative text, and examine the ways in which aspects of this performance are built into the narrative. A pre-condition of a performance as participatory as *jārigān* is the audience's familiarity with the narrative. As with most folk or fairy tale-based performances, the audience is supposed to already know the details of the story such that they know when to clap or chant or display the pathos appropriate for the scene.[81] From the preface to *Biśād Sindhu*, it becomes

---

[80] Those published shortly after *Biśād Sindhu* are *Ejidbadh kābya* (1899) and *Moslembadh kābya* (1901) by Matiur Rahman Khan, and *Kāsembadh kābya* (1905) by Abdul Ma'ali Muhammad Hamid ali.

[81] This familiarity is a generic feature of most folk performative forms in Bengal, including *jātrā*, *pālā gān*, and *pāncālī*.

Another World of Reading   177

apparent that Mosharraf Hossain's primary audience are Bengali Muslims intimately familiar with the story of Muharram, and for whom the details of the battle need little explanation. The novel, then, assumes a reader who not only knows the story, but knows its details well. The novelist repeats this supposition throughout the narrative, occasionally addressing the reader directly, and at other points delegating this task to the characters themselves. For example, at a critical juncture in the narrative, once Hasan has been killed, and Ejid's chances of marrying Jaynab are once again alive, the reader is taken into Ejid's court along with the traitorous Jayda and Maymuna, her co-conspirator. Ejid initially rewards both women by marrying the first and paying the second more than her promised share of gold, thus fulfilling his promise. At this moment, however, there is an abrupt change in tone as Ejid alters his attitude mid-sentence; he accuses Jayda of being a monster ("*rākkhasi*") capable of killing her own husband, and cuts her in half, dramatically spraying her blood all over his court.[82] The narrative does not stop to explain Ejid's behavior as it details the punishment meted out to Maymuna—being partially buried and then stoned to death—and then addresses the reader by suggesting this to be an opportune moment to leave the court of Damascus for Medina.

The untrained reader is left flummoxed. What happened to Ejid suddenly, they wonder? Yet the novelist can effect such an abrupt shift in the narrative without worrying about losing the reader because the novel's primary readers, those familiar with *jārigān* performances, have received their textual cues already. As *jārigān* audiences, they are attuned to moments in the narrative when generic feature peculiar to an oral performance takes over those of a print text. Thus at the start of this scene, Ejid addresses the members of his court twice, the first time when he reminds them that "all of you already know that Hasan was [his] archenemy,"[83] and next when, having invited Jayda to share his throne as his queen, he asks the audience to "carefully listen"[84] to his words. The reader, familiar with *jāri* performances of the story, knows to be attentive to calls to listen carefully or to moments when basic narrative facts are repeated as those are clues telling them of what comes next in the narrative. Thus when they are reminded of Ejid's enmity with Hasan, they are implicitly reminded of the reason behind this dispute, Ejid's love for Jaynab.

---

[82] *Biśād Sindhu*, 144–5.
[83] Ibid., 142.
[84] Ibid., 144.

178   *The Novel in Nineteenth-Century Bengal*

Given that knowledge, they know now to expect the overture to Jayda to be a false one. Alongside this narrative reminder, the ploy of asking the audience to listen carefully is one found frequently in oral performances to mark key plot points, so the reader is also alerted that something significant is about to take place. The shock of the execution, then, is lessened for the knowing reader through these narrative techniques borrowed from *jāri* performers, and the novelist can confidently transport the reader out of Damascus toward Medina.

One finds this welding of reading and performance in the *jāris* themselves, which begin to draw directly from the novel, capitalizing both on its popularity with readers and on its narrative structure. Given the largely oral nature of these performers, dating *jāris* is a particularly difficult task. To add to this, the border between various folk performances is a porous one, with performers of one genre not only singing other genres but building songs using elements of multiple genres. Thus a *jāri* performer will also sing *bāul* songs and weave in well-known *bāul* compositions into *jārigān*, and vice versa. The audience expects this and usually knows the conventions of different genres, thus making this melange a regular part of folk performances in rural Bengal. We have a sizeable collection of *jārigān* thanks to the efforts of the Bangladeshi poet Jasimuddin who first collated extant *jāris* in his work *Jārigān* (1968). He later collaborated with a North American scholar of classical languages, Mary Frances Dunham, as she recorded and published *jāri* performances in an effort to capture a folk art form on the wane.[85]

Using the texts transcribed by Jasimuddin and Dunham, and comparing the same with recordings of contemporary *jāri* performances offers us one way of establishing when new material is added to existing songs. *Jāri* songs often begin with an invocation in which the performer praises the various entities that have aided in their success. The singer is called the *boyati*, the term coming via the Arabic *bayt* or couplet, thus identifying the singer as a composer of couplets. Jainuddin Boyati, a contemporary *jāri* singer, begins his 2008 performance of "*Śahidnāmār jāri*" ("The *jāri* of the Martyr") by first thanking God, then the Prophet, and then his master or *ustād*, Meghu Boyati. The *jāri* itself depicts Hosen's son Ali Akbar dying of thirst, which leads Hosen to promise never to drink till he has killed Ejid, and then finally being killed himself. In his final moments, Hosen begs Simar to let him breathe before desecrating his body

---

[85] Her compilation, both textual and aural, is titled *Jārigān: Muslim Epic Songs of Bangladesh* (1997).

by beheading him.[86] The *jāri* is interesting on two fronts here: the first, in its use of the same sequence of events as that of *Biṣād Sindhu* to narrate Hosen's encounter with Simar. While this is a common story, this particular ordering of narrative events becomes consolidated in the nineteenth century based on Heyat Mahmud's *Jārijungnāmā*, which then finds itself in Mosharraf Hossain's *Biṣād Sindhu*. The detailed description of Hosen's death, and most notably the language of this scene closely follows that of the novel. The novel and the *jāri* song both begin the scene by describing Simar as jumping onto Hosen's chest to cut his head off. In *Biṣād Sindhu*, the moment is described as "*Simār khanjarhaste eklamphe Hosener bakkher upor giyā basila,*" while "*Ṣahidnāmār jāri*" narrates it as, "*ei lāph diyā uthilā Simār bakkherō upare.*"[87] The similarity in language is remarkable, with both genres emphasizing *lampha* or its more colloquial form *laph* (to leap) and Hosen's *bakkha* or chest. The rest of the scene is closely mirrored in both texts such that if one were listening to the song and using the novel as its transcription, one would be able to follow not only the song's meaning but its words as well.[88]

This brings me to the second point of note, Jainuddin naming his *ustād*. Meghu is one of the *boyati*s who gets transcribed by Jasimuddin in the 1950s and 1960s as one of the most notable performers of his time. Meghu Boyati begins his career sometime in the 1920s and performs "*Ṣahidnāmār jāri.*" In this oral tradition, the task of the disciple is to hear and memorize the *ustād*'s performance, and while the former will frequently give the song their own touch, the basic narrative and its words will remain mostly unchanged. Thus one can assume that Jainuddin learns "*Ṣahidnāmār jāri*" from Meghu, and even though the former, as an established *boyati* himself, now adds elements to his performance, he retains the core of the narrative. By tracing "*Ṣahidnāmār jāri*"

---

[86] The recording of the *jāri* can be found here: http://www.thetravellingarchive.org/record-session/ambikapur-faridpur-bangladesh-31-march-2008-jainuddin-boyati-and-team/. I base my comments on the *jāri* on my transcription of this recording.

[87] The line from *Biṣād Sindhu* can be translated as "Carrying a sword, Simar leapt onto Hosen's chest" (p. 271) while in "*Ṣahidnāmār jāri,*" the line says, "With a leap, Simar got on [Hosen's] chest" (17:30–17.33). Both translations mine.

[88] Another unnamed *jāri* is also of interest here given its use of the same introduction as that of the novel. This *jāri*, though performed as part of a *bāul* repertoire by Selim Baul, begins with the Prophet Mohammad revealing his vision foreshadowing Hasan and Husayn's death to his followers, mirroring the opening of *Biṣād Sindhu*. Selim Baul replaces Mosharraf Hossain's Sanskritized honorifics for the Prophet and the Imams with their Arabic counterparts, but barring this substitution, the structure remains the same. I place this discussion in a footnote because while a recording of the performance is readily available (https://www.youtube.com/watch?v=sUCZjeJH2i8&ab_channel=AroundTvAroundTv), I have not been able to trace the original *jāri* or its affiliations.

180   *The Novel in Nineteenth-Century Bengal*

to Meghu Boyati, then, one discovers that the influence of *Biśād Sindhu* was felt on *jārigān* performances at least by the 1920s, and possibly earlier, assuming that Meghu himself learned the song from his *ustād* whose identity we do not know clearly. Thus within a few decades of *Biśād Sindhu*'s publication, the narrative had made its way back into the *jāri* tradition which had originally served as its own inspiration.

My argument here is not to suggest that either Meghu or Jainuddin came to their version of "*Śahidnāmār jāri*" by a close reading of *Biśād Sindhu*—though that remains a possibility—but to remark on the social context in which the novel's text permeates the oral performance. While *jāri* as an art is no longer a living tradition in rural Bengal, in the immediate aftermath of *Biśād Sindhu*'s entry into print it was still very much a part of Bengali village life, particularly of Bengali Muslims. The novel's late-nineteenth- to early-twentieth-century reader's contribution, though not documented, can be seen in the transference of the text's language and form into *jāri* songs. The world of reading the novel runs parallel to that of watching *jāri* performances, and those moments when they intersect are revealed in these examples of one genre profoundly influencing the other. The exchange suggests that in places such as Kushtia, where Mosharraf Hossain was from and where he wrote *Biśād Sindhu*, or Ambikapur and Faridpur, where Jainuddin Boyati performs, neither the novel nor *jārigān* supplanted each other as the preferred mode of telling the Karbala story. Rather, through interactions between readers, performers, authors, and printers, they complemented each other, allowing these individuals to comfortably transition between genres. This network of people living within a shared context is integral to the Perso-Arabic reading practice as removing any one element—whether it is the *jārigān* performers, or the text of the novel, or a printer such as Kangal Harinath straddling both world—would render the experience of reading *Biśād Sindhu* incomplete. Thus regardless of how much the nineteenth-century urban Hindu intelligentsia debated over the chastity of Mosharraf Hossain's Bengali or his ability to make accessible an Islamic narrative to the Bengali (read Hindu) reader, it is the Bengali Muslim reader coming from the villages who is able to fully appreciate the linguistic and narrative play enacted by the novel.[89]

---

[89] It is also worth noting here the lack of distinction drawn between high and low culture by the audience of *Biśād Sindhu* and of the *jāri* performances. As I document here, the language of both freely intermingle, and even though Mosharraf Hossain uses a more refined (Sanskritized) form of Bengali, in its references and cadences, this language finds easy affinities with that of the popular oral performances.

Another World of Reading　　　181

Writing nearly sixty years after *Biśād Sindhu*'s publication, the Bangladeshi novelist Abul Bashar comments on the persistence of this merger of reading and watching narrativization of the Karbala event in the context of rural Murshidabad.[90] The novel, Bashar notes while drawing on his childhood memories, occupied a place in the *cāngāri*[91] alongside religious texts, effectively blurring the line between fiction and religious belief. While literate Muslims read the text of the novel as building on the stories they had heard as children, semi-literate Muslims read the book by relying on how they had heard oral performers speak the lines. Bashar recounts an amusing moment when as a child he corrected the local *ketāb-pāthak*[92] while the latter was reciting a line from the novel. Isa, the *ketāb-pāthak*, mistook the word *"hānkiyā"* (to call out) for *"hāntiyā"* (to walk) resulting in him reading the line as the messenger walked while riding his horse. Bashar as the literate young man pointed out the impossibility of walking while also riding a horse, while Isa replied that he was reading what was written in the text, and also that was how everyone had spoken the lines when he had heard them. The printing error is soon resolved by Isa scratching out *"hānkiyā"* and writing *"hāntiyā,"* and Bashar remarks "that this was 'Biśād-Sindhu' of the semi-illiterate world."[93] What is interesting here is that Isa as the reader does not rely on the printed text as his ultimate guide but rather on his memory of the text's performance. In those performances, individual letters of words, or occasionally entire words and phrases, are misplaced because tone and rhythm are of greater importance than lexical clarity. As long as the performance's rhythm remains consistent, the audience comprehends the gist of the story. So, for Isa, reading the text is less about the fidelity of the printed book and more about *telāyat* or recitation which is faithful to a rhythm. That the wrong printed word creates a confusion in meaning does not strike Isa because his relationship to the print text is founded on his familiarity with oral performances, and it is the latter that turns his reading into a performative act.

---

[90] The following discussion is based on Bashar's reading of *Biśād Sindhu* published as an online article which can be found here: http://www.amarboi.com/2015/11/bishad-sindhur-bishadmoy-torongo-abul-bashar.html.

[91] A receptacle for sacred texts in a Muslim household.

[92] The literal translation of the phrase is *ketāb* or book *pāthak* or reader. However, Bashar reminds us that in this context the particular kind of book referred to by *ketāb* is a *punthi* or a manuscript.

[93] Bashar, *"Biśād-sindhur biśādmay taranga,"* translation mine.

182   *The Novel in Nineteenth-Century Bengal*

Isa is far from being alone in his fluid interaction with texts and reading; Bashar remembers his aunt Ashura Khatun[94] who inhabited a world in which the novel was indistinguishable from *jārigān* performances of the battle of Karbala, and of going with her to these performances during Muharram to watch the ritualized mourning commemorating Hasan and Husayn. The uniting factor for Bashar is that *Biśād Sindhu* was not for the elites of either religion, but for the Bengalis living in rural areas such as Lalbagh and Kapasdanga in Murshidabad. What fascinates me is the time of which Bashar speaks in this article. He mentions being fifteen or sixteen when he corrected Isa, and given that he was born in 1951, this would have in the mid-1960s. As late as the mid-twentieth century then, one finds examples of this porous relationship between reading and performance, suggesting not just its longevity as a mode of consuming texts but also how profoundly it had become a part of rural Bengali life from the early nineteenth century onwards when *jāri* performers brought to life Heyat Mahmud's handwritten *punthi* of *Jārijungnāmā*.

Mosharraf Hossain's investment in the rural Bengali reader attests to the proximity of this knowing reader of *Biśād Sindhu* to *jārigān* performances. In his essays, the agricultural news covered in the periodical *Hitakarī* which he edited, and prose texts such as *Gāji Miyār Bastāni*, Mosharrah Hossain demonstrates his continued interest in placing the rural Bengali reader over their more urban counterparts from Kolkata and Dhaka. His familiarity with this reader's interests and tastes is well documented in his collaboration with the Bengali reformer Harinath Majumdar, popularly known as Kangal Harinath. As I discuss elsewhere in this work, Mosharraf Hossain had a close professional and personal relationship with Harinath, the former beginning his journalistic career in the latter's periodical *Grāmbārtāprakāśikā* (*Publisher of Rural News*). As the publication's name suggests, both Harinath and the novelist sought to highlight the realities of living in rural Bengal which were often ignored by the urban Bengali intelligentsia, be they Hindu or Muslim. They both wrote repeatedly about the plight of not just the agricultural worker, but also of the middle classes living under tyrannical landlords, first in *Grāmbārtāprakāśikā* which was one of the first investigative periodicals

---

[94] Bashar reads the novel and the Karbala story as uniting Shias and Sunnis such that even a Sunni woman would be named Asura after the tenth day of Muharram despite the festival and its religious connotations being Shia in nature rather than Sunni.

Another World of Reading

in Bengali, and then Mosharraf Hossain continued to dwell on the problem at length in *Gāji Miyār Bastāni*. Coming from the same district of Kushtia, Harinath and Mosharraf Hossain shared a similar socio-cultural context in which folk performers such as *jāri* and *bāul* would have been part of their quotidian life. Harinath was himself a *bāul*, and a friend and disciple of the famous *bāul* singer Lalon Fakir, and arranged to publish Lalon's songs from his own Mathuranath press in Komarkhali in Kushtia, the same venue where *Biśād Sindhu* was composed and later published.[95] The fluidity of genres meant that *bauls* would often sing *jāri* songs and vice versa, a tradition which continues till date,[96] and that Mosharraf Hossain himself was part of the folk performance culture through his friendship with Harinath.

It is, then, of little surprise that as a man from rural Bengal, Mosharraf Hossain would draw on those genres which were a part of his own life to create a novel that would appeal to readers within his context. When conceptualizing the first Bengali Muslim novel, he thus draws on not just a story whose contours these readers would have known, but does so by incorporating elements of a form through which the narrative returned every year. Hasan, Hosen, and their family fought and bravely died in the songs of *jārigān* performers, marking the cyclical passage of time for Muslims just as the *āgōmanī* songs marked the annual advent of Durga for the Hindus. In integrating such a communal and familiar story into the relatively new form of the novel, Mosharraf Hossain ensures that the Bengali Muslim can navigate their way through the genre using these recognizable markers. This reader knows the story, knows how the story is performed, and thus in reading it in print, can rely on their knowledge of this shared performative experience to approach a genre hitherto marked as belonging to the domain of the Hindus and Anglicized Bengalis. What remains truly remarkable about *Biśād Sindhu* is its ability to be read without any knowledge of its inner world, but it is only when one returns to rural Bengal via the textual markers encoded in it, that the novel's relationship with its Muslim readers becomes apparent through the vernacularized Perso-Arabic reading practice. It is here that *Biśād Sindhu*'s existence as text and performance acquires special significance; the

---

[95] https://www.thedailystar.net/country/150-years-old-press-still-works-1213822; also see Carola Erika Lorea's "'Playing the Football of Love on the Field of the Body': The Contemporary Repertoire of Baul Songs."

[96] One such example can be found here: http://www.thetravellingarchive.org/record-session/ambikapur-faridpur-bangladesh-31-march-2008-jainuddin-boyati-and-team/.

Perso-Arabic reading practice requires not only a familiarity with the tenets of Islam and a lived performance of the faith, but also an intimate relationship with the context of its production in rural Bengal. The Bengali Muslim emerges as a better reader of the Perso-Arabic practice than their Hindu counterpart because the former comprehends the text as aestheticizing the ethical through the concept of *adab*, and because this *adab* is presented in a text whose story is a significant part of the immediate cultural life.

Conclusion: The Novelty of Reading

I. The Novelty of Women Reading

What lies behind the remarkable popularity achieved by the Bengali novel by the end of the nineteenth century when it had only been a part of the print industry for a little over three decades? How did Bengali readers take to the genre so quickly when few of them had access—material or educational—to novels imported from England? What means did networks of authors, readers, printers, publishers, distributors, and reviewers in Bengal use to popularize a genre so far removed from its originary context in Victorian England? How did existing aesthetic, linguistic, and ethical structures engage with Bengali novels creating practices of reading unique to the region? And what does it mean for the scholar to take the life of a genre and its readers on their own terms?

These are the questions I have sought to answer in this book, and in the course of doing so, I've looked at the struggles over forming not just a genre but the modern Bengali language itself. From the Islamicate world via Persian, Arabic, and Urdu, to the debates between Sanskritists and Anglicists, this work has traced the contours of multiple, often competing and frequently contradictory, practices of reading. As I studied these conversations, they compelled me to reflect on the male-dominated nature of the book market in nineteenth-century Bengal, and to ask where were the women who were certainly reading and being read to, if not actively producing Bengali prose? That they were active readers becomes apparent in *battalā* satires such as Durgadas De's "*Miss Bino Bibi B.A.*" or the anonymous "*Nabhel nāyikā*" which bemoan the fate of women who read novels, and assume this act to be widespread enough to be a cause for moral concern. Their contribution to Bengali prose was not minor, especially when one considers how many women were editing and writing in periodicals and publishing monographs. Thakomoni Debi became the first woman to edit a periodical when she began editing *Anāthinī* in 1875, and Kailasbashini Debi

published a book of prose titled *Hindu mahilāganer hinabasthā* (*The Lowly State of Hindu Women*) as early as in 1863. The women of the Tagore family including Swarnakumari Debi and her daughters Hiranmoyi Debi, and Sarala Debi Chaudhurani were editors and contributors to the periodical *Bhāratī*, highlighting the condition of women in Bengal. While there were fewer Muslim authors, Faizunnesa Khatun or Nawab Faizunnesa was notable not only for her narrative poem *Rupjālāl*, but also for her work on educating young Muslim women in Bengali rather than in the Persianate languages, the latter being the norm for Muslims in colonial Bengal.

Rich though this body of work is, there are few allusions to women as readers not constrained by the dictates of social or religious morality. With the notable exception of Binodini Dasi,[1] discussions of women reading frequently merge into conversations debating the benefits or ill-effects of educating women. The didactic nature of documents both proposing and opposing women's education restrict the female reader to the role of a real or potential student, and simultaneously position reading as primarily a pedagogical instrument. The concept of the female novel reader, when it does appear, becomes associated with the question of educating women such that aesthetic or ethical concerns not related to education are rendered invisible.[2] Thus either one finds examples such as the satires mentioned above in which the act of reading novels serves as the vehicle for remarking on the moral dangers of giving women the power of literacy, or in a book of religious guidance such as Maulana Ashraf Ali Thanawi's *Behishti Zewar* where the author provides women with a curated list of books they may and may not read so as to be educated as good Muslims.[3] Yet other examples are the various social treatises—Kailashbashini's *Hindu mahilāganer hinabasthā* being a prime example—in which reading as a means of educating and thus ameliorating the domestic conditions of women is a recurring trope.

However, there is a handful of texts in which women engage with the act of reading without entering into conversations about education, and in these concluding remarks, I draw on two such works—Rassundari Debi's autobiography *Āmār jīban* (*My Life*) and Faizunnesa's *Rupjālāl*, both published

---

[1] See introduction.

[2] The nuances of nineteenth-century educational debates as pertaining to women have been examined at length by scholars such as Tanika Sarkar, Sumit Sarkar, Ghulam Murshid, Sujata Mukherjee, and Sonia Amin, to name only a handful.

[3] Book 10 of *Behishti zewar* provides such lists. I discuss this with reference to the concept of *adab* in Chapter 4.

Conclusion   187

in 1876. I stage these two texts as sites of reading to demonstrate the range of concerns women brought to the practice of reading. My aim in doing so is not to provide an exhaustive overview of women readers across the nineteenth century in Bengal, or to even suggest that Rassundari or Faizunnesa is representative of their gender. Rather it is to highlight the improbable, messy, and impossible ways in which these women practice reading knowing that it is an act first and foremost forbidden for them. As these two examples show, women read and misread, with Rassundari reading for divine solace, and Faizunnesa inviting her reader to read so that the author may mitigate the effects of black magic and heartbreak. Both women comment on the lack of a community that might support them *as* readers, or even be able to condone their desire to read, and it is through this profound sense of isolation that they express their relationship to texts. The act of reading itself is presented as novel as each author positions it as incompatible with the domestic space within which the woman is supposed to remain confined. They pay little attention to generic characteristics, both as readers and writers, and so the conclusion does not discuss the practice of reading novels but rather aims at unearthing what reading looked like for the few women who documented the process.

II. "Dayamadhav teach me how to read"

The predominant emotion structuring the first Bengali autobiography, Rassundari's *Āmār jīban*, is fear. The author narrates how this fear is instilled in her at a very young age by her mother's cautionary tale of *cheledharā* or kidnappers who abducted naughty children. From then on, she recounts, she lived in perpetual terror, even afraid of reporting bullies lest they be kidnapped for being bad children. As she grows older, she learns from her mother the efficacy of chanting the name of their household deity Dayamadhab in moments of distress. Rassundari thus adds Dayamadhab to her narrative, calling on him to protect her from the evils of the world. Growing up in the mid-1810s in an affluent family running a school for boys, Rassundari has the rare opportunity to not only be near an educational institution, but to be allowed to attend school, if only to keep her out of the reach of village bullies.[4] I say attend here, but the verb

---

[4] Rassundari, *Āmār jīban*, 3–6.

must be taken quite loosely because while she sits near the *mem* or the English teacher, she is not given any instruments of learning such as a stick which the boys use to draw letters of the alphabet on the ground. She is merely allowed to sit in the company of students as she recounts being terrified of even that context. Through her fog of fear, however, she manages to learn the sound of the alphabet, even though she does not learn to recognize the shape of the letters.

This mix of a girl child's fear and reliance on divine protection creates an intimate picture of domestic life in nineteenth-century rural Bengal, affording the reader access to a world in which women are constrained behind layers of physical and religious barriers. As she describes the school, she notes her lack of agency in participating in the process of learning. Rassundari comments on being taken to and from the school, placed there in the morning, taken inside by relatives to shower and lunch at midday, and then finally taken back in the evening when school closed for the day.[5] She adds to this sense of helplessness when she describes herself at age eight as a "*sōnār putuli*" or a golden doll who would cry if anyone even spoke to her aggressively.[6] It is within this discourse of fear and vulnerability that she places her act of starting to memorize both the Bengali and the Persian alphabet. Yet this learning happens in secret even though she is publicly sitting in the schoolhouse, as Rassundari remarks, "that I had learnt all these lessons in my mind (*mane mane*), no one else knew that."[7] As a young Bengali Hindu girl, she knows well the stigma associated with women even contemplating the act of reading, and while she presents her childhood self as blissfully unaware of social norms, she nonetheless demonstrates an acute awareness of reading as a forbidden act for women. Reading, for her, is a practice that must be secreted away from even her beloved mother because there is no room for it in the rigidly defined domestic sphere—the only space allocated to her.

Yet that Rassundari wishes to make reading a part of her domestic life becomes apparent in her description of how she learns to perform everyday chores such as cooking and cleaning. She follows the same format of representing herself as a frightened child living for a brief while in the care of her aging paternal aunt (*khurimā*), and learning *kāj*[8] without the knowledge of others. She does her work in secret for the fear of being chastised—an unusual fear for most women

---

[5] *Āmār jīban*, 6.
[6] *Āmār jīban*, 6, translation mine.
[7] *Āmār jīban*, 6.
[8] Work in general, and in this instance, household work.

Conclusion 189

given that they were expected to take up domestic chores at a fairly young age, but more justified in Rassundari's case as a thoroughly pampered child. Once she is found out, the women in the household laugh at her irrational fear, and the author is proud to have secretly learned something useful. That she represents *parā* (lessons, but also the infinitive form of "to read") and *kāj* using the same narrative pattern[9] suggests that she draws on the natural fit between the latter and the domestic space to incorporate the former into her life as well. She learns her *kāj* in the same way that she learns her *parā*, secretly and on her own, fearing discovery and censure, and in this, she brings together both parts of her world.

The connection between household work and reading is reinforced as Rassundari narrates the first time she comes across a book. By this time, she is married to an affluent man, Satinath Sarkar, and the mother to several children. As in her paternal home, so also in her marital home, Rassundari describes the process of learning to not only perform domestic duties, but also assume the responsibility of running her household. Initially, she is spared the task of doing anything by her mother-in-law who, according to the autobiography, treats her like her own mother, shielding her from the pressures of domesticity. Once Rassundari's mother-in-law dies, however, the burden of running a sizeable household falls entirely on her. Even if one leaves aside the focus on reading for a moment here, one cannot help but be amazed at the detailed description of a Bengali home provided in *Āmār jīban*. From waking up before dawn to cook meals for the household deity, to looking after her husband's needs, to tending to the children and the many servants and dependents, the Bengali housewife frequently has no time to eat, let alone time to read.[10] At the same time as Rassundari begins charting her increasing domestic duties, she reintroduces her desire to read. She recounts the pressure of work being such that she had no idea of the passage of time, and yet in the midst of this she reminds us that her "desire to be educated so as to be able to read *punthi*s became uncontrollable." The author rails against the fate of her gender being confined to an animal-like state, so far removed from learning that even the sight of a piece of paper was seen as "*biruddha karma*" or unnatural.[11] To counter the unnaturalness of her desire, Rassundari relies on divine protection again as she calls on god to teach her how to read. During this time, she dreams of reading *Caitanya Bhagabat*, a

---

[9] *Āmār jīban*, 15–17.
[10] Such descriptions appear frequently in *Āmār jīban*, notably on pages 34–6 and 56.
[11] *Āmār jīban*, 39.

hagiography of Chaitanya written in Bengali by Brindaban Das Thakur in 1535.[12] Her dream overjoys her and as if by coincidence, she overhears her husband instructing her oldest son Bipin that he was leaving his copy of the *punthi* in a place from where she then manages to steal a page. She completes her collection of texts by stealing a page from her son's *tāl pātā* or manuscript on which he had practiced the alphabet.[13]

This, then, is the first moment when we see Rassundari trying to read. She begins by consoling herself that she must remember some elements of the alphabet from her rote memorization days, but immediately follows this assertion with a plea unto god who must take the responsibility of teaching her because no one else will. The back and forth between human agency and divine intervention positions reading as an act guided as much by human endeavor as by divine agency. Her first instance of reading occurs not when she is awake but rather in her dream, in what is ostensibly a vision, given that she chances upon the same text soon after. The act of dream reading is a profoundly embodied one:

> One day I dreamt while sleeping—that I was reading the book *Caitanya Bhagabat*. On seeing this dream, I woke up. Then my mind and body were simultaneously filled with a joy (*ānandarase*) … I kept thinking, how strange! I have never seen this *Caitanya Bhagabat* book and I don't even know it; nonetheless in the dream I read that book. I don't know how to read or write at all, and on top of that this is an important (*bhāri*) book. That I could read this book is impossible. Anyway, that I read this book in my dream filled me with gratitude.[14]

Reading, here, occurs as an act that is both real and unreal. She claims to be pleased with reading it in her dream, which she takes to be a fact, but at the same time, she admits to the impossibility of her reading the book outside the dream. It is this moment of reading so secret as to be possible only in one's dream, coupled with the presence of the divine, that I take to be emblematic of women practicing reading. As a householder, the only space available to Rassundari where she can be truly outside the purview of social constraints is either in her dreams or in her relationship with god. In *Āmār jīban*, she brings both these spaces together to allow her access to not just a text but to the act of reading itself. Divine sanction, both in the form of god answering her

---

[12] The text is sacred to the Vaishnavas who, as members of a reformist Hindu sect worshipping Vishnu, take Chaitanya as their spiritual leader.

[13] *Āmār jīban*, 39–43.

[14] *Āmār jīban*, 40–41, translation mine.

Conclusion   191

prayers through her dream, and in the sacred nature of the text, legitimizes her otherwise aberrant desire to read. As a woman striving to read in the nineteenth century, Rassundari needs to remind her reader of not just force of her passions but of their chastity as well.

Outside her dream, the other two spaces left for her where she can continue to realize her ambition to become a reader are under her veil and beneath her kitchen pantry. She takes a leaf out of her husband's copy of the manuscript—which she recognizes as being an old-fashioned *punthi* with a wooden spine—but then becomes unsure of where to store this contraband object.[15] She hides it under her pantry, with the narrative reverting to her fear of reproach (*katū kathā*) and discovery, and reminding the reader of her previous attempt at learning to read as a child. When she finally presents herself as reading the page, she does so in the guise of a heavily veiled housewife, holding the page in her left hand under her veil while cooking with the other. At this point, she cannot recognize the letters, so her act of reading is one of looking at the page without comprehending the text. She begins to compare the *punthi*'s page with her son's *tāl pātā*—still under her veil, still while cooking—and gradually teaches herself to make sense of the marks on the page. This is a scene of reading unique for many reasons, not least of which is the window it opens into the world of the housewife. What further interests me is the marriage the author effects between learning to read and preparing meals for her family. The latter is a quotidian task, one which she feels enchained by, while the former is both aspirational and titillating in being outside the bounds of the permissible. The veil which isolates her from others here becomes the refuge within which she can begin to decipher letters, and she reads as she cooks. Reading, which is the domain of the educated man, enters not only the domestic sphere of the woman, but the very intimate space within her veil.

Rassundari thus instantiates a practice of reading that belongs exclusively to the woman, while removing the man from even the position of the teacher by according that role to her personal god. The men in her life are presented as agents of god, helping her achieve a power that god has decided to give her. Thus her husband coincidentally leaves a copy of *Caitanya Bhagabat* within her reach, and her son's *tāl pātā* is there for her taking. It is worth noting here that she does not claim to want to read for a higher purpose; this is not a narrative

---

[15] *Āmār jīban*, 42.

of self-improvement. The author continues to be frightened of censure and of overstepping her social role even as she expresses her wish to become a reader. Rassundari wants to read for the sake of learning to read, not because she associates reading with a higher sense of self. That she develops as a person is presented almost incidentally in the text, independent of her activities as a reader. She does not shy away from remarking on the social condition of women,[16] but she positions reading as her own aspiration unconnected from the narrative of the benefits of educating women. Having eventually taught herself to read, she gathers around her a secret group of women to whom she reads, always in a low voice, and always fearing the intrusion of others. In describing this, she remarks on people both suggesting women should read, and on those condemning it, but ultimately exclaims that all this discussion made her terribly afraid, so she continued to read secretly.[17] Once she reveals to her sisters-in-law that she can read, they try to learn from her for a little while, but are mostly content with letting her read to them.[18] The emphasis for her, then, is on being a reader *as* a reader; not as a social reformer, not even as a tireless teacher of other women, but as an individual capable of discovering the few loopholes within a housewife's life wherein she can practice reading on her own terms.

As the first Bengali autobiography, *Āmār jīban* occupies a significant space in literary history. For the scholar of reading practices, Rassundari's work is one of the few texts documenting the entry of reading into the life of the average Bengali woman, and into the inner chambers of the house via religious *punthis*. In her description of how she learns to read we find traces of a practice of reading unique to women across the nineteenth and a major portion of the twentieth century. Mundane objects such as lids in the pantry, and the veil extending to the woman's chest leaving her free to look only at her own feet, become key to fashioning oneself as reader, as the *punthi* gets secreted into these spaces in disjointed parts. A page here, a pause while cooking there—Rassundari strings her practice of reading onto these elements creating something that does not aspire to be either perfect or whole but reflects instead the multifaceted and creative existence led by women inside ordinary Bengali homes.

---

[16] We find several examples of this in the text, in particular at the start of Chapter 6 before the narrator begins to describe reading in her dream.

[17] *Āmār jīban*, 56–7.

[18] Ibid., 56–7.

III. The Magic of Reading

Faizunnesa's *Rupjālāl* tells the story of Prince Jalal and Rup Banu's romance, drawing on Hindu and Islamic fairy tales and folklore. The text, a combination of verse and prose, mythologizes the author's life, reimagining her as the chaste but helpless woman at the mercy of the brave man frequently ensnared by monsters and other women. The narrative brings together a wide array of genres, from the novelistic to *jārigān*, as well as Faizunnesa's knowledge of at least five languages, including Persian, Urdu, Arabic, English, and Bengali. In narrating Jalal's adventures, Faizunnesa frequently relies on *misra bhāśā* or a language born of mixing Persianate languages with Bengali, creating a text that is a repository of all three reading practices—Sanskritist, Anglicist, and Perso-Arabic—discussed in this book. Yet that is not the reason why I chose *Rupjālāl* to be the final text I mention in my work. My interest lies in the brief preface Faizunnesa provides at the start of *Rupjālāl*, giving her readers a brief autobiographical sketch through which she explains her rationale for writing her text. It is this preface that I wish to examine as a site of a reading practice exclusive to women in the nineteenth century, and in order to do so, one needs to follow her direct addresses to the reader.

The text begins with an invocation to Allah and his prophets, a convention followed by *jārigān* as well, and like the *jāri* performers, Faizunnesa saves her final set of thanks for her mentor or *ustād* Tazuddin Mian. She gives credit to him for having taught her to be "patient, pious and wise" before begging the reader's indulgence, excusing "the ignorant mistakes of a novice."[19] From the very opening of the narrative, then, the reader is invited to be a part of the creative process, and to see its inner workings. Doing so allows Faizunnesa to alert the reader to her unorthodox upbringing—as a Muslim woman, she is an exception in having not only having access to education, but doing so via a male tutor. Well before the narrative begins, it is already intimated to the reader that Faizunnesa is not only a competent reader herself, having been taught by a man, but also confident enough to assert her identity as an author. Thus as the reader transitions to the author's family history, they are primed to expect the exceptional, and that is what Faizunnesa appears to initially deliver. She traces her family back to the court of the Mughal Emperor, Shah Alam, who ruled in

---

[19] *Rupjālāl*, 42.

Delhi from 1761 to 1805. During this time, her ancestor Agwan Khan is sent by Shah Alam to Bengal where the former then establishes his household.

The royal connection foreshadows the narrative's own engagement with royalty even as it positions Faizunnesa as someone who would plausibly know of the inner workings of a courtly family. Her own happy childhood under parents who let her be tutored and play with friends continues to anticipate the romance and its happy ending, but the author interrupts this positive depiction of family life to abruptly transition to her own unhappy marital life. As soon as this transition occurs, the reader is invoked once again as Faizunnesa exclaims, "Now dear reader, listen to my sighs."[20] From being the distant audience addressed at the end of the opening invocation, the reader is now placed as the narrator's confidante; they are no longer the judge who will forgive the novice author's mistakes, but rather a sympathetic entity whom Faizunnesa can call on to narrate her troubles. These troubles arise because an older man, Mohammad Gazi Chowdhury, becomes besotted with Faizunnesa when she is a mere child, and offers to marry her. Mohammad Gazi's proposal is rejected by Faizunessa's mother, leaving the man to suffer from a broken heart which even his first marriage cannot cure. He returns once Faizunnesa is older and her father has died leaving her mother as the sole guardian of both Faizunnesa and the estate. The repeated proposal from Mohammad Gazi leads the mother to finally give in and assent to their marriage, "easily overlook[ing]" her "doomed future" and sacrificing her "in the name of marriage."[21] The sympathetic reader is made aware of the mother's failure—a trope which returns in the opening sections of *Rupjālāl* when Jalal's mother fails to find him a suitable bride—gradually moving into the intimate space of Bengali family life and into the *zenānā*.[22]

Having invited the reader into a private conversation, the author pours her heart out, asking the reader to "feel the pain [she] went through" when after a few short years of being happily married, she has to endure losing her husband's affection.[23] Faizunnesa blames her co-wife, Chowdhary's first wife Nazmunnesa, for conspiring to break her own marriage out of jealousy. As Faizunnesa describes how Nazmunnesa effected this break, the reader is drawn into a world in which black magic and the work of *tāntrics*[24] can disrupt material reality

---

[20] Ibid., 45.
[21] Ibid., 45.
[22] The women's quarters.
[23] *Rupjālāl*, 46.
[24] Practitioners of esoteric Hindu rituals using chants or *mantras*.

Conclusion

through spells and mantras. This is a place where the rational and the magical cohabit in comfort, causing no dissonance to those called on to believe that a marriage can be broken by casting spells from afar. As the author's confidante, the reader is assumed to share not just in the former's pain and heartache, but to also assent to this piece of information provided by here, that the marriage was broken unnaturally by another woman. Within a few short paragraphs, we have moved away from the world of Mughal emperors and the world of men in general, to that of women, gossip, and a sharing of emotional trauma. This space is reminiscent of the secret community to women to whom Rassundari reads *punthi*s in that it involves those matters deemed feminine by nineteenth-century social norms. Both women position reading within concerns of raising children, keeping one's husband happy, and performing the task of a good housewife. Rassundari steals moments within her happy domestic scene to learn to read, while Faizunnesa has the misfortune of inviting the reader into her broken home, but in either case, reading is aligned with the practice of sharing and understanding a woman's fate.

The intervention of the supernatural or the divine—and the two are frequently conflated—is a necessary part of the domestic sphere as it is only through such interruptions that the woman can find moments of escape from rigid social expectations. While for Rassundari, god alone can help her learn to read and have access to reading material, Faizunnesa needs to invoke the supernatural to explain the reason behind the outrageous act of a woman not just reading but writing a text and addressing the reader directly. Thus the reference to black magic and *tantra* achieves a threefold purpose. The first is to incorporate the reader into a space that is exclusively feminine in which this magic has a material impact on the woman's prospects of domestic bliss; the second is to undergird the act of reading and writing by entities beyond human control and thus outside even the scope of patriarchal regulations; and finally, to serve as a bridge the preface and the narrative through magical spells and *mantras* which acts as the conceptual foundation for both. Reading *Rupjālāl*, then, happens as an act located in the inner quarters of the home, where women have relative freedom to share their troubles with others of their gender, and to seek supernatural explanations for such womanly events as heartbreaks and unloving husbands. Invited into this space, the "dear readers" addressed by Faizunnesa are made privy to stories that can only be shared within its intimacy, and as they learn of the author's sorrows, they also learn to read the tale of Rup and Jalal as allegorical of her own life. To transmit the pain she feels, she offers the reader a

brief poem narrating her heartbreak and unhappiness at losing her husband to another woman, asserting that the reader's "heart will ache, and [the reader] will shed some tears after reading the following poem."[25] The happy ending to Rup and Jalal's love story becomes Faizunnesa's wishful projection of a closure denied to her, which the reader now knows to read as such because they too have felt the author's pain.

The final section of the preface is the abovementioned poem in which the author bemoans the fate of an abandoned wife, suggesting that black magic turns her life into an unnatural one as she cannot be with her mate unlike "[a]ll beasts and birds [who] have their mate/ to share the joys of nature."[26] Her final confession to her reader is that her husband has made her "a miserable mother" by taking with him their oldest daughter to live with his first wife.[27] What one is reading is no longer a justificatory piece but an expression of deep personal grief which Faizunnesa can share with her reader having placed reading as a domestic, womanly practice.

I should note that this intimate form of reading is far from the only one advocated by her. Having reconciled herself to her family life, Faizunnesa goes on to establish a school for Muslim girls in 1873 in Comilla where they are taught in Bengali, so the education they are provided is tellingly not religious.[28] She also enters into long discussions with the colonial government, going as far as petitioning Queen Victoria to demand that she be awarded the title of *Nawab* (an honorary title accorded to male *zamindārs* or landlords during the colonial period) rather than the politically insignificant title of *Begum* which is what she was granted originally.[29] Faizunnesa wins her petition, becoming one of the very few women to be accorded the title of *Nawab* and the concomitant prestige of having her rule of her estate be officially recognized. Yet the practice of reading instantiated in the preface to *Rupjālal* is worlds away from these more public forms of reading. It is familiar and personal, placing the reader in a position of being both receptive to, and affectively affiliated with, the vulnerability

[25] *Rupjālal*, 46.

[26] Ibid., 46.

[27] Ibid., 47.

[28] Woman, if at all educated, would have been taught the basics of Arabic, providing them with enough literacy to be able to read the Qur'an. Thanawi's *Behishti zewar*, for example, advocates for teaching women only Arabic so that they can read religious texts alone. Given that most Islamic religious texts such as the Qur'an and the *Hadīth* did not exist in Bengali translation till the end of the nineteenth century, the choice of teaching students in Bengali suggests the desire to provide a secular rather than a religious education.

[29] For a detailed discussion of this event, see Fayeza S. Hasanat's English translation of *Rupjālal* (2009).

Faizunnesa expresses. Like Rassundari, Faizunnesa also relies on the mundane to achieve this relationship with her reader, but since she has the relative luxury of not having to account for her own progress toward literacy, she can condense it into a short preface, leaving both the reader and the author free to enter the world of the story they have come together for.

IV. The Practice of Reading

I have been concerned in this book with practices of reading which occur within a network of people and institutions, each entity seeking to define the relationship between the individual and the text. In doing so, I have focused on what it means to read, be a reader, and consume a genre as newly arrived in colonial Bengal as the novel. My goal has been to highlight the many life worlds subtending these practices while consciously avoiding the logic of the colonial as the site of hybridity and multiplicity. Instead of celebrating difference, I have tried to be attentive to the lived realities of the book market within which readers exist, largely to demonstrate how aesthetic, linguistic, and religious affiliations create points of reference for producers, distributors, and consumers of the novel. Each chapter has sought to map the contours of particular practices of reading using as guides the literary and non-literary material produced by those seeking to define these practices.

The readings I have offered in this chapter are two examples of the real conditions within which reading happened, conditions which the scholar has to parse with and through the text. There is a certain irony in this—my only access to nineteenth-century reading practices has been through the act of reading material produced therein. But as I have made my way through this book's argument, I have found this irony to be a productive one; for one thing, it has heightened my awareness of my own practices of reading and, along with it, it has enabled me to question what it means to read literature. In my mode of analysis, then, I have tried to suspend categories such as the literary, being literate, and the reader of literature, to investigate instead reviews, critiques, opinions, and literary history as sites struggling to produce and fix categories relevant to them. The process has been necessarily circular, often messy, requiring me to revisit the same set of texts with different questions, from the perspective of the various *dramatis personae* in the book market. Yet this circularity has also revealed the literary myopia inherent in any practice of reading which normalizes its own

peculiar points of reference to the extent that all others are either made invisible or incomprehensible. Thus the reading of literature performed by Rassundari in which the divine is not just the procurer of texts but also of literacy requires the twenty-first-century reader situated in the Anglo-American world to reorient her perception of what it means to read, and to ask how the material and cultural reality we live in impacts our experience of engaging with a text. *The Novel in Nineteenth-Century Bengal* asks us to step away from the certainties we hold as readers about reading, and to truly examine where these beliefs originate and what they implicitly and explicitly require of readers.

In concluding with Rassundari and Faizunnesa, I have attempted to highlight that reading is not a universal faculty, capable of being transported, even from one domestic space to another. This is not to make a claim for radical relativism but to prioritize the experiences of the reader as they begin to conceptualize the shape of the verb "to read." How these two women participate in their practices of reading is representative of how other nineteenth-century Bengali readers learned to read the novel—hesitatingly, looking over their shoulder for those who would object, looking around for guides and mentors, and ultimately making sense of it all using what they had around them.

Bibliography

Acharya, Poromesh. "Bengali Bhadralok and Educational Development in 19th Century Bengal." *Economic and Political Weekly*, vol. 30, no. 13, Apr. 1, 1995. https://www.epw.in/journal/1995/13/perspectives/bengali-bhadralok-and-educational-development-19th-century-bengal.html.

Adam, William. *Reports on the State of Education in Bengal and Behar (1835 & 1838)*. 1835, 1838. ed. Ananthnath Basu. Calcutta: Calcutta UP, 1941.

Ahmad, Mohammad Reazuddin, ed. *Islam Pracārak*. Kolkata: Reyaz ul-Islam Press, 1891–1893, 1899–1900.

Ahmad, Nazir. 1869. *Mirat al-Arus*, translated by G. E. Ward as *The Bride's Mirror: A Tale of Domestic Life in Delhi Forty Years Ago*. London: Henry Frowde, 1903.

Ahmad, Rafiuddin. *The Bengal Muslims 1871–1906*. Delhi: Oxford UP, 1981.

Allan, Michael. *In the Shadow of World Literature: Site of Reading in Colonial Egypt*. Princeton: Princeton UP, 2016.

Al-katib, Abd al-Hamid. "Epistles to the Secretaries." *The Muqaddimah* by Ibn Khaldun. 747. Translated by Franz Rosenthal, edited by N. J. Dawood. Princeton: Princeton UP, 2015.

Amin, Sonia. *The World of Muslim Women in Colonial Bengal 1876–1939*. Leiden: Brill, 1996.

Anisujjaman. *Muslim-mānas ō Bāṅglā Sāhitya*. Dhaka: Charulipi, 2012.

Anjaria, Ulka. *A History of the Indian Novel in English*. New York: Cambridge UP, 2015.

Anjaria, Ulka. *Reading India Now: Contemporary Formations in Literature and Popular Culture*. Philadelphia: Temple UP, 2019.

Anjaria, Ulka. *Realism in the Twentieth-Century Indian Novel: Colonial Difference and Literary Form*. Cambridge, MA: Cambridge UP, 2012.

Anjum, Tanvir. "Sufism in History and Its Relationship with Power." *Islamic Studies*, vol. 45, no. 2, 2006, pp. 221–68.

Anonymous. "*Bishabriksha.*" *Ārya Darśan*, edited by Jogendranath Bidyabhusan. *Māgh* edition, 1878. *West Bengal Public Library Network*. DSpace Software, 2002–2010. Web, Apr. 4, 2014, p. 436.

Anonymous. "*Young Bengal Khudra Nabab.*" *Battalār Boi: Unish Śataker Duśprāpya Kuriti Boi*, edited by Adrish Biswas, vol. 1. Kolkata: Gangchil, 2011, pp. 295–310.

Arondekar, Anjali. *For the Record: On Sexuality and the Colonial Archive in India*. Durham: Duke UP, 2009.

Austen, Jane. *Northanger Abbey*. 1817. Cambridge: Cambridge UP, 2006.

200 *Bibliography*

Bagal, Jogeshchandra. "*Upanyās-prasanga.*" *Bankim Racanābalī: Pratham Khanda Samagra Upanyās*, edited by Jogeshchandra Bagal. Kolkata: Sahitya Samsad, 1953. Rpt. 2001.

Bagchi, Jasodhara. "Positivism and Nationalism Womanhood and Crisis in Nationalist Fiction Bankimchandra's *Anandamath.*" *Economic and Political Weekly*, vol. 20, no. 43, Oct. 26, 1985, pp. 58–62.

Banabhatta. *Banabhatta's Kādambarī.* trans. Caroline Mary Ridding. Mumbai: Jaico, 1956. Rpt. 1960.

Banabhatta. *Kādambarī.* ed. Kasinath Paṇḍuranga Paraba. New Delhi: Naga Publishers, 1985.

Banabhatta. *Kadambari: A Classical Sanskrit Story of Magical Transformations.* trans. Gwendolyn Layne. New York: Garland Pub., 1991.

Banabhatta. *The Kadambari of Banabhatta (the portion prescribed for the B.A. Examination in 1912 and 1913).* trans. and pub. P. V. Kane. Mumbai, 1911.

Bandopadhyay, Bhabanicharan. *Dutī bilās.* Kolkata: Indian Union Press, 1825.

Bandopadhyay, Bhabanicharan. *Kalikātā Kamalālay.* Kolkata: Samacharchandrika Press, 1823.

Bandopadhyay, Indranath. *Kalpataru* (1874). Kolkata: Jogeshchandra Bandopadhyay, 1874.

Banerjee, Sumanta. "Bogey of the Bawdy: Changing Concept of 'Obscenity' in 19th Century Bengali Culture." *Economic and Political Weekly*, vol. 22, no. 29, 1987, pp. 1197–206.

Banerjee, Sumanta. *The Parlour and the Street: Elite and Popular Culture in Nineteenth-Century Calcutta.* Chicago: U of Chicago P, 2018.

Bashar, Abul. "'*Biśād-Sindhur' Biśādmoy Taranga.*" *Amar Boi.* http://www.amarboi. com/2015/11/bishad-sindhur-bishadmoy-torongo-abul-bashar.html.

Basu, Chandranath. "Bankimchandra." 1898. *Bankimchandra: Essays in Perspective*, edited by Bhabatosh Chattarjee. New Delhi: Sahitya Academy, 1996.

Basu, Chandranath. "Nobel bā Kathāgranther Uddeśya." *Bangadarshan, Boishakh*, vol. 7. Kolkata: Radhanath Bandopadhyay, 1880.

Basu, Jogindrachandra. *Cinibās caritāmrita* (1886). Second ed. Kolkata: Biharilal Sarkar, 1886.

Basu, Jogindrachandra. *Model bhaginī* (*Model Sister*, 1886–87). Fourth ed. Kolkata: Arunoday Ray, 1890.

Basu, Ram Ram. *Lipimālā* (*Collection of Letters*). Serampore, 1802.

Basu, Swapan. *Sambād-sāmayik Patre Uniś Śataker Bāngālī Musalmān Samāj.* Kolkata: Books Space, 2019.

Bengal Library: Catalogue of Books Received during the Quarter Ending 1877. 1830–1954, British Library. London, Shelfmark: Asia, Pacific & Africa ORW, 1986.b.149/3.

Bentley, John. *Essays Relative to the Habits, Character and Moral Improvement of the Hindoos.* London: Kingsbury, Parbury & Allen, 1823.

Bibliography 201

Best, Stephen and Sharon Marcus. "Surface Reading: An Introduction." *Representations*, vol. 108, 2009, pp. 1–21.

Bhadra, Gautam. *"Bāngāli pāthak ō tār bānglā boi parā."* *Mudraner Sanskriti ō Bānglā Boi*, edited by Swapan Chakravorty. Kolkata: Ababhash, 2007, pp. 138–63.

Bhadra, Gautam. *Nyarā battalāy jāy k'bār?* Kolkata: Chhatim Books, 2011.

Bhamaha. *Kāvyalankāra*. ed. Raman Kumar Sharma. New Delhi: Vidyanidhi Prakashana, 1994.

Bhamaha. *Kavyalankara of Bhamaha*. trans. P. V. Naganatha Sastry. New Delhi: Motilal Banarasidass, 1970.

Bharata. *Bhārata Nātyāśastra*. trans. Suresh Chandra Banerji. Kolkata: Nabapatra Prakashana, 1917. Rpt. 1980.

Bharata. *Nātyaśāstram. Sanskrit Documents in Devanagari*. Sanskrit Documents in Devanagari, 2016. Web, Apr. 4, 2016.

Bharata. *Natyashastra: English Translation with Critical Notes*. trans. Sriranga. Bangalore: IBH Prakashana, 1986.

Bhatt, Rajeshwari. *Kādamvarī kā Kāvya-Śāstriya Adhyan*. Jaipur: Publication Scheme, 1991.

Bhattacharya, Amitrasudan. *Bankimcandra Jibanī*. Kolkata: Ananda Publishers, 1998.

Bhattacharya, Nandini. "Anglicized-Sanskritzed-Vernacularized: Translational Politics of Primer Writing in Colonial Bengal." *Language Policy and Education in India: Documents, Contexts and Debates*, edited by M. Sridhar and Sunita Mishra. London: Routledge, Forthcoming.

Bhattacharya, Nandini. "Ecce Homo—Behold the Human! Reading Life Narratives in Times of Colonial Modernity." *Religions*, vol. 11, no. x, 2020.

Bhattacharya, Sunayani. "How Not to Read Like a Victorian: Reimagining Bankim's Reader in Nineteenth-Century Bengali Novels." *Comparative Literature*, vol. 73, Mar. 1, 2021, pp. 84–109.

Bhattacharya, Tithi. *The Sentinels of Culture: Class, Education, and the Colonial Intellectual in Bengal (1848–85)*. Oxford: Oxford UP, 2005.

Biswas, Adrish and Anil Acharya. *Bāngālir battalā*. Kolkata: Anustup, 2013.

Bose, Hrishikesh. *Kādambarī ō Gadya-Sāhitye Śilpa-Bicār*. Kolkata: Jadavpur University, 1968.

Boyati, Jainuddin. *"Śahidnāmār jāri."* Mar. 31, 2008. http://www.thetravellingarchive. org/record-session/ambikapur-faridpur-bangladesh-31-march-2008-jainuddin-boyati-and-team/.

Bray, Julia. *"Adab."* *Medieval Islamic Civilization: An Encyclopedia*, edited by Josef Meri. Oxford: Routledge, 2006, p. 13.

Brouillette, Sarah. *UNESCO and the Fate of the Literary*. Stanford: Stanford UP, 2019.

Brown, Peter. "Late Antiquity and Islam: Parallels and Contrasts." *Moral Conduct and Authority: The Place of Adab in South Asian Islam*, edited by Barbara Daly Metcalf. Berkeley: U of California P, 1984, pp. 23–37.

Carey, Eustace. *Memoir of William Carey, D. D. Late Missionary to Bengal; Professor of Oriental Languages in the College of Fort William, Calcutta.* Boston: Gould, Kendall and Lincoln, 1836.

Carey, William. *A Dictionary of the Bengalee Language, In Which the Words Are Traced to Their Origin, And Their Various Meanings Given.* Serampore: Mission Press, 1825.

Chakrabarti, Arindam. "Play, Pleasure, Pain: Ownerless Emotions in Rasa-Aesthetics." *Project of History of Indian Science, Philosophy and Culture Vol XV Part III*, edited by Amiya Dev. New Delhi: Centre for Studies in Civilizations, 2009, pp. 189–202.

Chakrabarti, Kunal and Shubhra Chakrabarti. *Historical Dictionary of the Bengalis.* Lanham: The Scarecrow Press, 2013.

Chakrabarty, Dipesh. *Provincializing Europe: Postcolonial Thought and Historical Difference.* Princeton: Princeton UP, 2000.

Chanda, Ipsita. *Tracing Charit as a Genre: An Exploration in Comparative Literature Methodology.* Kolkata: D.S.A. Department of Comparative Literature, 2003.

Chandy, Anish. "Making Words Count: The Indian Publishing Industry in the New Decade." *The Hindu Business Line*, Jan. 3, 2020. https://www.thehindubusinessline.com/blink/cover/how-the-indian-publishing-industry-is-set-to-evolve-in-the-coming-decade/article30469070.ece.

Chatterjee, Chandrani. *Translation Reconsidered: Culture, Genre and the 'Colonial Encounter' in Nineteenth Century Bengal.* Newcastle: Cambridge Scholars Publishing, 2010.

Chatterjee, Partha. *The Nation and Its Fragments: Colonial and Postcolonial Histories.* Princeton: Princeton UP, 1993.

Chatterji, Suniti Kumar. *The Origin and Development of the Bengali Language.* Kolkata: Calcutta UP, 1926.

Chattopadhyay, Bankimchandra. *Ānandamath* (*The Abode of Bliss*). 1882. *Bankim Racanābalī: Pratham Khanda Samagra Upanyās*, edited by Jogeshchandra Bagal. Kolkata: Sahitya Samsad, 1953. Rpt. 2001, pp. 653–726.

Chattopadhyay, Bankimchandra. "A Popular Literature for Bengal." n.d. *Bankim Racanābalī—III*, edited by Jogeshchandra Bagal. Kolkata: Sahitya Samsad, 1969. Rpt. 1998, pp. 97–102.

Chattopadhyay, Bankimchandra. "Advertisement." *Sahaj Racanā Śikkhā.* n.d. *Bankim Racanābalī: Dwitya Khanda Samagra Sāhitya*, edited by Jogeshchandra Bagal. Kolkata: Sahitya Samsad, 1954. Rpt. 1998, p. 963.

Chattopadhyay, Bankimchandra. *Anandamath.* trans. Aurobindo Ghosh and Barindra Kumar Ghosh. Kolkata: Basumati Sahitya Mandir, 1940.

Chattopadhyay, Bankimchandra. *Bangadarśan.* Kolkata: Radhanath Bandopadhyay, 1872–1888.

Chattopadhyay, Bankimchandra. "*Bāngālā bhāśa.*" *Bibidha Prabandha: Dwītya Khanda.* 1892. *Bankim Racanābalī: Dwītya Khanda Samagra Sāhitya*, edited by Jogeshchandra Bagal. Kolkata: Sahitya Samsad, 1954. Rpt. 1998, pp. 317–20.

Bibliography 203

Chattopadhyay, Bankimchandra. "Bengali Literature." n.d. *Bankim Rachanavali—III (Collected Works of Bankim Chandra Chattopadhyay—Vol III)*, edited by Jogeshchandra Bagal. Kolkata: Sahitya Samsad, 1969. Rpt. 1998, pp. 103–24.

Chattopadhyay, Bankimchandra. *Biśabriksha (The Poison Tree)*. 1873. *Bankim Racanābalī: Pratham Khanda Samagra Upanyās*. ed. Jogeshchandra Bagal. Kolkata: Sahitya Samsad, 1953. Rpt. 2001, pp. 205–84.

Chattopadhyay, Bankimchandra. *Durgeśnandinī (The Chieftain's Daughter)*. 1865. *Bankim Racanābalī: Pratham Khanda Samagra Upanyās*. ed. Jogeshchandra Bagal. Kolkata: Sahitya Samsad, 1953. Rpt. 2001, pp. 1–83.

Chattopadhyay, Bankimchandra. *Kriśnacaritra. Bankim Racanābalī: Dwītya Khanda Samagra Sāhitya*. ed. Jogesh Chandra Bagal. Kolkata: Sahitya Sangsad, 1954, pp. 353–524.

Chattopadhyay, Bankimchandra. *Rajmohan's Wife*. 1864. n.d. *Bankim Racanābalī—III*. ed. Jogeshchandra Bagal. Kolkata: Sahitya Samsad, 1969. Rpt. 1998, pp. 1–88.

Chattopadhyay, Bankimchandra. "Sāmya." *Bankim Racanābalī: Dwītya Khanda Samagra Sāhitya*, edited by Jogesh Chandra Bagal. Kolkata: Sahitya Sangsad, 1954, pp. 328–51.

Chattopadhyay, Bankimchandra. "Uttarcaritra." *Bankim Racanābalī: Dwītya Khanda Samagra Sāhitya*, edited by Jogesh Chandra Bagal. Kolkata: Sahitya Sangsad, 1954, pp. 141–63.

Chattopadhyay, Purnachandra. "*Bankimcandra ō Dinabandhu*." 1914. *Bankim-Prasanga*, edited by Sureshchandra Samajpati. Kolkata: New Age Printers, 1922.

Chaudhuri, Rosinka. "Bankimchandra Chattopadhyay and the Inauguration of the Modern Indian Novel." *Wiley Blackwell Companion to World Literature*, edited by Ken Seigneurie, Wen-chin Ouyang, Christopher Lupke, Frieda Ekotto, and B. Venkat Mani. Oxford: Wiley-Blackwell, 2019.

Chaudhuri, Rosinka. "Cutlets or Fish Curry?: Debating Authenticity in Late Nineteenth-Century Bengal." *Modern Asian Studies*, vol. 40, no. 2, 2006, pp. 257–72.

Chaudhuri, Rosinka. *Gentlemen Poets in Colonial Bengal: Emergent Nationalism and the Orientalist Project*. Kolkata: Seagull Books, 2002.

Chaudhuri, Rosinka. *The Literary Thing: History, Poetry and the Making of a Modern Cultural Sphere*. New Delhi: Oxford UP, 2013.

Chaudhuri, Supriya. "Beginnings: Rajmohan's Wife and the Novel in India." *A History of the Indian Novel in English*, edited by Ulka Anjaria. Cambridge: Cambridge UP, 2015.

Cheah, Pheng. *What Is a World?: On Postcolonial Literature as World Literature*. Durham: Duke UP, 2016.

Choudhury, Munir. *Mirmānas*. Dhaka: Bangla Academy, 1968.

Collins, Wilkie. "The Unknown Public." *Household Words*, vol. 18, 1858, pp. 217–22.

Dace, Wallace. "The Concept of 'Rasa' in Sanskrit Dramatic Theory." *Educational Theatre Journal*, vol. 15, no. 3, 1963, pp. 249–54.

Dames, Nicholas. *The Physiology of the Novel: Reading, Neural Science, and the Form of Victorian Fiction.* Oxford: Oxford UP, 2007.

Dani, Ahmad Hasan. *Dhaka: A Record of Its Changing Fortunes.* Dhaka: Asiatic Society of Bangladesh, 2009.

Das, Sanjanikanta. *Bānglā gadyasāhityer itihās.* Kolkata: Mitralaya, 1946.

Das, Sisir Kumar. "Comparative Literature in India: A Historical Perspective." 1987. *Journal of the Comparative Literature Association of India,* vol. 1, 2011, pp. 18–30.

Das, Sisir Kumar. "The Akhyayika and the Katha in Classical Sanskrit." *Bulletin of the School of Oriental Studies,* vol. 3, no. 3, 1924, pp. 507–17.

Das, Trina. "Sanskrit Learning in Bengal under Foreign Invasion and in British Rule." *Pratidhwanī the Echo,* vol. 4, no. 4, Apr. 2018, pp. 267–73.

Dasi, Binodini. *Āmār kathā ō anyānya racanā.* Kolkata: Subarnarekha, 1969.

Dasi, Binodini. *My Story and My Life as an Actress.* trans. Rimli Bhattacharya. New Delhi: Kali for Women, 1998.

Datta, Kalinath. "*Bankimcandra," Bankim-Prasanga,* edited by Sureshchandra Samajpati. Kolkata: Nabapatra Prakashan, 1922. Rpt. 1982, pp. 130–53.

Datta, Rameshchandra. "Bankimchandra and Modern Bengal." trans. Indrani Halder. *Bankimchandra: Essays in Perspective,* edited by Bhabatosh Chattarjee. New Delhi: Sahitya Academy, 1996.

De, Durgadas. *Miss Bino Bibi B.A. (Honor, In A, Course).* Barisal: Student Friend and Co., 1898.

Debi, Kailashbashini. *Hindu mahilāganer hinābasthā.* Kolkata: Gupta Press, 1863.

Dhananjayan, V. P. *A Dancer on Dance.* Chennai: Bharata Kalanjali, 1984.

Digby, Simon. "The *Tuhfa I nasaih* of Yusuf Gada." *Moral Conduct and Authority: The Place of Adab in South Asian Islam,* edited by Barbara Daly Metcalf. Berkeley: U of California P, 1984, pp. 91–123.

Dodell-Feder, David and Diana I. Tamir. "Fiction Reading Has a Small Positive Impact on Social Cognition: A Meta-Analysis." *Journal of Experimental Psychology: General,* vol. 147, no. 11, 2018, pp. 1713–27.

Dubrow, Jennifer. *Cosmopolitan Dreams: The Making of Modern Urdu Literary Culture in Colonial South Asia.* Honolulu: U of Hawai'i P, 2018.

Dunham, Mary Frances. *Jarigan: Muslim Epic Songs of Bangladesh.* Dhaka: The University Press, 1997.

Dunn, Ross E. *The Adventures of Ibn Battuta: A Muslim Traveler of the 14th Century.* Berkeley: U of California P, 2012.

Dutta, Akshay Kumar. *Cārupāth.* 1853. Kolkata: Prabodhchandra Majumdar and Brothers, rpt. 1930.

Ekti Ālōkprabāha: Uniś theke Ekuś Śatak. Uttarpara: Uttarpara Joykrishna Library, 2009.

Eliott, George. *Silly Novels by Lady Novelists.* 1856. London: Penguin Books, rpt. 2010.

Faizunnesa, Nawab. *Nawab Faizunnesa's Rupjalal,* translated and commented by Fayeza S. Hasanat. Leiden: Brill, 2009.

Ghosh, Anindita. *Power in Print: Popular Publishing and the Politics of Language and Culture in a Colonial Society, 1778–1905.* New Delhi: Oxford UP, 2006.

Ghosh, Aurobindo. *Early Cultural Writings (1890–1910). The Complete Works of Sri Aurobindo,* vol. 1. Pondicherry: Sri Aurobindo Ashram, 2003.

Ghosh, Harachandra. *Bhānumati Cittabilās.* Kolkata: Purnachandraday Press, 1853.

Ghosh, Harachandra. *Cārumukhcittaharā.* Kolkata: Canning Press, 1864.

Gnoli, R. *Aesthetic Experience According to Abhinavagupta.* Rome: ISMEO, 1956.

Gupta, Abhijit. "Popular Printing and Intellectual Property in Colonial Bengal." *Thesis Eleven,* vol. 113, no. 1, Dec. 2012, pp. 32–44.

Gupta, Abhijit and Swapan Chakravorty, ed. *Print Areas: Book History in India.* New Delhi: Permanent Black, 2004.

Gupta, J. N. *Life and Work of R.C. Dutt.* London: J. M. Dent and Sons, 1911.

Halder, Epsita. "Reading the 'Cheapness' of Cheap Prints: Karbala Narrative in the Early Print Culture." *Sahitya,* Jan. 2015, nos. 4 & 5. http://www.clai.in/webjournal2015.html.

Halder, Radhabinod. "*Pāś karā māg.*" Kolkata: Great Town Press, 1902.

Higgins, Kathleen Marie. "An Alchemy of Emotions: Rasa and Aesthetic Breakthroughs." *The Journal of Aesthetics and Art Criticism,* vol. 65, no. 1, 2007, pp. 43–54.

Hossain, Mir Mosharraf. *Āmār Jībanī.* ed. Debipada Bhattacharya. Kolkata: Kolkata General Printers and Publishers, 1908–10. Rpt. 1941.

Hossain, Mir Mosharraf. *Basantakumāri Nātak.* 1873. Mymensingh: Umakantha Rakshit. Rpt. 1887.

Hossain, Mir Mosharraf. *Biśād Sindhu.* 1891. Dhaka: Kitab Mahal. Rpt. 2014.

Hossain, Mir Mosharraf. *Gāji Miyār Bostāni.* 1899. Dhaka: Ahmad Publishing House, rpt. 1982.

Hossain, Mir Mosharraf. *Hitakarī.* 1890–1895. ed. Abul Ahsan Choudhury. Kolkata: Bangiya-Sahitya-Parishat, 2015.

Hossain, Mir Mosharraf. *Jamidār Darpan.* 1873. Dhaka: Afsar Brothers. Rpt. 1973.

Hossain, Mir Mosharraf. *Ocean of Sorrows.* trans. Fakrul Alam. Dhaka: Bangla Academy, 2016.

Hossain, Mir Mosharraf. *Ratnabati.* 1869. Dhaka: Bangla Academy. Rpt. 1976.

"Indian Book Market to Touch 739 Billion by 2020: Survey." *India Today,* Dec. 1, 2015, https://www.indiatoday.in/pti-feed/story/indian-book-market-to-touch-739-billion-by-2020-survey-522296-2015-12-01.

James, Louis. *The Victorian Novel.* Malden: Blackwell Publishing, 2006.

Jasimuddin, *Jārigān.* Dhaka: Kendriya Bangla-Unnyayan-Board, 1968.

Jayadeva. *Gītagōvinda: Love Songs of Rādhā and Krsna by Jayadeva.* trans. Lee Siegel. New York: New York UP, 2009.

Jayadeva. *Srijayadevakaviviracitam Gītagōvindamahākāvyam : Sanjivani, Padadyotanika, Jayanti ityakhyātikatrayopetam.* ed. K. Kamala. Hyderabad: Osmania University, Sanskrit Academy, 2003.

Jayadeva. *The Gita Govinda of Jayadeva.* trans. Monika Verma. Kolkata: Writer's Workshop, 1968.

Joshi, Priya. *In Another Country: Colonialism, Culture, and the English Novel in India.* New York: Columbia UP, 2002.

Kalidasa. *Abhijnaśakuntalam.* ed. A. B. Gajendragadkar. New Delhi: New Bharatiya Book Corp, 1892. Rpt. 2004.

Kalidasa. "Shakuntala." *Great Sanskrit Plays in Modern Translation*, translated by P. Lal. New York: New Directions, 1964, pp. 12–74.

Kaviraj, Sudipta. "The Perfume from the Past: Modern Reflections on Ancient Art, Bankimchandra, Rabindranath, and Abanindranath Tagore." *The Bloomsbury Research Handbook of Indian Aesthetics and the Philosophy of Art*, edited by Arindam Chakrabarti. New York: Bloomsbury Publishing, 2016, pp. 167–94.

Kaviraj, Sudipta. "The Sudden Death of Sanskrit Knowledge." *Journal of Indian Philosophy*, vol. 33, no. 1, 2005, pp. 199–42.

Kaviraj, Sudipta. "Two Histories of Literary Culture in Bengal." *Literary Cultures in History: Reconstructions from South Asia*, edited by Sheldon Pollock. Berkeley: U of California P, 2003, pp. 503–66.

Khan, M. Siddiq. "Early History of Bengali Printing." *The Library Quarterly: Information, Community, Policy*, vol. 32, no. 1, Jan. 1962, pp. 51–61.

Khan, Maryam Wasif. *Who Is a Muslim? Orientalism and Literary Populisms.* New York: Fordham UP, 2021.

Khastagir, Ashish, ed. *Bānglā primer sangraha 1816–1855.* Kolkata: Pashchimbanga Bangla Academy, 2000.

Kia, Mana. "*Adab* as Ethics of Literary Form as Social Conduct: Reading the *Gulistan* in Late Mughal India." *No Tapping Around Philology': A Festschrift in celebration and honor of Wheeler McIntosh Thackston Jr's 70th Birthday*, edited by Alireza Korangy and Daniel J. Sheffield. Wiesbaden: Harrassowitz, 2014, pp. 281–308.

Kia, Mana. "Indian Friends, Iranian Selves, Persianate Modern." *Comparative Studies of South Asia, Africa and the Middle East*, vol. 36, no. 3, 2016, pp. 398–417.

Kopf, David. "Fort William College and the Origins of the Bengal Renaissance." *Proceedings of the Indian History Congress*, vol. 24, 1961, pp. 296–303.

Lapidus, Ira M. "Knowledge, Virtue, and Action: The Classical Muslim Conception of *Adab* and the Nature of Religious Fulfillment in Islam." *Moral Conduct and Authority: The Place of Adab in South Asian Islam*, edited by Barbara Daly Metcalf. Berkeley: U of California P, 1984, pp. 38–61.

Leavis, Q. D. *Fiction and the Reading Public.* London: Chatto and Windus, 1939.

Long, James. *Adam's Reports on Vernacular Education in Bengal and Behar, Submitted to the Government in 1835, 1836, and 1838. With a Brief View of Its Past and Present Condition.* Kolkata: Home Secretariat Press, 1868.

Long, James. *A Descriptive Catalogue of Bengali Works, Containing a Classified List of Fourteen Hundred Bengali Books and Pamphlets, Which Have Issued from the Press*

during the Last Sixty Years, with Occasional Notices of the Subjects, the Price, and Where Printed. Kolkata: Sanders, Cones and Co., 1855.

Long, James. *A Return of the Names and Writings of 515 Persons Connected with Bengali Literature, Either as Authors or Translators of Printed Works. Chiefly during the Last Fifty Years.* Kolkata: Tros. Jones, 1855.

Long, James. *Returns Relating to Native Printing Presses and Publications in Bengal.* Kolkata: Tros. Jones, 1855.

Lorea, Carola Erika. "'Playing the Football of Love on the Field of the Body': The Contemporary Repertoire of Baul Songs." *Religion and the Arts.* Jan. 1, 2013, pp. 416–51.

Love, Heather. "Close Reading and Thin Description." *Public Culture*, vol. 25, no. 3, 2013, pp. 401–34.

Macaulay, Thomas Babington. "Minutes on Indian Education." 1835. *Internet Archive*, Internet Archive, 1999. Web, Mar. 6, 2016.

Majumdar, Rochona. *Marriage and Modernity: Family Values in Colonial Bengal.* Durham: Duke UP, 2009.

Mallya, Vinutha. "Nielsen Values Indian Publishing at $3.9 Billion." *Publishing Perspectives*, Oct. 21, 2015. https://publishingperspectives.com/2015/10/nielsen-values-indian-publishing-at-3-9-billion/.

Mansel, Henry "Sensation Novels." *Quarterly Review.* Apr. 1863, *Varieties of Women's Sensation Fiction: 1885–1890*, edited by Andrew Maunder. London: Routledge, 2004, pp. 483–91.

Marcus, Sharon. *Between Women: Friendship, Desire, and Marriage in Victorian England.* Princeton: Princeton UP, 2007.

Masson, J. L. and M. V. Patwardhan. *Aesthetic Rupture: The Rasadhyaya of the Natyasastra in Two Volumes Vol. II: Notes.* Poona: Deccan College, 1970.

Masud, M. Khalid. "*Adab al-Mufti*: The Muslim Understanding of Values, Characteristics, and Role of a *Mufti*," *Moral Conduct and Authority: The Place of Adab in South Asian Islam*, edited by Barbara Daly Metcalf. Berkeley: U of California P, 1984, pp. 124–51.

McKeon, Michael. *Origins of the English Novel, 1600–1740.* Baltimore: Johns Hopkins UP, 1987.

McKeon, Michael. *The Theory of the Novel: A Historical Approach.* Baltimore: Johns Hopkins UP, 2000.

Metcalf, Barbara Daly. "Introduction." *Moral Conduct and Authority: The Place of Adab in South Asian Islam*, edited by Barbara Daly Metcalf. Berkeley: U of California P, 1984, pp. 1–20.

Mitchell, Rebecca N. *Victorian Lessons in Empathy and Difference.* Columbus: Ohio State University, 2011.

Mitra, Pearychand. *Ālāler Gharer Dulāl.* 1858. ed. Brajendranath Bandopadhyay and Sajanikanta Das. Kolkata: Bangiya Sahitya Parishat, 1940. Rpt. 1947.

Mitra, Royona. *Akram Khan: Dancing New Interculturalism.* New York: Palgrave Macmillan, 2015.

Mitra, Samarpita. "Periodical Readership in Early Twentieth Century Bengal: Ramananda Chattopadhyay's Prabasi." *Modern Asian Studies*, vol. 47, no. 1, Jan. 2013, pp. 204–49.

Monier-Williams Sanskrit-English Dictionary. 1899. *Cologne Digital Sanskrit Dictionaries.* DFG-NEH Project 2010–2013. Web, Apr. 4, 2016.

Moore, Grace. *The Victorian Novel in Context.* Sydney: Bloomsbury, 2012.

Muhammad, Sahidullah. "Bāṅglā Sāhityer Kathā." *Bāṅglā Sāhityer Itihās*, vol. 1. Kolkata: Eastern Publishers.

Mukherjee, Meenakshi. "Anandamath: A Political Myth." *Economic and Political Weekly*, vol. 17, no. 22, 1982.

Mukherjee, Meenakshi. *Realism and Reality: The Novel and Society in India.* New Delhi: Oxford UP, 1985.

Mukherjee, Sujata. *Gender, Medicine, and Society in Colonial India: Women's Health Care in Nineteenth- And Early Twentieth-Century Bengal.* Delhi: Oxford UP, 2017.

Murshid, Ghulam. *Nāripragatir Ekśō Bachar: Rāśsundarī Theke Rōkeyā.* Dhaka: Pratik Prakashana Sangstha, 1993.

Nabhel nāyikā bā śikkhit bou (The Novel Heroine or the Educated Wife), pub. Nabakumar Dutta. Kolkata: Sahitya Prachar Karyalay, n.d.

Naim, C. M. "Prize-Winning *Adab*: A Study of Five Urdu Books Written in Response to the Allahabad Government Gazette Notification." *Moral Conduct and Authority: The Place of Adab in South Asian Islam*, edited by Barbara Daly Metcalf. Berkeley: U of California P, 1984, pp. 290–314.

Nandi, Tapasvi. "Rasa-Theory: A Catholic Application." *Annals of the Bhandarkar Oriental Research Institute*, vol. 82, no. 1/4, 2001, pp. 113–23.

Nayar, Pramod. K., ed. *Colonial Education in India 1781–1945*, vol. 1–5. Oxford: Routledge, 2020.

Nyayratna, Ramgati. *Bāṅglār Itihās.* Hooghly: Bodhodoy Jantra, 1867.

Orsini, Francesca, ed. *Before the Divide: Hindi and Urdu Literary Culture.* Hyderabad: Orient Blackswan, 2010.

Orsini, Francesca. "Between Qasbas and Cities: Language Shifts and Literary Continuities in North India in the Long Eighteenth Century." *Comparative Studies of South Asia, Africa and the Middle East*, vol. 39, no. 1, 2019, pp. 68–81.

Orsini, Francesca. "Present Absence: Book Circulation, Indian Vernaculars and World Literature in the Nineteenth Century." *Interventions: International Journal of Postcolonial Studies*, vol. 22, no. 3, 2019, pp. 310–28.

Orsini, Francesca. *Print and Pleasure: Popular Literature and Entertaining Fictions in Colonial North India.* New Delhi: Permanent Black, 2009.

Pare, Bireswar. "*Adbhut swapna bā strī purusher dwanda*" (*A Strange Dream or a Battle between the Sexes*, 1888), *Battalār Boi: Uniś Śataker Dūṣprāpya Kuriti Boi*, edited by Adrish Biswas, vol. 2. Kolkata: Saptarshi Prakashan, 2011, pp. 145–216.

Perneau, Margrit. "The *Delhi Urdu Akhbar*." *The Annual of Urdu Studies*, 2003. https://minds.wisconsin.edu/handle/1793/18325.

Pollock, Sheldon. "The Death of Sanskrit." *Comparative Studies in Society and History*, vol. 43, no. 2, Apr. 2001, pp. 392–426.

Pollock, Sheldon. *The Language of the Gods in the World of Men: Sanskrit, Culture, and Power in Premodern India*. Berkeley: U of California P, 2006.

Price, Leah. *What We Talk about When We Talk about Books: The History and Future of Reading*. New York: Basic Books, 2019.

Pritchett, Frances. *Marvelous Encounters: Folk Romance in Urdu and Hindi*. Delhi: Manohar, 1985.

Priyolkar, Anant Kakba. *The Printing Press in India: Its Beginnings and Early Development*. Mumbai: Marathi Samshodhana Mandala, 1958.

Raman, Bhavani. *Document Raj: Writing and Scribes in Early Colonial South India*. Chicago: U of Chicago P, 2012.

Rao, Parimala V. *Beyond Macaulay: Education in India, 1780–1860*. Oxford: Routledge, 2020.

Rassundari, Srimati. *Āmār Jīban*. Kolkata: Indian Associated Publishing Co. Private Ltd., 1876.

Ray, Deeptanil, and Abhijit Gupta. "The Newspaper and the Periodical Press in Colonial India." *Journalism and the Periodical Press in Nineteenth-Century Britain*, edited by Joanne Shattock. Cambridge: Cambridge UP, 2017, pp. 245–62.

Regmi, Acharya Shesharaja Sharma. *Kādamvarī (Hindi ebam Sanskrit Anuvād)*. Varanasi: Chaukhamba Surabharati Prakashan, 2016.

Ricci, Ronit. *Islam Translated: Literature, Conversion, and the Arabic Cosmopolis of South and Southeast Asia*. Chicago: Chicago UP, 2011.

Richards, J. F. "Norms of Comportment among Imperial Mughal Officers." *Moral Conduct and Authority: The Place of Adab in South Asian Islam*, edited by Barbara Daly Metcalf. Berkeley: U of California P, 1984, pp. 255–89.

Roy, Tapti. *Print and Publishing in Colonial Bengal: The Journey of Bidyasundar*. Oxford: Routledge, 2019.

Ryan, Vanessa L. *Thinking without Thinking in the Victorian Novel*. Baltimore: Johns Hopkins UP, 2012.

Rudrata. *Kāvyalankāra*. ed. Satyadev Chaudhary. New Delhi: Parimal Sanskrit Series, 2015.

Russell, Ralph. *The Pursuit of Urdu Literature: A Select History*. London: Zed Books Ltd., 1992.

Sarkar, Akshaychandra, "*Bankimcandrer Pratham Gadya Racanā*" (1901), *Bankim-Prasanga,* edited by Sureshchandra Samajpati. Kolkata: New Age Printers, 1922.

Sarkar, Akshaychandra. *Kabi Hemcandra*. Kolkata: Bangiya Sahitya Parishat, 1911.

Sarkar, Akshaychandra. *Pitā-putra. Bangabhashar Lekhak*. ed. Harimohan Mukhopadhyay. Kolkata: Nutbihari Ray. Vol. 1, 1904, pp. 465–659.

Sarkar, Tanika. *Hindu Wife, Hindu Nation: Community, Religion, and Cultural Nationalism*. New Delhi: Permanent Black, 2001. Rpt. 2005.

Sastri, Haraprasad. *A Descriptive Catalogue of Sanskrit Manuscripts in the Government Collection under the Care of the Asiatic Society of Bengal.* Kolkata: Asiatic Society of Bengal, 1917.

Saxena, Akshya. *Vernacular English: Reading the Anglophone in Postcolonial India.* Princeton: Princeton UP, 2022 (*forthcoming*).

Scott, Walter. *Ivanhoe.* 1820. Oxford: Oxford UP, 1955. Rpt. 1996.

Sedgwick, Eve Kosofsky. "Paranoid Reading and Reparative Reading: Or, You're So Paranoid, You Probably Think This Introduction Is about You." *Novel Gazing: Queer Readings in Fiction.* Durham: Duke UP, 1997.

Sen, Amiya P. *Bankim Chandra Chattopadhyay: An Intellectual Biography.* New Delhi: Oxford UP, 2008.

Sen, Amiya P. *Hindu Revivalism in Bengal 1872–1905: Some Essays in Interpretation.* Delhi: Oxford UP, 1993.

Sen, Dinesh Chandra. *History of Bengali Language and Literature: A Series of Lectures Delivered as Reader to the Calcutta University.* Kolkata: Calcutta University, 1911.

Sen, Sukumar. *Battalār chāpā ō chabi.* Kolkata: Ananda Publishers, 1984.

Sen, Sukumar. *Bāṅglā sāhityer itihās.* Vols. I–IV. Kolkata: Pragati Prakashani, 1965.

Sen, Surendra Nath. *Prāchīn bāṅglā patra sankalan.* Kolkata: U of Calcutta P, 1942.

Sen, Surendra Nath. *Studies in Indian History.* Kolkata: U of Calcutta P, 1930.

Shaikh, Abdul Khaer. *"Musalmānī" Punthi Sāhitya.* Kolkata: Books Space, 2016.

Shaw, Graham. "South Asia." *A Companion to the History of the Book*, edited by Simon Eliot and Jonathan Rose. Oxford: Blackwell Publishing, 2007, pp. 126–37.

Singha, Kaliprasanna. *Hutam Pyancār Nakśā.* 1868. ed. Arun Nag. Kolkata: Ananda Publishers, 2008.

Smith, George. *The Life of William Carey, D.D. Shoemaker and Missionary Professor of Sanskrit, Bengali, and Marathi in the College of Fort William, Calcutta.* London: John Murray, 1885.

Spivak, Gayatri. *An Aesthetic Education in the Era of Globalization.* Harvard: Harvard UP, 2013.

Sripantha. *Battalā.* Kolkata: Ananda Publishers, 1997.

Sripantha. *Jakhan chāpākhānā elō.* Kolkata: Pashchimbanga Bangla Academy, 1977.

Subandhu. *Vāsavadattā.* ed. Bhattacharya Jivananda Vidyasagar. 1933. Digital Library of India, 2006. Apr. 4, 2016.

Subandhu. *Vasavadatta: A Sanskrit Romance by Subandhu.* trans. Louis H. Gray. New York: Columbia UP, 1913.

Subramani, Vijaya. "Rasa: Aesthetics of Belonging *Unbelongingly* in Theory and Practice." *Consciousness, Theatre, Literature and the Arts*, 2012, pp. 242–55.

Tagore, Rabindranath. *"Bankimcandra,"* Bankim-Prasanga. edited by Sureshchandra Samajpati. Kolkata: Nabapatra Prakashan, 1922. Rpt. 1982, pp. 1–12.

Tagore, Rabindranath. "Viśwa Sāhitya." *Rabindra Rachanabali*, vol. 13. Shantiniketan: Viswa Bharati, 1994.

Tarkalankar, Madan Mohan. *Śiśu śikshā*. Kolkata: Sanskrit Press and Depository, 1849.

Temple, Richard. *James Thomason*. Oxford: Clarendon Press, 1893.

Thackeray, William Makepeace. *Roundabout Papers*. Leipzig: Bernhard Tauchnitz, 1869.

Thanawai, Maulana Ashraf Ali. *Behishti zewar,* translated as *Perfecting Women* by Barbara Daly Metcalf. Berkeley: U of California P, 1990.

"The Nielsen India Book Market Report 2015: Understanding the India Book Market." *Nielsen*, Oct. 10, 2015, https://www.nielsen.com/in/en/press-releases/2015/the-nielsen-india-book-market-report-2015-understanding-the-indian-book-market/.

Trevelyan, Charles E. *On the Education of the People of India*. London: Longman, Orme, Brown, Green, and Longman's, 1838.

Vidyasagar, Iswarchandra. *Barnaparicay*. 1855. Kolkata: Chokher Aloy Books, rpt. 2017.

Viswanathan, Gauri. *Masks of Conquest: Literary Study and British Rule in India*. New York: Columbia UP, 1989.

Warner, Michael. "Uncritical Reading," *Polemic Critical or Uncritical*, edited by Jane Gallop. New York: Routledge, 2004, pp. 13–38.

Yusuf, Ananta. "150 Years Old Press that Still Works." *The Daily Star*, Apr. 24, 2016. https://www.thedailystar.net/country/150-years-old-press-still-works-1213822.

Index

Abraham, Thomas 2
adab 43
   aesthetic structures of 156
   Biśād Sindhu, reading practice 152–61
   concept of 158–9, 167
   ethical and social implications of 167
   informative and entertainment 161
   Islamic classics 160
   literariness of 158–9
   literary examples 157
   moral virtue of 162
   principle of 150
   in shaping Islamic culture 162–3
   technicalities of 159
   as window to the world 161–71
ādālatī bhāśā 11
Adam, William 53–4, 92
   on practice of reading 54–6
   reading, memorizing, repeating
      formula 57
   Reports on Vernacular Education in
      Bengal and Bihar 41, 52, 54–5,
      57–8, 75
   textbooks 55–8
   translation of European works 58
   vernacular school books series 56
Ādarinī 156
adīb 162, 163, 166, 167
Adventures of Amir Hamzah 18, 169
agricultural community 61, 64, 82, 182
Ahmad, Muhammad Reazuddin 75–81
   Islām Pracārak 15 n.38, 78–81, 149
   Sudhakar 149
Ahmad, Nazir 155–6, 164
   Banat-an-nāsh (Daughters of the Bier)
      155
   Mirat-al-arus (The Mirror of the Bride)
      24, 155, 156, 160
   Taubā-an-nāsuh (The Repentence of
      Nasuh) 155, 164
Ahmad, Rafiuddin, *The Bengal Muslims*
   51 n.14

Ahmed, Moulvi Sirajuddin 76
Aina-e-Sikander 76, 156
Ajimuddin, Sheikh 149
ākhyāyika 43, 122, 139–45
ākhyāyikābarnita kāl 124
alamkār (ornaments) 131, 144
al-Baghdadi, Abd al-Qadir ibn Umar,
      Khizānat al-adab wa-lubb lubāb
      lisān al-Arab (Library of Literature
      and the Door of the Heart of the
      Arab Language) 162
Ali, Rajab 77
Allan, Michael 28, 29
almanacs 17, 24, 55, 91
Āmār kathā 33
Ānandamath (The House of Bliss) 43, 120,
      122, 139, 142, 143
Anāthinī 185
andarmahal 14
Anglicist reading practice 32, 37, 40–4,
      90–4, 96–9, 103–5
Anglo-centric education 96
Anisujjaman 50 n.12
   Muslim-manas o bangla sahitya 51 n.14
Anjaria, Ulka 5 n.13
Ansari's *Mukhtasar fi adab assufiyya* 158
anti-novels 25
Arabic *bayt* 178
Arabic language 49–50
Āryadarśan 108–9
Association of Publishers in India 1
Avadh Punch 76
azadari 171

Bagal, Jogeshchandra 119
Bāhabā cŏddŏ āiyin (Kudos to the
      fourteen laws) 19
Banabhatta's *Kādambarī* 110, 126
Banat-an-nāsh (Daughters of the Bier)
      155
"*Bande Mātaram*" ("I bow to thee,
      Motherland") 142–4

Index 213

Bandopadhyay, Bhabanicharan 17, 24, 68
   Kalikātā kamalālay 45–7
Bandopadhyay, Indranath, *Kalpataru* 25
Bangabāsī press 15 n.38
Bangabhāśār Lekhak 107
Bangabhāsi 83
Bangadarśan 53, 69, 83, 117, 148
"*Banga o Bihār bijay*" ("Conquering
   Bengal and Bihar") 81
"*Banga o Bihār biśay*" ("On the Subject of
   Bengal and Bihar") 81
Bangiya Mussalmān Sāhitya Samiti
   (Bengali Muslim Literary Society)
   78
Bangiya Sahitya Parishat (the Bengal
   Academy of Literature) 98
Bānglār pāthak parāna brata 72
Basak, Bhubanchandra 22
Basak, Nilmani, *Nabanāri nay nārir jīban
   carit* (*Lives of Nine Women*) 23
Bashar, Abul 181
Basu, Jogendrachandra 15 n.38
   Model bhaginī (*Model Sister*) 25
Basu, Ram Ram 11
   Lipimālā (*Collection of Letters*) 24
   Pratāpādityacaritra 23
battalā publications 14–15, 15 n.38, 63, 65
   n.47, 118, 119
   access to rural Bengal 16
   Battle of Karbala tales 18
   Bengali reader and 15
   book industry 63
   Hindu and Muslim presses 17
   Islamic works 18
   languages 17, 19
   and literacy growth 23
   naksās (sketches) 24
   paper quality 16, 19
   reading practices 21
   satires 18–20, 185
   textbooks 22
   trading 16, 17
   Vidyāsundar 17–18
   woman's reading practice 23–5
Battle of Plassey 6, 9, 10, 48, 160
bāul 178, 179 n.88, 183
Bengali folk performances 173. *See also*
   jārigān
Bengali Hindus 14, 48–52, 85

Bengali language 7–10, 74
   British intervention in 7–13
   and literary history 11
   manuscripts in 10–12
   textbooks 12, 64–5
   transition to 49–52
Bengali literacy/literature 10–11, 13, 19,
   23, 24, 47, 65–6, 71–3, 89, 92, 118,
   148
Bengali Muslims 48–53. *See also* Muslim
   reader
   Muharram rituals 151
Bengali novel/novelists 4, 5, 27, 87,
   90, 119–20, 145–9, 166. *See also
   Durgeśnandinī* (*The Chieftain's
   Daughter*)
   national literature 6
   in nineteenth century 6, 185
   reader 27, 88, 93, 96, 104 (*see also*
   reading practice/readers)
Bengali primer 12, 74–5
Bengal Library Quarterly Report 1875 16
Bengal Renaissance 12, 65, 74 n.77
bhāb 33, 34–5
Bhadra, Gautam
   Bāngāli pāthak ō tār bānglā boi parā
   65–6
   Nyara battalāy jay k'bar? (*How Often
   Does Nyara Go to the Battalā?*) 118
bhadralōk (gentleman) 13 n.35, 14, 18, 19,
   25, 52, 63–5
bhasha texts 1, 153–4
Bhaskar press 63
Bhattacharya, Amitrasudan 118
Bhattacharya, Gangakishore 17–18, 47
Bhattacharya, Tithi 18 n.52
bhāva 34
bhrātribhāśā 155
Bidyabhushan, Jogendranath 92
biraha 126
Biśabṛksha (*The Poison Tree*) 33, 43,
   109–10, 122, 137–8, 141, 142
Biśād Sindhu (*Ocean of Sorrows*) 43, 82,
   84, 147–8
   concept of *adab* 152
   didacticism 167
   Ejid badh parba of 152
   jārigān performance and 148, 150,
   171–84

Muharram parba of 152, 153
mukhabandha 151
  narrative of 151–2
  practice of reading 149 152–3
  public imagination 155
  qissā and *dāstān* 169–70
  rasa, aesthetic principles of 153
  reading as performance 150–1
  Sanskritist reading practices 15.
  self-identified Islamic Bengali novel
    149
  source texts of 173–4
  Uddhar parba of 152, 170
  upakramanika 152
book(s)
  market 2, 48
  usage of 45–6, 67–8
boyati 178
Bramho Samaj 92
Bramho woman 25
British intervention in Bengali language
  7–13, 52
British novel readers 94–6, 102–3, 119,
  145–6
British pedagogical approach 53–62. *See
  also* Adam, William
Brouillette, Sarah 28, 29
Burra Bazar Family Literary Club 95
Byron, Lord, *Complete Poetical Works* 74

Caitanya Bhagabat (*The Life of Chaitanya*)
  23, 189–90
Calcutta Gazette 16 n.39
Calcutta Public Library 95
Calcutta Review 153, 157
Calcutta School Book Society 21
Carey, William 9–12, 10 n.24
charit (life narratives) 23
Chattopadhyay, Bankimchandra 4, 6, 21
  n.60, 25–6 n.78, 53–4, 87, 150
  Akshaychandra's criticism of Bankim's
    prose 106–8, 111, 112
  Ānandamath (*The House of Bliss*) 43,
    120, 122, 139, 142, 143
  "A Popular Literature for Bengal"
    69–70, 73
  Bangadarśan 15 n.38, 69, 117, 120,
    154

bankimī novels 14, 121
Biśabṛksha (*The Poison Tree*) 33, 43,
  109–10, 122, 137–8, 141
  and British pedagogical approach 53
  commitment to *rasa* aesthetics 122–3
  Durgeśnandinī 13, 32–3, 38, 41–3,
    67 n.54, 87–94, 115
  encoding future events 141–2
  Kapalkundalā 33, 109
  Kṛṣnacaritra (*The Life of Krishna*) 24,
    102, 120
  "*Lalita,purākalik galpo, tathā mānas*"
    106, 119 n.8
  model reader 123–34
  Mrinālinī 33
  as novel reader 88–90
  novels and essays 115–16
  pāthak's perception of 128–9
  Rajmohan's Wife 119, 145–6
  rasa in prose 128–34
  on reading and culture 64–75
  revolutionary politics 143
  Sahaj Racanāśikkhā (*An Easy Guide to
    Composition*) 74–5
  sahṛdaya pāthak 134–8
  Sanskrit as lived experience novels
    117–23
  and Sanskrit pundits 105–13
  as Scott of Bengal 89, 94–105
  use of verse 140–2
  uses rhyming ideophones
    (*dhyanātmakśabda*) 133–4
  works and modern Bengali literature
    118
  writing for *sahṛdaya pāthak* 134
Chattopadhyay, Purnachandra 88
  "*Bankimcandra o Dinabandhu*"
    ("Bankimchandra and
    Dinabandhu") 87
  Durgeśnandinī review 87, 106
Cheah, Pheng, *What Is a World* 28
cheap popular presses 13 n.35, 14–16, 118.
  See also battalā publications
Chowdhury, Ali 78
Collins, Wilkie
  "The Unknown Public" 19 n.54
  "Unknown Public" 96
Colonial Library series 115

colonial pedagogical policies 52, 104, 119, 121
commercial publication 3, 6, 7
compounding words (*samās*) 144
cookbook, *Pākrājeśwar* 63
Coombe, George 13
couplets 178

Daly, Barbara Metcalf 159
Dames, Nicholas, *The Physiology of the Novel* 26 n.80
Dasi, Binodini 33–4, 186
dāstān (Persian) 169
Dāstān-e-amir Hamzah (*Adventures of Amir Hamzah*) 18, 169
Datta, Kalinath 100–2
Datta, Michael Madhusudan 103
Datta, Rameshchandra 98
    review of *Durgeśnandinī* 99–100
Debi Chaudhurāni 139
Debi, Kailasbashini, *Hindu mahilāganer hinabasthā* (*The Lowly State of Hindu Women*) 185–6
Debi, Rassundari
    Āmār jīban (*My Life*) 44, 186, 187
    autobiography 187–90
    on girl child's fear 188
    parā and *kāj* 189
    process of learning 188
    reading practice 188–91
    religious *punthi*s 192
Debi, Thakomoni, *Anāthinī* 185
De, Durgadas 32
    Miss Bino Bibi. B.A. Honour in a Course 35, 185
Derasulla, Mohammad 17
Dhananjayan, V. P. 128
didacticism 167
dissemination of Christianity 9, 12
Drain-er pāncālī (Song of the drain) 19
dramatis personae 25
Dubrow, Jennifer 51
    Cosmopolitan Dreams 26 n.80
Dunham, Mary Frances 178
durbyabahār (bad behavior of readers/subscribers) 79
Durgeśnandinī (*The Chieftain's Daughter*) 87
    as *ākhyāyikā* 139

Anglicist 90–4
    Aurobindo's review of 103–4
    financial and literary success 88
    Kalinath's review of 100–2
    of modern Bengali literature 123–6
    national identity, representation of 97–8
    Rameshchandra's review of 98–100
    rasa aesthetics 122
    reading practice 87–9
    Sanskrit grammar 107–8
    Sanskritist reader 105–13
    Sanskritized Bengali 144–5
    Scott's *Ivanhoe* and 97–9
    śṛṅgāra rasa in 123, 127–30, 142
    Western influence in 100, 105
Duti bilās 24
Dutta, Akshay Kumar, *Cārupāth* 13, 13 n.34
Dutt, Michael Madhusudan 119 n.7
    Śarmiṣṭhā 33

East India Company 6–9, 50, 52, 160
education
    agricultural community 61
    debate over 57
    Indigenous Books 59–60
    native institutions 54–6
    print text books 55–8
    prison curriculum 60–1
    reading practice 54
    schooling systems 53–5
    vernacular education in Bengal 61–2
The Education Gazette 148, 152 n.14, 153
Ekei bale pole 19
English Education Act of 1835 22, 49, 50
English language
    literacy 4 n.10
    readers 95
    transition to 49–52
European printer-publishers 7

Faizullah, Sheikh, "*Jaynaber Cautisā*" 172, 174, 175
Faizunnesa, Nawab 149
Federation of Indian Publishers 1
fictional works 94–6, 99, 115, 140–1

filter down education 53, 72
folktales 148, 175 n.78, 178
Fort William College 7–13
  Bengali text book 14, 49
funds, publication 6, 22
future events, encoding of 141–2

Gada,Yusuf, *Tuhfa i nasaih* 158
Gagging Act 77
Gāji Miyār Bastāni 182, 183
Ghosal, Ashutosh 16
Ghosh, Anindita 18 n.52
  Power in Print 26 n.80
Ghosh, Aurobindo 90, 102–4
Ghosh, Girishchandra 32–5
Ghosh, Kashiprasad 91
Ghosh, Kshetramohan, *Kākbhuśundir*
  kāhinī 24
Gilchrist, John 11
Gītgōvinda 73, 126, 144–5
Gō jīban (Life of Cows) 170
Gopalchandra De of Puran Prakash Press
  16
government funds 22
Grāmbārtāprakāśikā (*Publisher of Rural*
  News) 31, 182–3
Gray, Louis H. 130–1
Gunanidhi, Narayan Chattaraj,
  Kalikutuhal 24
Gupta, Abhijit 5 n.12, 6 n.15, 7
Gupta, Iswar 70, 71 n.67
Gyanratnākar Press 22

Hachette India 2
Hadith 151
hagiographic texts 23
Halder, Radhabinod, *Pās karā māg*
  (Educated Woman) 25
harmful books 163
Hastings, Warren 10
Hemlatā-Ratikanta 118
Hindu- and Muslim-run newspapers 75–6
Hindu Bengalis. *See* Bengali Hindus
Hindu epics 64
The Hindu Intelligencer 91
Hindu intelligentsia's critique 62
  Bengali primer 74–5
  British-inspired institutions and 64
  good reading, pleasure/worship 68

literary celebrities 63–4
literary merit 69–70
literary revolution 66–7
print texts 63
reading practice 64–5
Hindu nationalism 6
Hindu newspapers 79
Hindustani Press 11, 17
Hitakarī 78–9, 81–4, 154, 156
Hossain, Mir Mosharraf 4
  Basantakumārī 157
  Bengali Muslim writing novels 149
  Biśād Sindhu 43, 82, 84, 147–8
  Gāji Miyār Bostāni 157
  Hitakarī 78–9, 81–4, 154, 156, 182
  Mirat-al-arus 158
  Musalmani bhasha 154
  Ratnabati 30–1, 35, 153, 156
  reading practice 149–50
Hossain, Rokeya Sakhawat, *Sultana's*
  Dream 149
Hussain, Golam 149
hussainiya 151
Hutam. *See* Singha, Kaliprasanna

Ibn Battuta 161–2
Ibn Juazzy 161–2
Imperial Library (National Library of
  India) 115
indexical of literary 28
Indian book market 2, 48
Indian nationalism 142, 143
Indian vernacular languages 1 n.1
India Today 1
Indigenous Books 59–60, 62
indigenous presses 7
Islamic Bengali 14, 16, 17, 43
Islamic rule 7, 8
Islamic tales 175 n.78
Islam Pracārak 78–81, 149
itihās 140
Ivanhoe 90, 96–8, 100

Jamidar Darpan (*A Mirror Held to the*
  Landlords) 153
jārigān 43
  azadari 171
  and *bāul* 179 n.88, 183
  Bengali folk performances 173

and *Biśād Sindhu* 171–84
    folk music performance 148, 150
    jāri performers/singer 178
    jāri text 172, 173
    marsiya/nauha poetry form of 173
    pak panjatan 150
    pāncālī form of 173
    reading as performance 150–1
    Śahidnāmār jāri 179
Jārijungnāmā 174, 175
    punthi of 182
jāri performers/singer 178
jāri text 172, 173
Jasimuddin 178
Jayadeva's *Gītgōvinda* 73, 126, 144–5
Jaynaber Cautisā 172, 174, 175
Jones, William 10
Joshi, Priya 7, 94–6

Kalidasa
    Abhijyanaśankuntalam 110, 121
    Śakuntalā 135
Kalikātā kamalālay 24
Kaminīkumār 118
Kangal Harinath 31. *See* Majumdar,
    Harinath
kanyālābha/kanyāharana 140
karuna (compassionate) *rasa* 154
Kashifi, Husain Waiz, *Maqtal Rawzat al-
    Shuhada* 148
kathā 43, 122, 139–45
Kaviraj, Sudipta 118
kāvya (poetry) 117, 139
Kāvyalamkāra (*The Ornaments of Poetry*)
    139–40
Kerāni purān 47
Khan, Maryam Wasif 51
    Who Is a Muslim 26 n.80
Khan, Muhammad, *Maqtul Husayn* 148
Khan, Shamsuddin 77
Khatun, Faizunnesa
    biography of 193–5
    jārigān 193
    mentor (*ustād*) 193
    on *misra bhāśā* 193
    reading practices 193, 195–7
    Rupjālāl 44, 149, 186, 193–6
kirtan 141–2
Kṛṣnacaritra 120

languages 7, 9–10. *See also specific*
    languages
    debate over 52
    lower/upper class 14
Lavandier, J. 11
Leavis, Q. D. 96
Lewes, G. H. 133
libraries 95, 115
literary history 4, 6, 13–15, 42, 89, 92, 93,
    118, 197
literary language 4 n.10, 7, 108, 114, 167
literary reading. *See* reading practice
literary revolution 66–7
literature's power 28
Long, James 41, 52, 62
    *A Descriptive Catalogue of Bengali
    Works Containing a Classified
    List of Fourteen Hundred Bengali
    Books and Pamphlets, Which Have
    Issued from the Press during the
    Last Sixty Years, with Occasional
    Notices of the Subjects, the Price,
    and Where Printed* 3, 3 nn.8–9, 7,
    62–3
    Quarterly Reports 17, 18
    Returns 15, 17, 18
lower/upper class languages 14
low rhymes 19

Macaulay, Thomas Babington, *Minute on
    Indian Education* 11
Macmillan 115
madhyabartinī bhāśā 107
madrasās 50, 55
Mahāriśī Prabhu Hajrat 170
Mahfouz,Naguib, *Palace of Desire* 29
Mahmud, Heyat 182
    Jārijungnama 150, 174, 179
Mahmud, Sufi pir Heyat, *Jungnāmā* 172
Majumdar, Harinath 31, 182, 183
Malatī-mādhava 110, 112
mangal kābyas 17, 41
manuscripts 10–12, 45. *See also punthis*
marginalization 48
Marshman, John 9–11
mātribhāśā 155
Meredith, George, *The Egoist* 103
middle-class intelligentsia 79
milan 126

218   *Index*

Mirat-al-arus (*The Mirror of the Bride*)
155, 156, 160
Mirza Ghalib, *Gul-e-Raana* 76
misrabhāśā (mixed language) 175 n.78,
176
Mission Press 6–13, 49
Mitra, Pyarichand 71
Ālāler gharer dulāl 118
modern Bengali 7–9, 7n.17, 12–14, 41
n.116, 72
Mohammadi Press 17
*Monier-Williams Sanskrit-English
Dictionary* 128
moral ramifications 23
Mouat, Frederic J. 60
Muharram rituals 151
Muir, William 155
Mukhopadhyay, Bhudeb 154
Mukhopadhyay, Rajiblochan,
*Mahārāj Kriśnacandra Rāyasya
Caritram* (*The Life of Maharaja
Krishnachandra Ray*) 23
munshis 12 n.32
Musalmani bangla (Islamic Bengali) 14,
16, 17, 153–4
Musalmani katha 154
Muslim Bengalis. *See* Bengali Muslims
Muslim intelligentsia 47, 48, 51, 78
Muslim presses 17
Muslim reader 75–85. *See also tabula rasa*

Nababābu bilās 24
Nababibi bilās 24
Nabaīiban 65
Nabhel nāyikā (*The Novel Heroine*) 4, 135,
185
naksās (sketches) 24
nātak-nabel (plays, novels) 139
native institutions 54–6
Nātyaśastra 33, 126–9
Nawab Faizunnesa 186
newspapers 75–6
Nielsen India Book Market Report:
Understanding the India Book
Market 1–3
nineteenth-century Bengal, British
colonial rule 3
N.L. Shil's press 22

Nobhel nāyikā 20
novels. *See also* Bengali novel/novelists
libraries 95
reading 88–9, 96–7
writing 4 n.10

obscene literature 65, 67, 70–3
online reading 2

Paine, Tom, *Age of Reason* 74
Pākrājeśwar 63
palm-leaf manuscript. *See punthis*
pāncālī 20
pandit/guru mahāśay 55
pan-Indian reading community 80
panjikās 24. *See also* almanacs
Pare, Bireshwar, *Adbhut swapna bā strī
purusher dwanda* (*A Strange Dream
or a Battle between the Sexes*) 25
pathapustak/hetochorā 19
pāthśālās 22, 55, 64, 68
paurānik kāhinī 17
Permanent Settlement of Bengal 50
Persian language 8, 14, 17, 22, 37, 49
Perso-Arabic reading practice 37, 40–4,
149, 152, 153, 158, 180, 183–4
pleasure/worship, good reading 68
poetry, composition of 139–40
Portuguese missionaries 8–9
Postal Act of 1854 16
pōurānik 33
Prabadh candrikā 66
Pradip 101
prahaśan 18, 19. *See also* satires
Press and Registration of Books Act of
1867 16 n.39
Price, Leah, *What We Talk about When
We Talk about Books* 26 n.80
Print Areas 6 n.15
printed books 46, 62–3
arrival of 6–7
battalā publications 14–16, 63
in Bengali language 7–12
Bengali readers and 13–14
college and press 7–14
commercial publication 6, 7
dissemination of Christianity 9, 12
East India Company 6–9

Index

Portuguese missionaries 8–9
  technology 7
  textbooks 55–6
printing press 31–2, 62–3
prison curriculum 60–1
Prophet Mohammad 170–1
prose 23, 24, 138
  ākhyāyika 43, 122, 139–45
  Bengali 66, 71, 103–8
  forms of Sanskrit 114, 139
  as inferior art form 139
  kathā 43, 122, 139–45
  poetic composition of 139–40
  writing 140
publishing industry 1–3, 6, 76
punthis (manuscripts) 17, 18, 45, 47, 69,
    148, 174 n.77
punthi sāhitya 175, 175 n.78
Puruś parikkhā 66

Qabusnāmā (Mirrors for Princes) 159
qissā (Arabic) 169
Qissā-e Gul-e bakavali 18
Qissā-e Hātim Tāi 18
qissās and *dāstāns* 18
Qur'an 49, 50, 151, 175, 196 n.28

Rahasya Sandarbha 153, 156
Rahmani Press 17
Rāmāyana and *Mahābhārat* 17, 18, 64, 109
rasas 110, 117, 120 n.9, 122, 126–34
  Bande Mātaram 143
  bankimī style of 144
  of *kathā* 141
  sahṛdaya and 134–8
rasik pāthak 122–5, 133–5
rasik sahṛdaya (empathetic) 134
Ray, Bharatchandra 49
  Annadāmangal 5 n.12, 17, 66–8,
    109–10
reading practice/readers 2, 13–14, 15,
    25–6, 26 n.79, 27 n.81, 54, 197–8.
    See also Durgeśnandinī, reading
    practice; Muslim reader
  as *adīb* 162
  Anglicist 37, 40–4
  animating theory 30
  bad readers 47, 53–62, 68

battalā presses and 15, 21
Bengali Muslims 43, 51–3
Bengali novel and 4–6, 27
Biśād Sindhu (Ocean of Sorrows) 149
book trade 32
British colonial rule and 3
British novel 94–6
concept and method of 27, 29, 32,
    47–8, 51–2
dramatizing the novel 32–4
Durgeśnandinī novel and 87–90
intelligentsia's 64–5
literary reading 29–30, 68–70
magic of 193–7
nineteenth-century readers 26–7
paper quality and 16, 19, 31
Perso-Arabic 37, 40–4
pleasure/worship, good reading 68
postcolonial novel 36
printing press and 31–2
rasik pāthak 134, 135
Rassundari's reading practice 187–92
readers experiment/investigation 28,
    36
reviewer identities 30–1
Sanskritist 37, 40–4
social and gender categories 38
symptomatic reading 40
twenty-first-century reader 31
UNESCO and world literature 28
women readers 44
realism 5 n.13, 13
Reynolds, G. W. M. 96
rhyming ideophones (*dhyanātmakśabda*)
    133–4
Ricci, Ronit 160
Rihla (Travels) 161
romantic fiction 140, 141
Royal Asiatic Society 10
Roy, Rammohan 11, 12
Roy, Tapti, *Print and Publishing in
    Colonial Bengal* 7 n.17
Rupjālāl 149

sacred texts 47–8, 99, 151
Sādhāranī 65, 106, 148
sādhu bhāśā 11
sahānubhūti 72–3

Śahidnāmār jāri 179–80
Sāhitya 107
sahṛdaya pāthak 134–8
samās 144
Sambad Prabhākar 70
Sāmya 120
Sanskrit 8, 11, 13, 17, 31, 37
  Bengali and 117–19
  compounding words (*samās*) 144
  as lived experience 117–23
  poetic composition 139
  prose narratives 139–45
  word meanings 117
Sanskritic/Sanskritized Bengali 51, 138–45
Sanskritist reading practice/readers 32, 37,
    40–4, 89–94, 146
  Āryadarśan show 108–9
  Durgeśnandinī and 105–8
Sanskrit Press 15 n.38, 22, 66–7
Sanyasis (ascetics) 143
sarasa vastu 140
Saraswati Bandana 55
Sarkar, Akshaychandra 91, 150
  criticism of Bankim's prose 106–8, 111,
    112
  "*Pitā-putra*" ("Father-Son") 65–8
śāstras 17
satires 4, 16–20, 18 n.52, 24, 35
Saxena, Akshya *Vernacular English* 5 n.14
schooling systems 53–5
Scott of Bengal, Bankim 89, 94–105
Scott, Walter 13
  Ivanhoe 90, 96–8, 100
Sensation novel 133
Sen, Sukumar 18 n.49
  Bānglā sāhityer itihās (*The History of
    Bengali Literature*) 118
  Battalār chapa o chabi (*The Prints and
    Images of Battalā*) 118
shādhāran (average) Bengali reader 52
Sharashar, Ratan Nath, *Fasana-e Azad* 76
Shaw, Graham 7
Shil, Benimadhav, "*grihinir guide*" 24
Shirazi, Shaykh Mushrif al-Din, *Gulistān*
    (*Rose Garden*) 167
Siddiqi, Shamsuddin Mohammad, *Uchit
    Sraban* 149
Sikdar, Ayen Ali 149
Singha, Kaliprasanna 14, 71

Hutam Pyāncār Nakśā (*Sketches by
    Hutam, the Owl*) 24, 71, 118
singular knowledge system 38
Śiśubōdhak 22
Śiśusebadhi Barnamālā 22
śiśu (child) textbooks 22
sketches. *See naksās* (sketches)
Smith, George 11
social aspiration 22
Sōmprakāś 156
Sripantha 24
  Battalā 118
sṛngāra (erotic) *rasa* 43, 110, 122, 123,
    126–31, 140
sthayibhāva 127, 136
Stone, *setta* 29
street books 19
Subandhu's *Vasavadatta* 126, 130–1,
    139
Subramani, Vijaya 135
Sudhākar 75–7, 149
Sufi pirs 151
Sufism 159, 172 n.69
Sultan ul Akhbar 77
sundar (beautiful) 128–31
Sundarkānda 131

tabula rasa 9, 78
Tagore, Debendranath 15 n.38
Tagore, Rabindranath
  Bankim Prasanga (*On the Subject of
    Bankim*) 122 n.17
  prose experiments 42, 72 n.69
  "*Viswa sahitya*" ("World Literature")
    104 n.45
tangled genealogy 37–8
Tarkaratna, Tarashankar, *Kādambari* 67,
    129–31, 139
tatsama/tadbhāva 145
Tatwabodhinī Patrikā 92
Tatwabōdhinī Press 15 n.38, 22
Taubā-an-nāsuh (*The Repentence of
    Nasuh*) 155
textbooks 11–13, 21–2
  Adam's 55–8
  battalā publications 22
  Bengali language 12, 64–5
  printed books 55–6
  William's 55–8

Thakur, Brindaban Das, *Caitanya Bhagabat* 189–90
thākurmā'r galpa (grandmother's tales) 156
Thakur, Tekchand 71
  Ālāler Gharer Dulāl (*The Pampered Brat*) 71
Thanawi, Maulana Ashraf Ali
  Bahishti zewar (*Heavenly Ornaments*) 24, 163–4, 186
Thomason, James 59–60
trading 8, 16
Treveleyan, Charles 92, 111
  On the Education of the People of India 111
  on learning languages 112

ucchvāsas (pauses) 140, 141
Unitarian Press 11
upakramanikā 164
Urdu literature 155–6
Urdu-Persian literary community 81

Vaishnava poems of Vidyāpati 41
Vasavadatta 126, 130
vernacular education 22, 54, 60–2
vernacular languages 1 n.1
Vernacular Literature Society 91
Vernacular Press Act 77
vernacular presses 3 n.9, 12–13
  of *battalā* 15, 21

vernacular school books series 56
verse compositions 139–42
Victorian novels 95–7, 100, 115, 118
Victorian texts 5
Victoria Press 16
Vidyalankar, Mrityunjay 12
Vidyasagar, Iswarchandra
  Barnaparicay 12, 13, 13 n.34
  Caritābali (*Collection of Lives*) 23
  editorial interventions 66–8
Vidyāsundar/Kālikāmangal 7 n.17, 16–17, 19, 67
vir (heroic) *rasa* 154

Walker's experiments on prison curriculum 60–1
Ward, William 9
Warwick Research Collective (WreC) 28
Wednesday Review 98, 100
Wellesley, Richard 10
women readers 23–5, 35, 44, 185–6
  education and restrictions 186
  lack of community 187
  practice reading 187
  social treatises 186
  Tagore family, women of 186

yellow pages 17
Young Bengal 74
Young Bengal Khudra Nabab 46
Yusuf-Zuleikhā 18

www.ingramcontent.com/pod-product-compliance
Lightning Source LLC
Chambersburg PA
CBHW052038300426
44117CB00012B/1880

The Novel in Nineteenth-Century Bengal